16.99

54546

D1626741

60522

L T

RETU

RETURN

RETURNED

RETURN

RETURN

17. OCT. 2

WITHDRAWN FROM
ST. HELENS COLLEGE LIBRARY

The David & Charles Manual of

# CONCRETE, BRICKWORK, PLASTERING AND TILING

Frank Spander

# The David & Charles Manual of

# CONCRETE, BRICKWORK, PLASTERING AND TILING

## Frank Spander

**David & Charles**

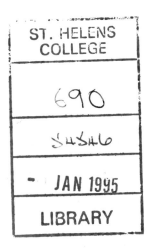

ST. HELENS
COLLEGE

690

34346

- JAN 1995

LIBRARY

*Unless otherwise credited, photographs*
*supplied by courtesy of the Cement &*
*Concrete Association*

**British Library Cataloguing in Publication Data**
Spander, Frank
    David & Charles manual of concrete, brickwork,
    plastering and tiling.
    1. Building——Amateurs' manuals
    Rn: Jan Woudhuysen    I. Title
    690    TH148

    ISBN 0-7153-8593-3

Text and line illustrations © Frank Spander 1987

First published 1987
Second impression 1988
Third impression 1990
Fourth impression 1992

All rights reserved. No part of this
publication may be reproduced, stored
in a retrieval system, or transmitted,
in any form or by any means, electronic,
mechanical, photocopying, recording or
otherwise, without the prior permission
of David & Charles Publishers plc

Typeset by ABM Typographics Limited, Hull
and printed in Great Britain
by Redwood Press Ltd, Melksham, Wilts.
for David and Charles Publishers plc
Brunel House   Newton Abbot   Devon

# Contents

# Introduction

This book is about the wet trades, as they are known among builders: laying bricks, casting concrete, setting tiles and applying plaster. They are called the 'wet trades' because all of them use a lot of water, though I prefer to call them the 'creative trades' because you really can start off with a pile of sand and a bag of cement and finish up with a garage or a swimming pool.

However, it is precisely this 'creativity' which causes most DIY people to leave the wet trades alone. There are no easy-to-use kits available for the job, no exact components which slot or bolt together and no special DIY tools that enable you to bypass the skill of the trained craftsman. It all seems a matter of skill and experience built up over the years — the steady hand and good eye of the expert.

Nevertheless, the amateur handyman (or woman) *can* learn to lay bricks, mix concrete, plaster walls and cover the plaster in tiles without years of apprenticeship — all by yourself, if necessary, though it is more enjoyable with other people's help. Nor do you require a contractor's yard full of mixers, tractors and scaffolding.

Once you have mastered the techniques, you can build almost anything with concrete and bricks. You need not confine yourself to garages and potting sheds: how about a gazebo, a Japanese water garden, a rock garden with a miniature cave?

You will need a few tools, most of which you probably have already or can hire or borrow (*see* Chapter 9). You will also need to buy sand, cement, bricks etc, which are not terribly expensive (*see* Chapter 10). The rest of the book tells you how to use these tools and materials to complete the job, and suggests projects for you to try or to adapt to suit your own requirements.

Of course, the best way of learning how to tackle most of these jobs is to watch a professional builder at work. Just standing around watching can be hard work if you are really trying to understand it all, so do not be ashamed to watch whenever you get the chance.

Now try to do it yourself. You will soon find out how hard it is to do a proper job, but you should also discover that, although you cannot manage quite as well as the expert, you can still finish up with something you recognise. That is the time to read this book again; you will soon spot all the tricky bits when you come to read about them.

You cannot expect to tackle major projects, such as building a whole house, without a lot more knowledge and experience than can be gained just from reading this book. The line has to be drawn somewhere, otherwise we would be in danger of collapsing walls, breaking lintels and cracking foundations. In fact, the line is drawn by an official known variously as the District Surveyor, Borough Engineer or Building Inspector. Almost all work involving brickwork or concrete has to be supervised and inspected by him at some stage. Listen to him carefully. He has usually been trained in the old school of 'belts and braces'. He will stop you doing anything dangerous, and will tell you when you are going out of your depth. Do not be ashamed to admit that there are things you cannot do yourself, and do not take short cuts — they are only for the experts. If there are large jobs you cannot tackle yourself, eg putting in a large beam or taking brickwork up above first-floor level, get a builder in for that part, and watch what he does. He may let you help and, if you choose your man carefully, he will almost certainly explain 'what and why'.

No single book can explain everything, but this book will certainly get you started and enable you to experience the joy of messing about with bricks, cement, sand and water — and the satisfaction of having done it yourself.

# 1 Concrete Mixes

Concrete is a mixture of four materials — cement, sand, stones (usually known as ballast) and water. It is important that these are mixed properly, using only clean material of the right type: both materials and mixing methods affect the final strength of the concrete. The mixture sets rock-hard within a few days, but only reaches its ultimate strength after a month's hardening, or curing as it is technically called.

Concrete used for foundations is the first structural material to make contact with the earth. If your foundations are to carry the structure above them adequately, they must be prepared properly. You must know how far down to dig, and how to prepare the ground to receive the concrete.

When just mixed, concrete is a plastic, almost fluid material, which cannot be shaped by hand like clay. It must be poured into a mould, and making this correctly is an important part of working with concrete. The mould is usually referred to as 'shuttering' and is made of softwood (sw) boards (or plywood for bigger areas) stiffened by softwood (sw) frames. Concrete then has to dry out and harden, a process that cannot be left to chance. It must not dry out too fast, nor must it be left to get too cold if there is a possibility of frost during the night.

You will need to pour concrete if you are going to build anything larger than a sundial. Mass concrete is used as a foundation for brick walls, as a combined floor and foundation for garages and extensions, and as the material for a path or driveway. It can be used to make your own paving stones, lintels over a doorway or window, small pools, intriguing water gardens; in fact, concrete

Water, fine and coarse aggregate, cement (right) and sand (front)

can be used for a thousand different purposes. It is a versatile material, though not particularly attractive for the exterior of your house. With a little ingenuity, however, you can learn to hide it underground or behind other materials.

## Materials

The water used must be clean, preferably of drinking water standard, as dirty water will make the concrete weaker. This matters less when concrete is used in mass foundations but, on the whole, dirty water should be avoided. Tap water is ideal, and on most jobs it should be readily available. However, if you have to make concrete away from the mains, feel free to use water from a stream or well, but remember that the concrete will not be as strong.

Much more important is the amount of water used — ideally, as little as possible. In theory, very little water is needed to combine with the cement to produce the strength needed, but a lot of extra water has to be added to make the concrete workable — plastic enough to pour, to settle into corners, to push into odd crannies — and all this extra water has to evaporate as the concrete dries.

As it evaporates, it may leave shrinkage cracks; or the extra water may wash the cement powder from between the aggregate, leaving you with stones in one part and cement in another. So, it is best to keep the water content as low as possible, often by using plasticisers. For small quantities, where strength is not of the utmost importance, ordinary washing-up liquid is sufficient. Larger quantities of concrete may require special plasticising agents.

Cement normally comes in 50kg bags of grey powder. It is produced in the United Kingdom to a standard set by the British Standards Institute — each bag is marked with the little kite mark (or the new BS logo) — so there is no need to worry about the quality. Use white cement if you are planning to colour the concrete (yes, this is possible) and rapid-hardening cement if you must do a job in the winter. (Try to avoid this, if possible, as serious doubts have arisen over the long-term strength of rapid-hardening cement.)

Sand for concrete needs a little more attention. Often it is combined with the ballast to give an all-in aggregate (the term used for the inert matter in concrete), ranging from fine particles of sand to large pebbles. However, it is important to know where the sand has come from. It can be dredged from the sea, in which case it will contain some salt — perfectly all right if you want a base for paving stones, but fatal if you are making concrete. This requires clean, river sand, which comes in two varieties: sharp sand for most concrete work, and builder's sand for mortar in brickwork. Sand ordered from a large and reputable company will be perfectly suitable. It is only less reliable sources that may try to make a little on the side by supplying sea instead of river sand — banking on your ignorance as a DIY customer.

Ballast is the last component. Depending on the purpose for which you are going to use the concrete, you will need either a fine or a coarse ballast. A fine ballast, used for garden paths or for casting paving stones, will have pebbles not exceeding 10mm, ie they will all pass through a mesh screen with 10mm square holes. Coarse ballast, used for foundations, will have pebbles up to 20mm. Ballast is sold as a mass of small, medium and large stones to be mixed with sharp sand, or as all-in aggregate (also known as all-in ballast) which contains everything needed for the concrete except the cement (and water, of course). Again, you can buy fine or coarse all-in aggregate.

## Quantities and proportions

Before you can pick up the telephone to ask the price or place an order, you will need to know how much concrete you require. Estimating concrete is a rough-and-ready science, but fortunately none of the materials is wildly expensive, and you will always be able to find a use for small amounts left over. It is better to order a little too much, than order too little — you could be left with a structural weakness where two different batches of concrete join.

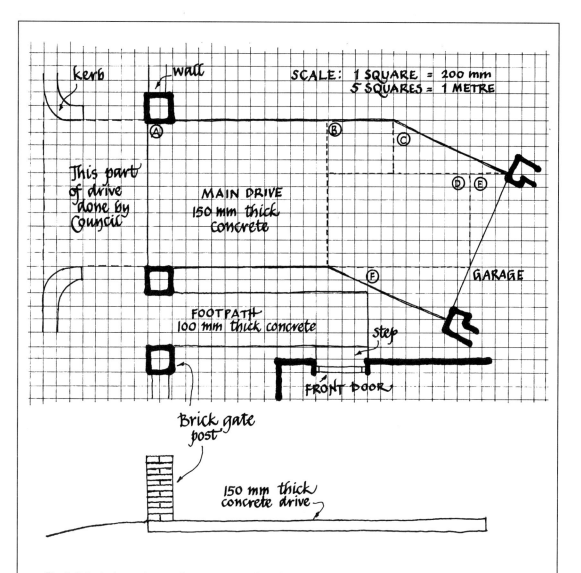

**Fig 1** Calculating volume of concrete required for main drive and footpath using graph paper plan

Area of main drive:
A 154
B 20
C 18
D 77
E 10
F 22

301 squares

Each square is ¹/₂₅th of 1sq metre
Therefore the area of the drive is 301sq metres
$$\frac{301}{25}$$
= 12.04sq metres

Volume is 12.04 × 0.15 cubic metres
= 1.806 cubic metres

Area of path 68 squares = 2.72sq metres
Volume is 2.72 × 0.1 cubic metres
= 0.272 cubic metres

All in all you will need  2.078 cubic metres
+10%  0.207 spare, just in case

2.285

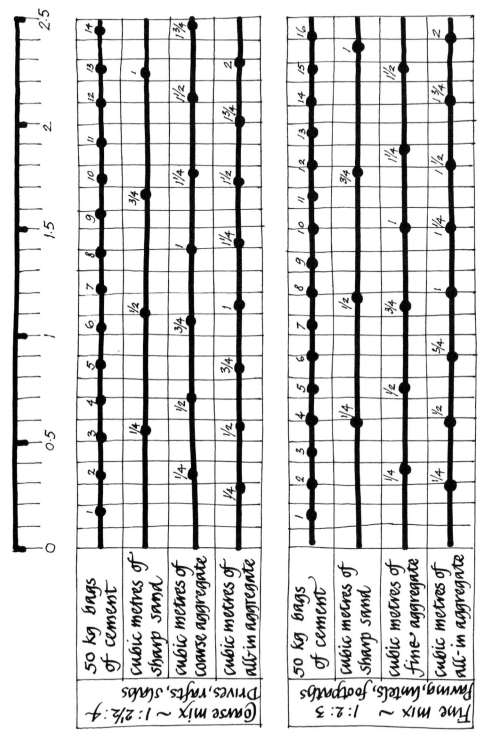

**Fig 2** Quantities of cement, sand and aggregate required for different volumes of concrete

Begin the process by calculating the *volume* of concrete you will need. This may involve making a plan (and possibly other drawings) of what you want to build (*see* Fig 1). Use graph paper or a school exercise book with the paper ruled in somewhat larger squares. Choose a scale such as 1 : 10 (1cm = 10cm) or 1 : 20. Draw everything in pencil first (so that you can make alterations) and then finalise the correct plan in ink.

Calculate the area (you may need to count the squares on the graph paper if you have an awkward curved area) and multiply this by the depth. If you are using metric units, be careful not to misplace a decimal point. As a guide, the average driveway to a house needs about 1.75 cubic metres of concrete. If you arrive at a figure between 1.3 and 2.2 cubic metres, it is likely to be correct; if you come up with a figure of 5.8 or 8.3 cubic metres, you either have a stately home or you need to check your calculations.

Next, choose your mix. The professional engineer who deals with bridges, office blocks and factories may use half a dozen different mixes; you need only know about two. The first, which I call the coarse mix, is used for foundations, drives and floors, and is referred to as a 1 : 2.5 : 4 mix, ie 1 part cement to 2.5 parts sand to 4 parts aggregate. The aggregate should be of the coarse variety (up to 20mm). The same mix can be made from a 1 : 5 mix of 1 part cement to 5 parts all-in mixed coarse aggregate. The second mix, a fine mix, used for paving stones, footpaths and other thinner concrete sections, is made from a 1 : 2 : 3 mix of 1 part cement, 2 parts sand and 3 parts fine aggregate (up to 10mm), or a 1 : 3.75 mix if using all-in fine aggregate. All these proportions are by volume, which is why you will need measuring buckets or boxes at a later stage. However, cement is sold by weight, so you should use the table given in Fig 2 to estimate how much you will need to buy.

To use this table, first find the amount of concrete (by volume) you need in the top line. Run your finger down till you come across the relevant mix, and you will cross the lines showing how much cement, sand and aggregate you need. For instance, for 1.8 cubic metres of coarse mix, you will need about 10.5 bags of cement, 0.8 cubic metres of sand and 1.35 cubic metres of aggregate. Allowing for a little extra and knowing that cement is sold in 50kg bags and that sand and aggregate are delivered in multiples of 0.25 cubic metres, you can now order 11 bags of cement, 1 cubic metre of sand and 1.5 cubic metres of aggregate. Or you can order 11 bags of cement and 1.75 cubic metres of all-in aggregate.

You can, of course, dispense with all this by ordering ready-mix concrete. It is simply a matter of ringing the local company, asking for a price and a minimum order (important) and arranging a delivery date and time. However, be warned — few companies will deliver much less than 3 or 4 cubic metres, which is usually enough for a 13 or 15 metre long drive. If you do need that much concrete it might be well worth while using ready-mix, especially if the alternative means paying for the hire of a mixer and a lot of extra work.

If you are going to mix your own concrete by hand, this is how to make a small quantity. Find a level space that can be washed down afterwards, eg a concrete path or yard. Alternatively, use a piece of hardwood, plywood or blockwood (although you will not be able to use this for anything else afterwards). Collect together three or more same-sized buckets, a shovel and, of course, water, cement, sand and aggregate.

Begin by cleaning up your mixing area. Run a hose over it, scrub it with a hard broom until it is clean — impurities always weaken

**Fig 3** Cement, sand and aggregate measured out onto the mixing area in separate buckets. They are mixed thoroughly with a shovel

Mixing the dry materials, adding water to the crater, and the final concrete mix. The mixture is just right – quite smooth but without any watery cement oozing to the surface

the mix. Now measure out each ingredient, using a separate bucket for each material (Fig 3). For a quantity to be mixed by hand, start with a bucket of cement and the appropriate number of buckets of sand and aggregate to suit the mix. Heap them out on the mixing area, and turn them over two or three times with the shovel to make an evenly grey heap. In the middle of the heap, make a crater, pour in about half a bucket of water (Fig 4), and start mixing the water into the heap without letting any water escape. The best method is to use the shovel to push the walls of the crater into the puddle in the middle (Fig 5).

When the heap is uniformly moist, but still not plastic, make a fresh crater, and add a little more water — about one-quarter of the bucket or a little less. Mix as before to obtain a nice plastic mixture — too soft, and the cement will wander off with the water; too hard, and you will not be able to push the concrete into shape. After mixing it as well as you can, turn it over and mix it again; as a final gesture, chop the shovel into the mixture at 30mm intervals, as if you were chopping it into slices.

Remember, it is easier to add a little water (using a plastic squeezy bottle) if the mixture is too dry, than to add more sand, cement and aggregate in the right proportions if it is all too wet. As a guide, pull the shovel over the mixture and press it in as you go to form a series of ridges. If the ridges fill in with a cement slurry quite quickly, the mixture is just right; if they fill in with a watery mix or even disappear, the mixture is too wet; if they do not fill up at all, the mixture is too dry.

Hand mixing is heavy work, and should be left for very small jobs — a small pond or bedding stones around it, a base for a barbecue or sundial. The moment you want to do more than that, you should hire a mixer. Using a mixer is very simple. It will probably be an electric one; plug the machine into a power socket or the socket of an extension lead, and make sure that the cable is not going to be in the way. Run it overhead by way of trees, clothes line or whatever; do not let it trail on the ground where it might be damaged and cause problems.

**Fig 4** Water is poured into a crater made in the middle of the heap

Start the machine running, and shovel in about half the required sand and aggregate. Add about half the water needed, and let it stir about for a minute. Now add all the cement and the rest of the aggregate and sand. Continue mixing, and gradually add the remainder of the water, checking as you go that you are not adding too much. Finally, leave the machine running another minute or two, and tip the drum out over a wheelbarrow. The machine is now ready for the next load. The machine works at its most efficient if there are two people (or more); one mixes and the other transports the concrete to the site and pours.

When you take a break of half an hour or more, throw in a couple of buckets of aggregate only, and let it turn around for about five minutes. Add water and let it run for another minute. Tip out the aggregate, and run a hose over the pile to wash away particles of partly dried cement. Never leave this cleaning up process for 'later'; cleaning out partly dried cement is very hard and difficult. The same applies to wheelbarrows, shovels, buckets and anything else that is dirtied by cement.

For very small jobs, it is often sufficient to carry the mixed concrete in a bucket (be warned — an ordinary plastic household

**Fig 5** Mixing the water in the heap without letting any water escape

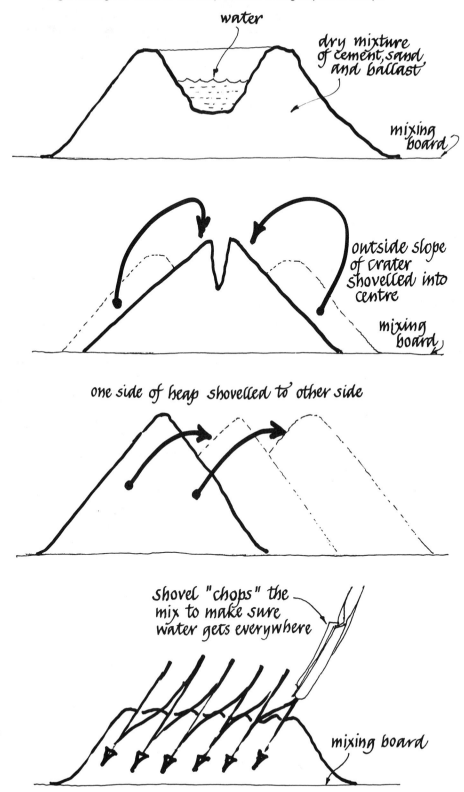

water

dry mixture of cement, sand and ballast

mixing board

outside slope of crater shovelled into centre

mixing board

one side of heap shovelled to other side

Shovel "chops" the mix to make sure water gets everywhere

mixing board

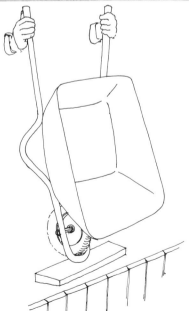

Fig 6 Use a plank as a ramp, if necessary, to tip the cement from the wheelbarrow straight into the mould

Arrange the mixer and materials to cut down wasted motion

bucket filled with cement weighs about 35kg). Most jobs, however, will require the use of a wheelbarrow. If you are using a concrete mixer, it is simple enough (usually) to stand the wheelbarrow under the mixer and tip the concrete into the wheelbarrow. If you are shovelling hand-mixed concrete into a wheelbarrow, you will find it easier to hold the shovel by the neck (very near the blade) with your left hand.

At the site, tip the contents of the wheelbarrow straight into the form or mould, if at all possible. Most wheelbarrows have a bent tube 'nose' in front of the wheel. Try to rest this 'nose' on a plank when you tip the barrow (Fig 6). If necessary, lay a plank as a ramp so that you can push the barrow right to the edge of the mould and tip in the concrete — rather than shovelling it out. Always try to save yourself work.

15

# 2 Mass Concrete

A mass concrete slab is usually laid for: a raft foundation; a solid floor to an existing room; a strip foundation for a brick wall; a driveway; a garden path. The first three items require the scrutiny and approval of the local building inspector. Before you start digging, go to see him or his assistant at your local council offices. If you are building a small conservatory, a garden shed or a garage, it is unlikely that he will want to see proper drawings. Usually an hour's discussion, during which you make a few notes of his requirements, will be quite sufficient. If you are thinking of building a home extension you may require the services of a draughtsman; if the inspector cannot recommend anyone, search the advertisement columns of the local papers for a 'building technician' or similar.

The building inspector will tell you the minimum size of the foundation, the thickness of the concrete required and a few other

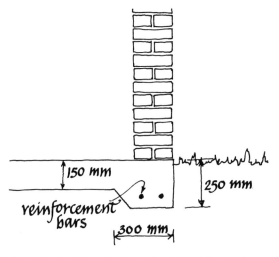

**Fig 8** Section through edge of typical raft foundation

details. As a general guide, a strip foundation will usually be sunk some 700–800mm below finished ground level, its width will be three times the thickness of the wall and its depth the same as the thickness of the wall (Fig 7). Most rafts (the ground floor slab of a garage or other small building) will be between 100 and 150mm thick (Fig 8). It is not possible to be more precise as it all depends on what you are building and on the views of the building inspector. Generally speaking, inspectors like everything to be solid; it is their responsibility if something falls down after they have approved it. If you feel strongly that the inspector's requirements spoil the appearance of the building, you will have to engage the services of an architect, surveyor or engineer — an expensive measure for a small extension.

## Clearing the site

The inspector will ask you to clear the site. By that, he means not merely removing odd bits of stone, bottles and bicycle frames, but stripping the top soil to a depth of about

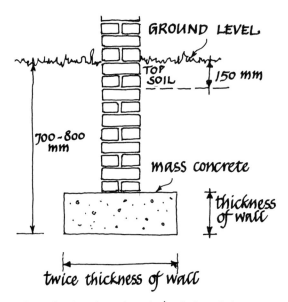

**Fig 7** Section through typical strip foundation to a brick wall

150mm. This stops plants growing through the concrete and cracking the foundations. In fact, if you suspect that any tree roots are growing under the planned site of the slab, it is wise to dig these out and remove them. It is much cheaper to do this now than later. Keep the top soil, once it is removed; it is valuable garden soil and could well be used elsewhere in your garden or your neighbour's.

For rafts and drives, remove enough soil over the entire area to accommodate the required depth of concrete plus whatever thickness of hardcore or rubble is needed. The rubble will be what is called 'clean selected' which means bits of old brick without any plaster attached (important), stones, chopped-up bicycle frames and anything else that is hard and strong. The total thickness of rubble and slab may be about 150–200mm; your building inspector will tell you the exact thickness. For foundations, the removal of top soil is only the beginning; how far down you must dig is discussed later (*see* p 23).

Once you have a clear site stripped over the total area of the foundation or slab, plus an extra 300mm all round, you can start marking out.

## Marking out

Begin by setting a datum peg at a convenient point near to but outside the foundation or slab area. The datum peg is a piece of 50mm square softwood batten pointed at one end. It is driven into the ground using a wooden mallet, if possible; if you have a metal hammer, use an off-cut between hammer and peg to cushion the shock and prevent the peg splintering or splitting.

When the peg is firmly driven into the ground, mark on it the level of the finished slab or a level which is a convenient distance above the top of the foundation. The convenient distance could be a multiple of 76mm (a brick course height) such as 912mm (12 brick courses). If this level is to be related to the floor level of your house, you may have to involve yourself with some long battens and a spirit level before you get it all correct (*see* Fig 9). The datum peg should be driven into the ground fairly near the house, and a long batten positioned with one end resting on the existing floor while the other end is held against the side of the datum peg. A spirit level is laid along the batten, and when

**Fig 9** Setting a datum peg

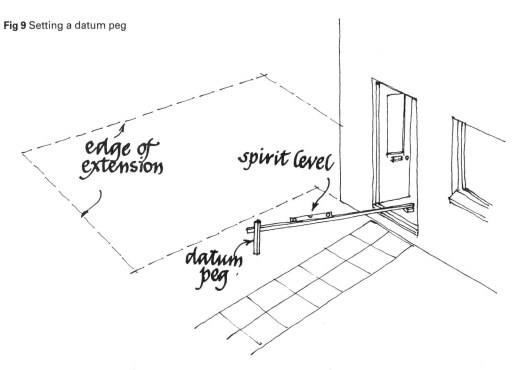

edge of extension

spirit level

datum peg

**Fig 10** Establishing datum level related to the existing floor of a house

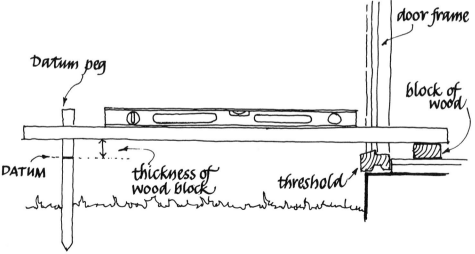

this indicates that the batten is perfectly horizontal, the datum peg can be marked (*see* Fig 10).

When the datum line is established, saw the peg off at this point so that the top of the peg is the datum. Take your time over establishing this datum; all vertical measurements will relate to it and a mistake now can lead to a lot of problems later on.

The datum peg is the basis for all vertical measurements; for horizontal measurements two main methods are used:

(1) *Pegs and twine:* the simpler method, suitable for rafts, drives, garden walls and simple structures like the barbecue shown in Project 3.

(2) *Profile boards:* more accurate, but more fiddly; use this method if you are building a home extension or load-bearing brick walls on a strip foundation.

*Pegs and twine*

Using long lengths of twine with a peg at each end, establish the base line of the wall or slab. The base line will be a line well outside the work area (to avoid it being trampled on) that relates easily to an existing feature as well as to the new structure. For instance, the base line might be taken as a line parallel to the kerb if you are building a garage (Fig 11*a*) or parallel to the wall of the house if you are building a home extension (Fig 11*b*). It will

be helpful to have two people to hold the pegs at each end of the line while you use the tape measure. Keep the line taut at all times and drive in the pegs when the line is accurately set. Each peg should be driven in about 1 metre beyond the planned corner of the slab (or end of the wall).

Next, set out the building lines. These are the lines that mark the actual position of the wall or slab. If you are building a garden wall you will need a single line, parallel to the base line, to mark one face (or the other) of the wall. If you are building a garage, outhouse or even a drive, you will first need building lines at right-angles to the base line.

To mark out a right-angle, either use a builder's square (*see* Chapter 9) or measure out a 3 : 4 : 5 triangle (or any triangle with the same proportions) as follows (Fig 12). Drive in a peg (Peg A) somewhere along the base line; when it sits firmly in the ground, knock a nail into the top directly next to (or even through) the twine of the base line. Then drive a second peg (Peg B) into the ground 3 metres further along the base line. Again, knock a nail into the top, and make sure that the distance between the nails is exactly 3 metres. Take a third peg (Peg C) and drive a nail into its top before the peg is hammered into the ground. Two pieces of string, one exactly 4 metres and the other exactly 5 metres long, are tied between the third peg and the first and second pegs. Move

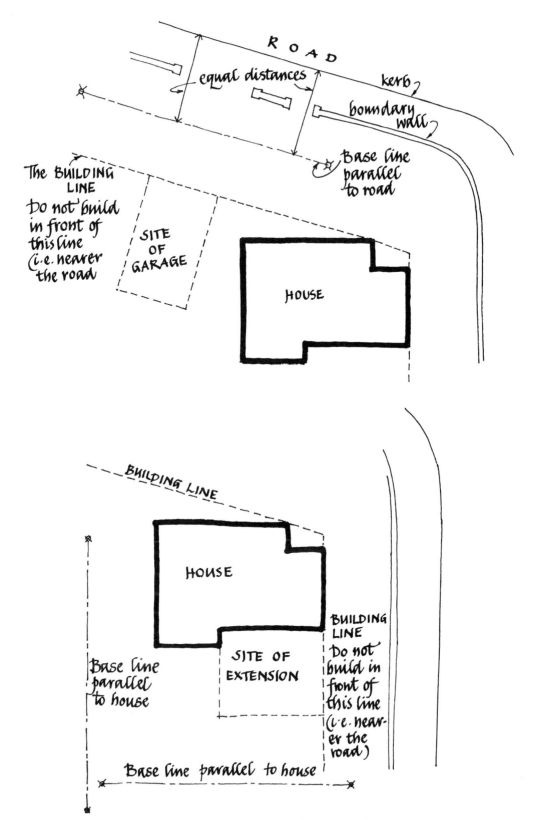

**Fig 11** Setting out baselines and building lines for (*a*) a garage and (*b*) an extension

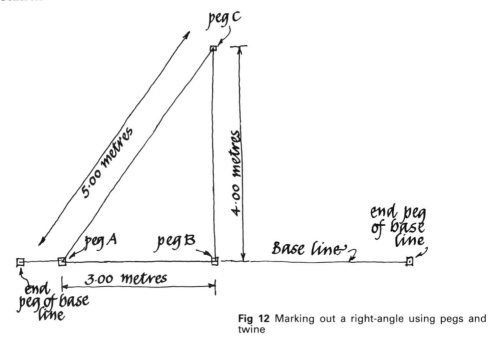

Fig 12 Marking out a right-angle using pegs and twine

Fig 13 Marking out a right-angle: the third peg (Peg C) is moved until the strings are taut

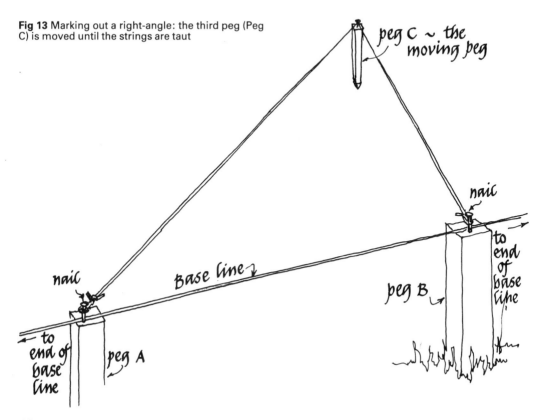

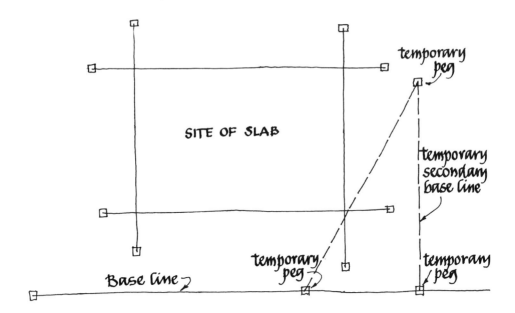

**Fig 14** Setting out building lines for a slab foundation

the third peg to such a point that both strings are taut, and then hammer it into the ground (Fig 13). The 4 metre long string will be at right-angles to the base line if your measurements are correct.

This line at right-angles can be used as a building line or as a secondary base line. From now on it is easy to lay all the building lines by measuring carefully and driving in further pegs and twine. Make sure that each peg is driven into the ground about 1 metre beyond the planned end of the wall or corner of the slab (Fig 14).

If you are laying a slab, you will have completed the marking out. If you are laying the foundation to a wall, you will need to go on to lay lines to mark the inner face of the wall, the outer line of the foundation and the inner line of the foundation. You should finish up with six lines to each wall — four along the length (two lines to mark the thickness of the brickwork and two lines to mark the width of the concrete foundation) and two to mark the ends (*see* Fig 15).

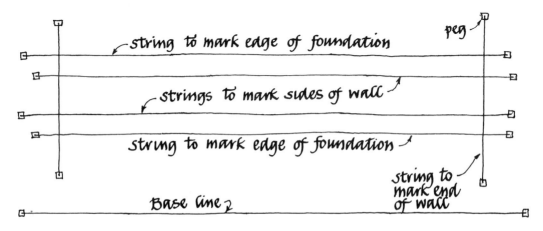

**Fig 15** Setting out building lines for a wall on a foundation

## Mass Concrete

**Fig 16** Profile boards to mark a wall

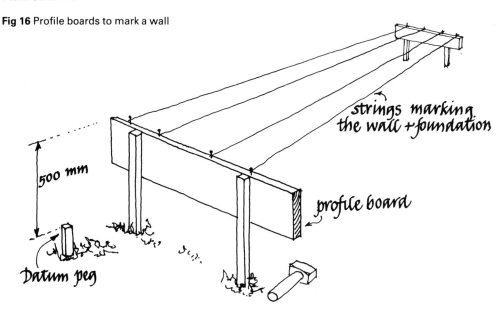

strings marking
the wall + foundation

profile board

500 mm

Datum peg

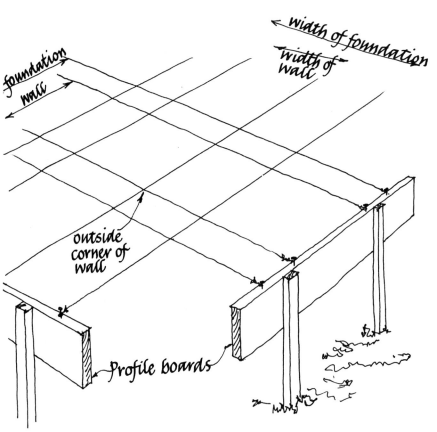

width of foundation

width of
wall

foundation

wall

outside
corner of
wall

Profile boards

**Fig 17** Profile boards to mark a corner in brickwork

22

## Profile boards

Building lines just above the ground are liable to be trodden on, tripped over or broken by spades or other tools. Official building practice is therefore to run these four lengths of string over 'profile boards'. These are 800mm lengths of softwood board nailed to two stout posts driven into the ground about 1 metre beyond the corner or end of the wall. Two profile boards are needed for each length of wall; the strings run parallel to each other between the profile boards, marking out the wall and foundation some 200–300mm up in the air (Figs 16 and 17).

The profile boards are put up before the building lines are laid out. No pegs and twine are needed; the two people holding the ends of the line keep it taut while you hammer in a nail on top of the profile board around which the line is wound and knotted.

To be really professional the top of the profile board should relate to the datum, and the top of each profile board should be level with the others. This allows you to set the level of the foundation using boning rods (*see* Chapter 9).

Profile boards prevent the twine lying on the ground and becoming dirty, frayed or even broken. However, if you are careful, you may omit the profile boards. They are a lot of extra work, and not really necessary for small jobs.

## Strip foundations

Strip foundations need to be laid quite deep to avoid soil movement disturbing the stability of the brickwork. For a garden wall not more than 1.5 metres high, a depth of 400mm is usually quite sufficient; but if the wall is part of a home extension, the foundation will have to go down some 700 or 800mm. A spade (not a shovel) and a fork are usually sufficient for digging out the trench. If the going gets harder, a pick-axe or mattock may be required, or a pneumatic drill for really rocky soil. The concrete footing will usually be about 450mm wide (Fig 18), but you will need to dig a wider trench — 600mm is stan-

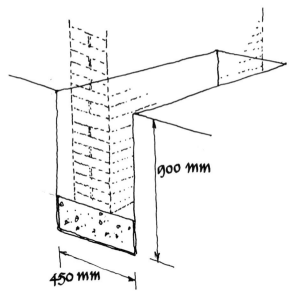

**Fig 18** Trench for strip foundation left by a machine excavation

dard — to allow you room to swing the spade and later to build the wall (Fig 19).

However you excavate, you will need to remove the spoil. If money is no object, hire a skip for a week or two. As you pay not only for each skipload but also for the length of time it stands outside your house, it is worth while trying to get a skipload (4.5 or 6.5 cubic metres) dug out at a time. Alternatively, if you are digging up fertile soil, you may well find someone in your area willing to take it away at no cost to yourself. I have heard of cases where a company took the soil and sent a bulldozer along to speed up the excavation! However, remember that although to clear the space for a foundation you will need to dig out about 5 or 6 cubic metres for a 10 metre wall, a lot of this will be used for backfill later; you will only have to remove about 2 cubic metres permanently.

Dig the trench down to roughly the level of the top of the strip foundation. You now have to set the first trench peg; this is similar to the datum peg, but some 700–800mm lower. The peg is driven into the ground somewhere along the trench where you are going to pour the concrete, near to the datum peg if possible. The top of the trench peg will mark the top of the concrete foundation.

**Fig 19** Trench for strip foundation for DIY footings

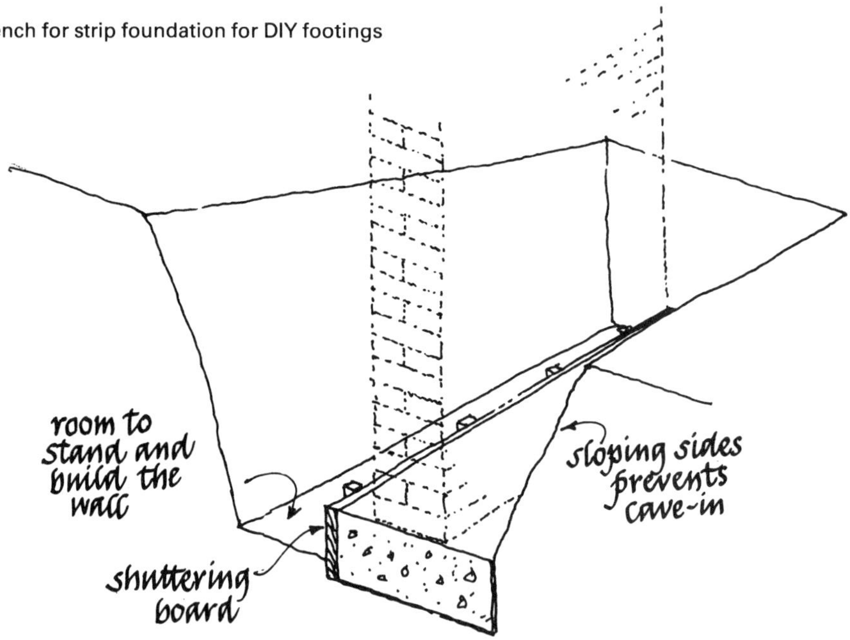

*room to stand and build the wall*

*shuttering board*

*sloping sides prevents cave-in*

There are two methods of establishing the trench peg datum:

(1) If you are using profile boards (Fig 20), mark off the required vertical distance between the top of the foundation and the top of the profile board on a softwood batten; this batten is called a 'boning rod'. Get an assistant to hold the rod upright with one end resting on the trench peg. Sight along the two profile boards marking the length of the wall; you can see the top end of the boning rod or an appropriate mark on it and thus determine whether the peg needs to go in further or has been hammered in too deep.

(2) If you are using pegs and twine to mark out your building lines, you will need to use battens and a spirit level (Fig 21). A long batten is rested at one end on the datum peg, while the other end is held in the air above the position of the trench peg. The spirit level rests on this horizontal batten. When the batten is exactly level, the vertical distance between the top of the datum peg and the top of the trench peg can be measured with an ordinary tape measure or a batten cut to length.

Whichever method is used, the exact level of the top of the foundation should be marked off. Again, the peg is driven into the ground to the exact depth or sawn off at this point. Further pegs are similarly set along the trench at 2 metre intervals.

If you come up against a pipe (and this applies especially to drainage pipes) take care in digging around and underneath it not to disturb it more than is necessary. Inform the building inspector, and he will tell you what steps to take to deal with the pipe. It is important to make sure that none of the weight of the new wall and foundation rests on the pipe. At the concreting stage, this means that the trench is stopped off either side of the pipe. When the brickwork is being built up, a pre-cast concrete lintel is laid over the pipe; each end of the lintel rests on brickwork which rests in turn on the concrete footing (Fig 22).

If the soil you are digging is very loose, it may threaten to cave in as you dig down. Officially you should use boards to form a retaining wall but, unless you are cramped for space, it makes better sense to dig your trench with slanting walls (*see* Fig 19). This saves the cost of boards, and the extra digging needed is more or less balanced by the

**Fig 20** Setting the first trench peg using a boning rod

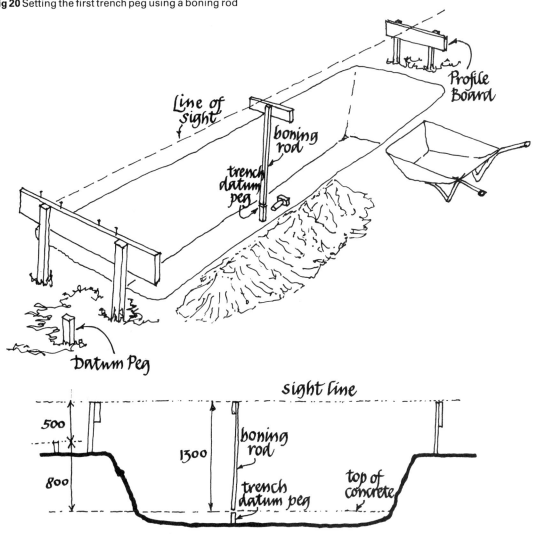

Line of sight

boning rod

trench datum peg

Profile Board

Datum Peg

sight line

500

1300

800

boning rod

trench datum peg

top of concrete

**Fig 21** Setting a trench peg using datum peg only

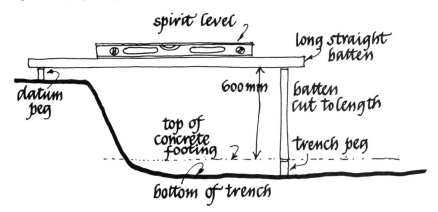

spirit level

long straight batten

600 mm

batten cut to length

datum peg

top of concrete footing

trench peg

bottom of trench

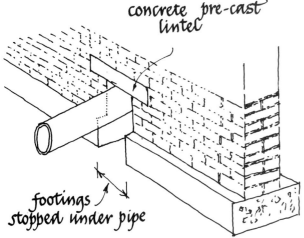

concrete pre-cast
lintel

footings
stopped under pipe

Fig 22 Lintel over existing pipe/drain in footings

extra work that putting up shoring would necessitate.

The side of the trench which lies immediately beneath one of the setting-out strings will act as shuttering to one side of the trench (*see* Fig 19); take care to leave this side clean and undisturbed. The near side of the trench, where you have been working from, will need a little more in the way of shuttering. An old floor board is generally used. The board is half-dug, half-driven into the ground so that the top edge of the board is level with the trench pegs. Check this with a spirit level. The outside of the board (not the side in

which the concrete is to be poured) is supported by pegs driven into the ground. For extra stability, the shuttering board is nailed to these pegs.

Now is the time to contact the building inspector, and invite him to visit the site. Ask him to come along about 10 o'clock in the morning. You will need to get up much earlier, however, to check the weather, since foundations cannot be poured if there is any chance of the bottom of the trench getting wet. Digging out the last bit of the trench should not be done more than a few hours before pouring the concrete.

If the day looks fine, dig out the last 70–80mm of the trench before the inspector arrives, taking care not to disturb the trench pegs or shuttering board. If the soil is very soft or wet, you will need to put down hardcore (old bricks and stones compacted with a rammer, *see* Chapter 9). A depth of about 50–60mm is sufficient.

A strip foundation for a 10 metre garden wall will need about 1 cubic metre of coarse mix concrete (*see* p 11). This is too small a quantity for ready-mix, but too great for hand mixing; so you will need a small electric mixer. If you use a large plastic bucket as the basic measurement, you will finish up with about 6 buckets of concrete per batch — a convenient wheelbarrow load. Run the wheelbarrow from mixer to foundation along

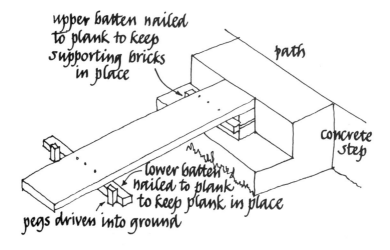

upper batten nailed
to plank to keep
supporting bricks
in place

path

concrete
step

lower batten
nailed to plank
to keep plank in place

pegs driven into ground

Fig 23 Wheelbarrow ramp up steps

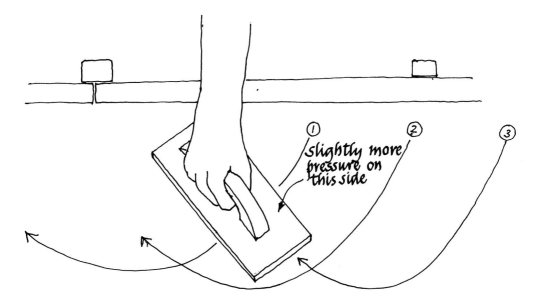

slightly more pressure on this side

Fig 24 Using a wooden float on fresh concrete

timber boards, especially if you have to cross a grass lawn or other delicate ground. Use planks as ramps to go up or down steps (Fig 23), and tip the wheelbarrow directly into the trench, using a small block of wood as a fulcrum (*see* Figure 6).

One person should mix and transport the concrete; another could be in the trench prodding the concrete into place with an old broom-handle. Try not to push the concrete too far from where it falls; the further it is pushed, the greater the chance that the solids and cement will separate, resulting in concrete which is leached of cement in places and therefore weak. Nevertheless, make sure that the concrete does go into all the nooks and crannies.

When the concrete is more or less level with the trench pegs, use a very small tamping board (*see* Chapter 9) to tamp the concrete level. One end of the tamping board rests on the trench peg, the other travels along the shuttering board. Once the concrete is roughly level, use a wooden float to smooth the surface.

The float is not difficult to use, once the concrete has been levelled with the tamping board. Hold the float in your right hand, and put it down flat onto the concrete to the left of your body. Then sweep it in a curve to the right, holding it down firmly onto the con-

crete at all times, with a little more pressure on the trailing edge than on the leading edge (Fig 24). You will be surprised to see that the float does most of the work. Try not to go over any part of the concrete twice: this brings up the cement and weakens the concrete.

As each length of the trench is filled with concrete, tamped and levelled, the trench pegs should be pulled out. This can be quite a difficult operation, which is often conveniently glossed over. I tackle it by taking precautions beforehand. Each peg, after being hammered into place, has a hole drilled into the top into which a stout coach screw is driven. The coach screw is then removed, and used on the next peg, and so on till all the trench pegs have a screw hole in the top. A piece of mild steel, about 250 × 30mm is bent into the form of a handle (Fig 25) and welded to a coach screw (you may have to get someone at a garage to do this). When a peg is to be pulled out, the coach screw is turned by the handle into the top of the peg, which can then be wiggled and pulled clear. The hole is then filled with a little extra concrete and smoothed flat with the wooden float.

When all the concrete for the footing has been poured, tamped and floated, cover it with polythene sheeting (sold in 6 metre or 9 metre wide rolls). In very cold weather, lay old blankets, hay or other insulating material on top of the polythene to prevent the water inside the concrete freezing; ice crystals disrupt the setting of the concrete. In hot weather, it may be necessary to sprinkle the concrete foundation with a watering can once every other day to prevent over-rapid drying out. After two or three days the shuttering board and pegs can be removed, and at the end of a week the concrete is strong enough to take a moderate amount of brickwork.

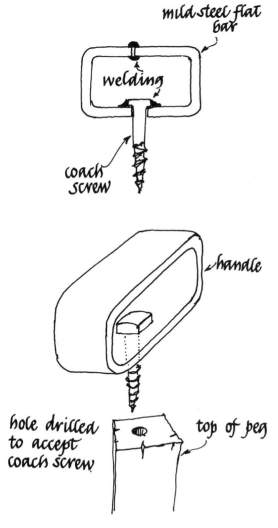

**Fig 25** Coach screw and handle to pull up trench pegs

## Rafts and slabs

There are two main types of slab foundation:

(1) The straightforward floor slab, where the slab only takes the weight of people and furniture.

(2) The raft slab, where the slab also takes the weight of the surrounding walls.

The first type is usually cast to replace a worn or badly laid concrete or suspended timber floor in an existing room. The floor does not need to take a lot of weight, and the weight is evenly distributed over the whole area. Settlement of the ground which takes place when walls are built on top of a strip foundation will have taken place long ago. There is therefore no need for reinforcement and, besides the fact that you are working in a fairly confined space, there are no special problems. For a detailed description *see* Project 5.

The raft foundation slab is more interesting. Combining the floor slab and the foundation to the walls provides an economic solution. There is no need to dig out a 700–800mm trench and build upwards, the shuttering is much simpler and you will need less in the way of materials.

If the raft slab is to be used for a structure, you will have to discuss the project with the local building inspector, who will tell you what thickness of concrete and what reinforcement he requires. By and large, if you are not building more than one storey, and the ground is not clay, you will need a 100mm thick raft with edges that are 200–250mm deep over a strip about 300–350mm wide. These thickened edges act as a ring beam to stiffen the whole raft (Fig 26).

In theory, the raft slab 'floats' on the soft and slowly moving soil; as the load is spread, there are no great pressures anywhere and so the whole structure can be kept light. To help the concrete distribute the load, nominal mesh reinforcement will be needed over most of the area, and possibly a few 100mm diameter mild steel bars near the edges. None of this is really complicated.

Mark out the site as already described (*see* p 17), and clear it to a depth of at least 150mm, digging a 300mm strip near the edges

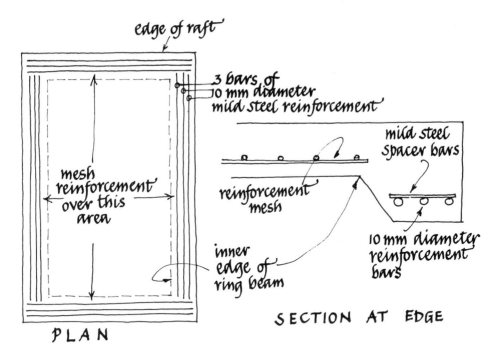

edge of raft

3 bars of
10 mm diameter
mild steel reinforcement

mesh
reinforcement
over this
area

mild steel
spacer bars

reinforcement
mesh

inner
edge of
ring beam

10 mm diameter
reinforcement
bars

SECTION AT EDGE

PLAN

to a depth of 250mm; this will form the ring beam. Cover the whole area with a layer of compacted hardcore about 50–60mm deep, and cover this in turn with sand to form an even surface with no hardcore corners protruding. Lay polythene sheeting over the sand to form a damp proof membrane (DPM) to stop damp rising through the concrete.

Use old softwood floor boards to form the shuttering all around the edges; the boards

**Fig 26** Raft foundation slab showing ring beam and reinforcement

are nailed to and held in place by pegs driven into the ground. If any part of the floor is more than about 2.5 metres wide, divide the floor into bays using softwood shuttering boards. Take care to make sure that the tops of the shuttering boards are horizontal and level with the top of the datum peg.

The reinforcement mesh is made of 5 or 6mm steel rod welded at 100mm intervals to

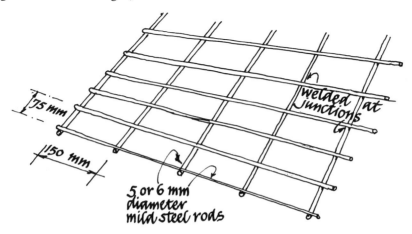

75 mm

150 mm

welded at
junctions

5 or 6 mm
diameter
mild steel rods

**Fig 27** Detail of reinforcement mesh

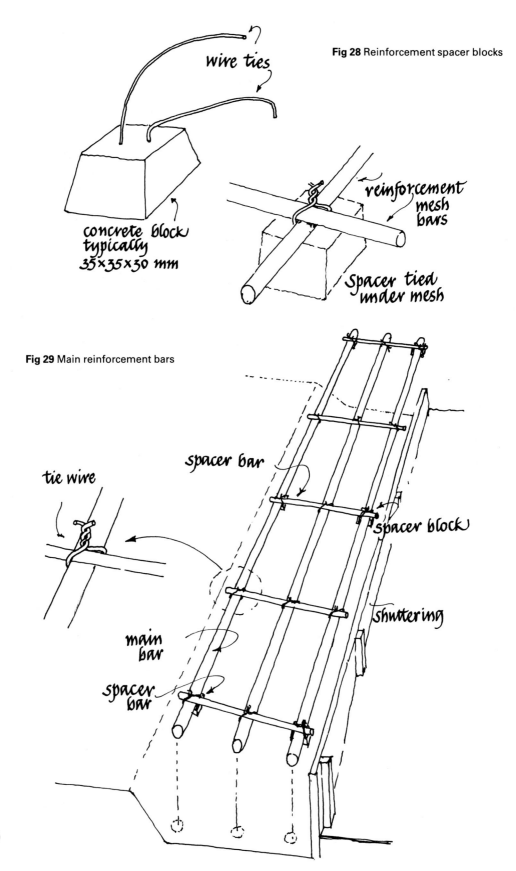

wire ties

**Fig 28** Reinforcement spacer blocks

concrete block
typically
35×35×30 mm

reinforcement
mesh
bars

Spacer tied
under mesh

**Fig 29** Main reinforcement bars

spacer bar

tie wire

spacer block

shuttering

main
bar

spacer
bar

form a grid (Fig 27). It can be cut using special cutters (which you will have to hire). The mesh should cover the whole area of the raft, and be suspended some 25mm above the ground. On a professional building site this is done with special concrete blocks called 'spacers' (Fig 28), which have wires to which the mesh is tied. It is almost as easy, and much cheaper, to drive a few large nails into the shuttering at the sides to hold up the edges of the mesh and lay a few brickbats under the mesh at about 600mm intervals. (Drive the nails in from the outside — the shuttering boards together with the nails can be prised off the concrete.)

If the building inspector requires extra reinforcement at the edges, this will have to be wired into place. Make up a grid with 10mm diameter mild steel reinforcement bars held some 40–50mm apart by wiring them at 1.5 metre intervals to steel cross-bars. The completed grid again rests on spacers or brickbats (Fig 29).

The concrete (use a coarse mix) is poured and poked into place with a broom-handle and then topped up and 'chopped' down using a tamping board (*see* Chapter 9). Make sure the concrete flows through the mesh reinforcement and fills up the space beneath; you will need to poke it around a little with an old broom-handle. Only when all the space below the mesh is filled should you top up.

After tamping the concrete into place, use a 75 × 40mm softwood batten to 'saw' the concrete floor as smooth as possible, and finish off with a steel float. Take care to use the float once only for each sweep, otherwise you will bring up too much cement, resulting in a permanently dusty floor.

Each bay should be completed — poured, tamped, sawed and floated — before starting on the next bay. As soon as a 300mm wide stroke of concrete has been poured into the next bay, the intervening temporary shuttering board (and pegs) can be pulled out.

The concrete is cured in the usual way using polythene sheeting and/or insulating materials, depending on the weather. The shuttering is taken away after a few days. Do not start building the brickwork for a week or ten days after pouring.

Using a tamping board

## Drives and paths

The driveway to your garage will have to be thick enough to take the weight of your car, which generally means a thickness of about 90–100mm concrete. However, if you are thinking of owning a heavy car or a small van, it is probably a good idea to use nominal mesh reinforcement over the whole area. Use a coarse concrete (*see* p 11). The surface of the drive should be fairly rough to allow the car's tyres to grip the surface in icy weather. The surface should also slope a little to stop puddles forming when it rains. Finally, and something that is often neglected, there should be no more than about 4 metres of continuous concrete without a movement joint.

Clear the site in the usual way, and put down hardcore if necessary. Using 150 × 25mm second-hand floor boards, form the shuttering to the sides of the drive. If the drive slopes naturally up to the garage, there is no need to build in a drainage gradient; if it does not slope, then the board on one side will have to be some 40mm higher than on the other side; aim at a slope of 1 in 6 or so.

**Making a concrete garden path:**
Setting the shuttering

In the path illustrated, a softwood lath is used to form the bays and is left permanently in place

Finishing the surface with a tamping board

Damp sacking being used to cure the concrete

A well-laid concrete path should remain weed and maintenance free all of its life

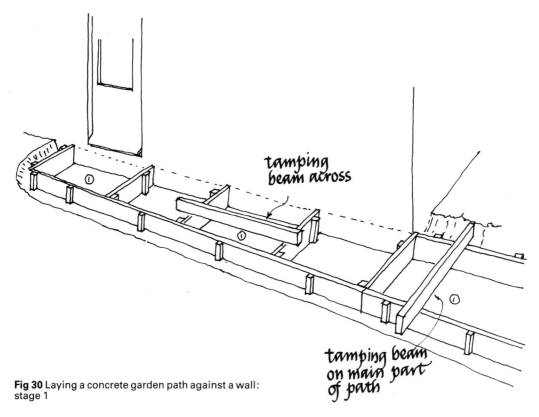

tamping
beam across

tamping beam
on main part
of path

**Fig 30** Laying a concrete garden path against a wall:
stage 1

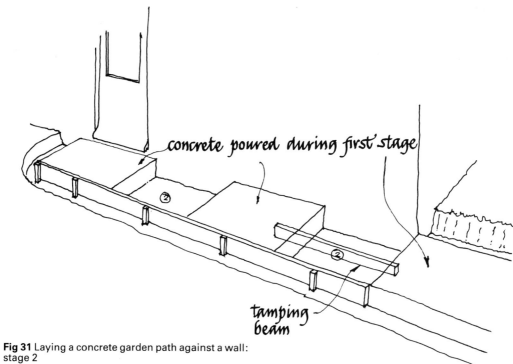

concrete poured during first stage

tamping
beam

**Fig 31** Laying a concrete garden path against a wall:
stage 2

Divide the drive into bays of about 3.0–3.5 metres each. This will allow for:

(1) Temperature movements in the slab as it gets alternatively heated (by day) and cooled (at night). Over twenty years of this treatment, the slab will tend to form weaknesses or even crack.

(2) Soil movements which sometimes take decades to develop. If combined with weaknesses caused by temperature changes, then the concrete slab is almost bound to crack eventually.

The division between bays should be made using 9mm plywood backed temporarily with a 25mm softwood board. The softwood board is taken away when the bays have been filled and smoothed, but the plywood is left and only removed after a few days. Its place is taken by an expanded-polystyrene board the same width as the path but about 15mm thinner than the concrete, to leave a cavity at the top between the two concrete slabs. This space is then filled with mastic sealant.

Finish each bay of the slab with a tamping board. The ridges left by bringing up the tamping board and slapping it down as you go along form a perfect surface for car tyres to grip in wet or icy weather. After casting each slab, cover it in polythene sheeting for the first week or so. (In hot weather, use a watering can to sprinkle the surface every other day; in cold weather, cover with additional insulat-ing materials.) After two days, take away all the shuttering. You can safely walk on the concrete by the end of the week, but leave your car on the road for about three weeks.

Concrete is frequently used for garden paths which are laid against a wall, either a garden wall or a wall of the house. Laying the path itself presents no problems, but laying it next to an existing wall means organising the work a little differently.

Clear the site as usual; strip down all plants and roots to a depth of 150mm. Then ram down a layer of hardcore to finish some 60–70mm below the planned level of the path. Use floor boards nailed to pegs driven into the ground to form the shuttering. The existing wall will act as shuttering on one side, so you will only need one length of softwood shuttering. Nor will you need reinforcement since the path will only need to take the weight of people, a lawn-mower or a wheel-barrow.

The length of the path is divided into bays, each about 1.2 or 1.5 metres long. Using a fine concrete mix (*see* p 11), pour each alternate bay and use the tamping board lengthwise along the path, resting it on the bay divisions (Fig 30). When the concrete has set for a couple of days (or longer), take out the divisions between the bays and pour fresh concrete into the empty bays (Fig 31). Remove the shuttering boards after a week or so. The concrete is cured in the normal way.

# 3 Screeds and Castings

## Screeds

Chapter 2 described how to lay concrete floors, paths and driveways where the final finish is just as the tamping board leaves it. Such a rough surface is exactly right for a driveway, so that car tyres can grip the surface even in wet weather, but it is not suitable for a kitchen. It therefore becomes necessary to lay a screed.

A screed is a layer of concrete (or mortar) which is not designed to have any structural strength but forms a smooth surface which can be swept clean or on which tiles or other covering can be laid. Screeds are usually 30–60mm thick and made from a mixture of cement and sand only. Small aggregate can be added to provide bulk, but it might make the smoothing process more difficult. The usual mix is 1 : 3 or sometimes 1 : 4 of

cement and sharp sand. It is mixed just like concrete, either by hand or, preferably, in a mixer. Since strength is not of great importance, there is not quite the same need to keep the water content as low as possible; nevertheless, try to keep the mixture dry to minimise shrinkage cracks.

Mixing should present few problems, but laying the screed is quite a difficult feat for the beginner since it must be finished perfectly horizontal and flat. Tackle the job by dividing the concrete floor into a number of bays (Fig 32). A room with a floor being screeded should have at least four bays; each one the length of the room, and no wider than about 1 metre. The edges of each bay are marked by timber battens of exactly the same height, when laid on the floor, as the desired screed. The edges of bays next to walls should be marked by a batten about 150–200mm away from the wall. The battens

**Fig 32** Dividing a room into bays ready for screeding

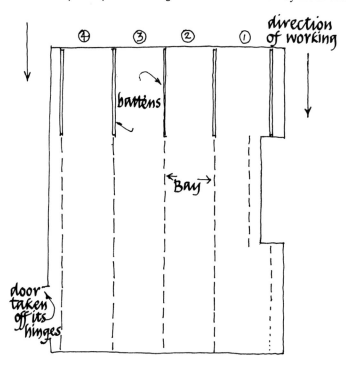

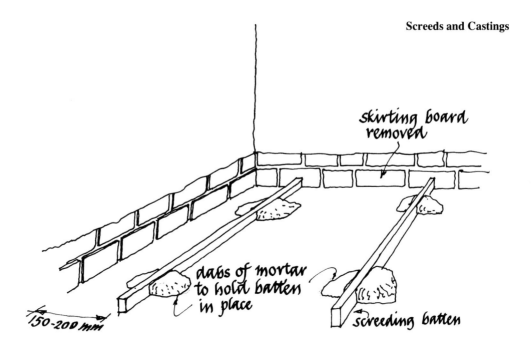

*skirting board removed*

*dabs of mortar to hold battens in place*

*150-200 mm*

*screeding batten*

should be short lengths of about 1.5–2.0 metres so that they can be pulled up out of the screed and the gap made good without having to walk on the wet screed.

There are two ways to keep the battens in place during the screeding process. One way is to nail them down into the concrete using masonry nails. This keeps the battens very firmly in place but a masonry nail can be awkward to get in, and it can damage plastic DPM sheeting (*see* p 41). Alternatively, the battens can be held in place by dabbing a little of the screed mix to each side at two or three intervals along their length just before you start screeding a bay (Fig 33). This avoids using masonry nails, but makes the screeding process a little messy.

Lay the battens on the floor roughly in the right position, and lay a levelling batten (*see* p 135) at right-angles across the battens to each side of a bay. Use a spirit level to check that the levelling batten is horizontal. Obviously, the levelling batten must be reasonably straight. To check the straightness of a board or batten, place it on the floor and draw a pencil line along its length. Turn over the batten or board and draw a second pencil line starting and finishing at the same points as the original line. There will be a gap between the two lines if the plank (or board) is not straight.

**Fig 33** Screeding battens temporarily held in place by dabs of mortar

If the spirit level indicates that two battens are not exactly of the same height, one of the battens will have to be raised. This can be done by nailing small squares of hardboard (use off-cuts) underneath the batten at 150 or 200mm intervals — if the original concrete floor was carelessly laid, this could be quite a long job. However you do it, when finished, all the battens should be exactly level. If you are nailing down your guide battens, this should be done before screeding begins. If you are holding them in place with dabs of screed mix, this is only necessary for the 2 or 3 metres of batten on each side of the section of the bay being filled.

Into each bay pour enough screed mix to fill about a 2 metre section of the bay. Use a wooden float to distribute the screed mix fairly evenly and a levelling batten (*see* Chapter 9) to 'saw' and move the screed sideways to provide a flat surface. If you have one or two hollows, add some more of the mix and use the levelling batten to smooth away the excess. The first 2 metres of the first bay should now be filled and reasonably flat.

The next step is to smooth the concrete. You will need a steel float and a basin of water large enough to dip the float into hori-

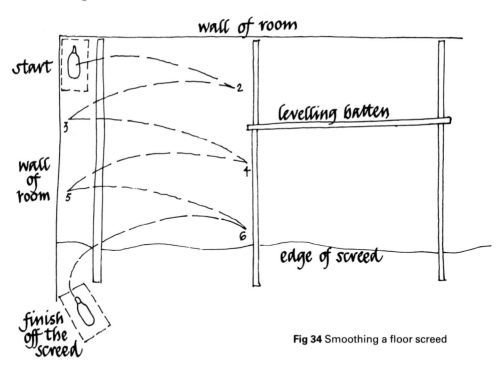

Fig 34 Smoothing a floor screed

**Fig 35** Holding the metal float

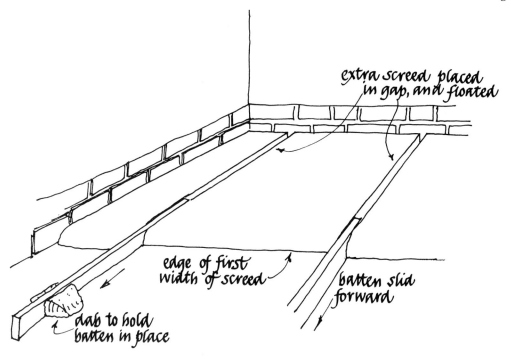

extra screed placed
in gap, and floated

edge of first
width of screed

batten slid
forward

dab to hold
batten in place

Fig 36 Removing battens as screeding proceeds

zontally. Kneel on the unscreeded floor next to the freshly screeded bay, dip the steel float into the water and lay it perfectly flat onto the fresh concrete. Sweep the float in broad arcs from left to right and back (Fig 34), putting very slightly more pressure on the trailing edge, and a fair amount of pressure on the float as a whole (Fig 35). You should find — probably to your own surprise — that the float does the work. Each sweep of the float will leave a whole trail of smooth concrete. Try to avoid smoothing any part of the screed more than once. Each sweep will bring up some of the cement/water part of the screed (leaving the sand behind). If too much is brought up, you will be left with a weak(er) floor and a constantly dusty surface.

Continue this action, dipping the float into the basin of water frequently, till eventually the whole screed is smooth. If at this stage anyone manages to leave a footprint in the fresh concrete, simply fill it in with a little fresh mix, use your tamping board to 'saw' off the excess, and re-smooth the area with the float.

Then start on the first 2 metres of the next bay, leaving the holding dabs, but pouring concrete everywhere else in the bay. When the length of batten separating this next bay from the first is held in place by the newly poured mix, then (and only then) take away the batten by sliding it horizontally towards you (ie without lifting it off the floor). Add a little extra screed mix to fill the space left by the batten. Now use the levelling batten to smooth out the new bay, and finish off with the steel float (Figure 36).

When the first 2 metre section of all the bays across the width of the room has been screeded, start on the next 2 metre section, and continue all the way down the length of the room, not forgetting the areas between the walls and battens. The whole area should now be covered with plastic sheeting (or plastic bags overlapping each other) to slow down the drying process and prevent shrinkage cracks. This is especially important in hot weather, when it may be a good idea to take up the plastic after one or two days, sprinkle the whole area with water, and replace the plastic. After a week or so the plastic can be removed. The floor will now be hard enough to walk on, though it takes about a month to reach its full strength.

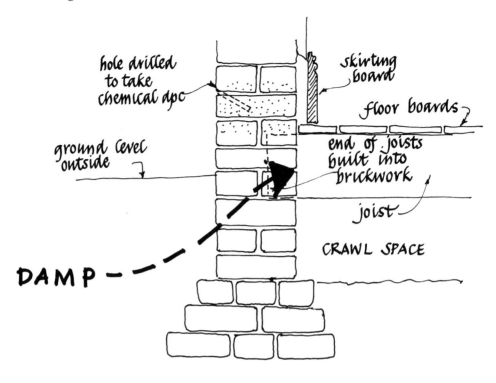

**Fig 37** Damp penetration in suspended timber ground floor

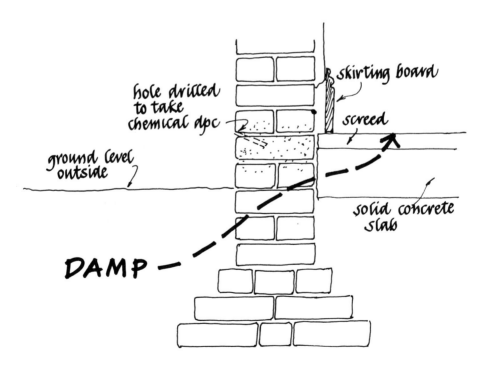

**Fig 38** Damp penetration in solid ground floor

Laying a simple screed is therefore quite straightforward. Unfortunately, screeds are rarely simple, but are complicated by what goes under and on top of them. When you are considering buying an old property, the first thing that any surveyor will do is to test the walls for dampness. Even new houses, if left empty for a few months, will show dampness, so you can expect a negative report and the suggestion that you should put in a damp proof course. The need for a damp proof course (or DPC) is caused by dampness rising from the soil and around the foundations and creeping up into the brickwork (Fig 37). When it has risen above floor level, you can expect damp patches on the plaster. Putting in a DPC in the brickwork stops the damp rising, but it does not prevent damp penetrating the house, especially if you have (or are going to lay) a solid floor (Fig 38). The dampness can quite easily go sideways through the solid concrete floor, bypassing the damp-proofed walls, and then continue on its way. And I have yet to experience a surveyor asking for the equivalent of a DPC to be put in a solid floor other than in a cellar.

If you want to avoid damp in the kitchen, hobby room or whatever, it is therefore important to damp proof the concrete floor by laying down a damp proof membrane (DPM) between the concrete floor and the new screed. This applies to any new solid floor, even if you think damp will not be any problem — it costs so little extra to put in at this stage. If the floor already has a screed, and you do not mind a little less headroom and a step at the entrance, you can damp proof an existing floor by laying down a new screed.

A DPM consists of a large sheet of 'building plastic' (usually sold in sheets of about 6 or 9 metres wide cut to length) which is thick enough not to tear if laid over slightly rough mass concrete. The sheet is laid on the floor before putting down the screeding battens. If you need two sheets to cover the floor, overlap them by about 400mm, fold the edges over twice and tape them down — the weight of the concrete screed will soon keep the fold down permanently.

The edges of the DPM are taken up around the edges of the room, and taped to the wall

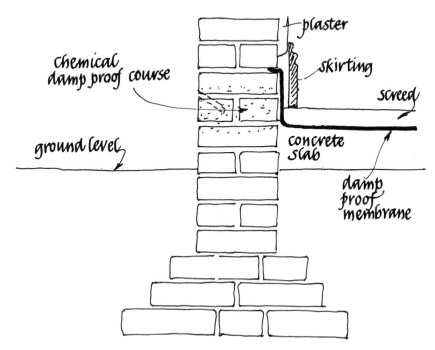

**Fig 39** Continuous damp proof course and damp proof membrane

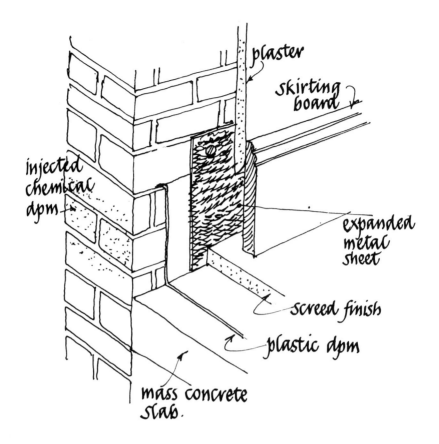

**Fig 40** Joining the damp proof membrane and damp proof course

at least 100mm above the DPC. To do this properly, the plaster on the wall below the level of the DPC should be hacked away so that the DPM is continuous across the floor and up the lowest part of the wall. It can then be tucked into the wall above the DPC (Fig 39).

Obviously, the screeding battens cannot be nailed down or they will penetrate the DPM — you will have to use the dab method. The screed is laid as previously described. When it is finished you will see a nice smooth floor with crinkled black plastic at the edges rising up the bottom 250mm of the walls. This can be covered over by skirting boards — it does not matter if the nails holding the skirting board penetrate the plastic. If you have to go higher than 250mm you may need to fix an expanded metal sheet (Expamet) over the

plastic (*see* Project 5) before finishing the wall in plaster (Fig 40).

The final finish of the floor is the other main consideration to bear in mind when laying a screed. If the floor is to be left bare, finished with a smooth coat of concrete paint or tiled, then finishing is merely a question of making sure that the floor is smooth and level, and that you have not brought up 'laitance' by using the float too much. If you want to finish up with a timber floor, simply leave in the battens used for screeding and nail the floorboards to them. These battens must be protected against rot by painting them with an anti-rot, anti-fungus chemical. Remember that if the battens are being combined with a DPM they cannot be nailed down so you must use the dab method, and you must also make sure that any nails used for nailing down the floor boards are short enough not to pierce the plastic membrane.

**(pages 43–6) Laying a concrete floor to replace a failed suspended-timber floor:**
Positioning the DPM

Tamping the concrete

Placing the last of the slab concrete from the doorway

Placing the screeding mix

Tamping the screed

Finishing with a steel float

Polythene sheeting being laid to cure the completed floor

# Casting concrete

Most of the work done around the house using concrete is for slabs, foundations, drives etc. However, concrete is a plastic material and lends itself to casting. It is merely a matter of making the original mould. This is useful for items like paving stones and lintels. (I am not concerned here with copies of Michelangelo's *David* to stand at the foot of your garden!) This might seem rather dull and, at first glance, totally unnecessary. After all, you can buy a great variety of ready-made paving stones and lintels — why bother making them? Yet a lot of satisfaction can be derived from making your own and, however great the variety, there are times when you need something special — in an unusual size perhaps — which you will be able to make exactly to order.

To begin with simple paving stones, they can be made to any size to suit your requirements. This will save you having to cut them to fit paths of an odd width or to turn an awkward corner — just measure carefully and cast. The mould for a rectangular paving stone is simplicity itself. For the standard size, you need four pieces of 50 × 25mm softwood batten, but vary this to suit your needs. Coat the battens with an anti-rot paint and join them together with a simple butt joint held by nails, screws or a metal plate at two opposite corners, a hinge at the third corner and a clip at the fourth (Fig 41).

The concrete used is a fine mix (*see* p 11) kept fairly dry to minimise shrinkage cracks at the drying-out stage. Colouring agents can be incorporated at the mixing stage. Lay the frame on a sheet of polythene on a flat surface, and pour a shallow layer of concrete about 20mm deep, evenly over the area of the mould. Cut a piece of heavy-duty chicken-

Paving slabs used attractively in a garden designed for the RHS Flower Show, Chelsea, 1981

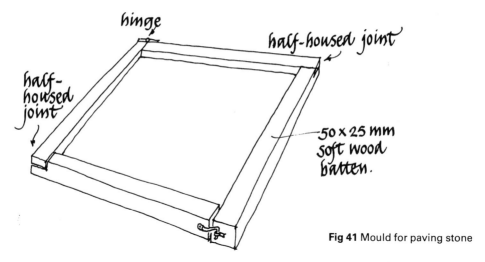

**Fig 41** Mould for paving stone

wire mesh to fit the mould (using ordinary pliers) and place it flat onto the wet concrete mess (Fig 42). Finally, fill the mould with more concrete. Use the levelling batten to 'saw' and tamp the concrete to achieve a flat surface, which can be finished several ways:

(1) It can be left with the tamping marks giving it a rough finish.

(2) It can be trowelled smooth using a wooden float.

(3) It can be trowelled smooth with a wooden float and then swept with a stiff brush to give a light striped surface.

(4) The concrete can be cast onto the back of a sheet of hardboard, and the pattern of the hardboard used as the finish.

(5) Small pebbles (pebbledash) can be scattered onto the wet concrete surface and pressed down into the concrete with a clean batten to obtain a flat surface.

(6) A variety of patterns can be 'printed' onto the surface, for instance using sticks.

After finishing the surface, leave the paving stone for an hour or so to dry, then unlatch the frame, move it carefully and use it for the next slab. If you cast four or five paving stones every evening using two frames, you will build up sufficient stock for the average garden path in the course of a fortnight. If you have to make one or two 'specials' — at the end of the path or where it turns a corner — these will need separate

**Fig 42** Pouring concrete into paving stone mould

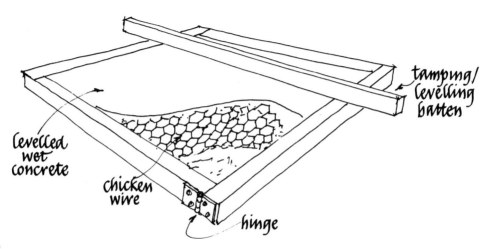

The *Daily Telegraph* and *Sunday Telegraph* garden
at the RHS Flower Show, Chelsea, 1974

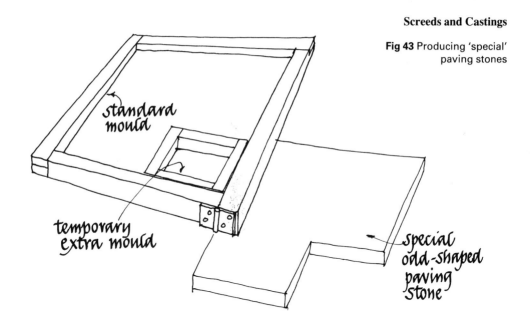

Fig 43 Producing 'special'
paving stones

standard
mould

temporary
extra mould

special
odd-shaped
paving
stone

frames. Since they will only be needed for one or two paving stones, they can be made more simply, without hinges and latches at the corners (Fig 43).

Casting lintels for use over door and window openings is not too difficult, and certainly allows much greater control over the final appearance of the building. You can buy ready-made lintels, but are somewhat restricted to standard lengths. I also find that the cross-sectional sizes rarely fit in with brickwork. When casting your own lintel, you can make it to match the thickness of the wall and the general brick course heights. It is also possible to make special lintels that can be faced with brick slips to imitate the flat arches found in old brickwork.

To begin with, the lintel must be calculated or estimated. Strictly speaking, this should never be left to the amateur; structural calculations must be done by a structural engineer and approved by the building inspector. However, when you are dealing with a simple window in a brick wall, and there are no floor joists built into the wall immediately above

Paving slabs around a small concrete pool at the RHS Flower Show, Chelsea, 1974

A DIY garden path made with paving slabs

the window, it is often possible to get the building inspector to tell you simply how much reinforcement he wants. He may ask for two or three times the amount that would be required if proper calculations were done, but this does not matter a great deal as the materials are cheap enough.

By and large, you should make the height of the lintel equal a whole number of courses; this means in practice that your lintel will be approximately 150 or 225mm high. Its thickness should equal the overall thickness of the wall if it is to be exposed on the face of the brickwork (or covered with plaster at a later stage). Alternatively, the thickness will be smaller by the thickness of any covering such as brick slips or tiles. The lintel should have a bearing at each end of at least 100mm onto supporting brickwork (ie it should rest on the brickwork by this amount) (Fig 44). It will also need reinforcement rods cast inside; the number and size of these will be decided by the building inspector or structural engineer.

As an example, imagine you need a small lintel for a window 914mm wide (equal to exactly four whole bricks). The lintel, allowing for minimum bearing, will have to be at least 1,114mm long. This is an odd length in brickwork; the nearest whole brick size will be 1,143. In fact, we will have to take off the thickness of one mortar joint to arrive at a final lintel net length of 1,134mm. Assuming

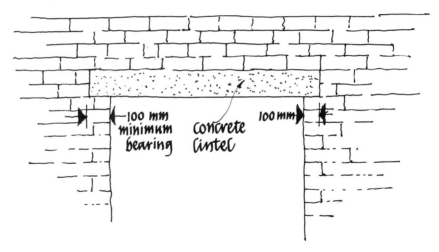

Fig 44 Minimum bearing of a lintel

the lintel is to be built into an internal 225mm wall, it will probably be 142mm high (to fit in with two courses of brickwork). The actual net size, taking into account the size of mortar joints, will be $225 \times 142 \times 1,134$mm. The engineer or building inspector might ask for three reinforcement rods of 12mm diameter steel (Fig 45).

The lintel should be cast on the ground, cured until it builds up a reasonable strength (about 2 weeks) and then lifted into place. Dry concrete weighs approximately 2,300kg per cubic metre, so the lintel would weigh about 83kg, which is something that can be manoeuvred into place by two adults.

To make the mould for the lintel, begin by making an overgrown flowerbox with internal dimensions of exactly $225 \times 142 \times 1,134$mm (Fig 46). The box can be made of second-hand floor boards reinforced with sawn $75 \times 40$mm softwood battens. When the timber is all nicely in place, paint the whole of the inside with releasing oil (obtainable from a good builders' merchant).

Fig 45 Section and bearing of internal lintel

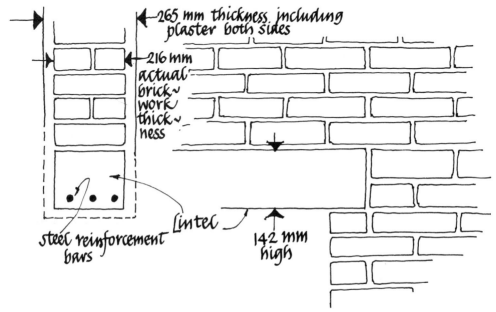

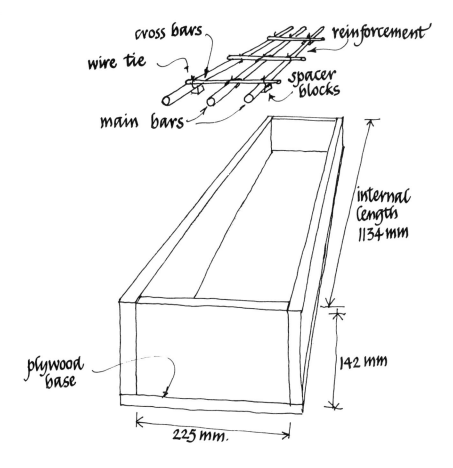

*cross bars*

*wire tie*

*reinforcement*

*spacer blocks*

*main bars*

*internal length 1134mm*

*plywood base*

*142 mm*

*225 mm.*

**Fig 46** Typical shuttering for lintel

The reinforcement bars are more of a problem. If the lintel will be taking up only a few courses of brickwork above, you will probably need only straight rods. However, at all points these rods must be covered with at least 30mm of concrete to stop the iron rusting over the years and weakening the whole lintel. Official building practice is to wire the rods into place using cross-pieces to form a miniature frame which is held above the bottom of the wooden mould by spacers. These spacers are small cubes of concrete into which a wire has been inserted before the concrete hardens. The wire is tied to the bottom of the reinforcement frame, and the concrete spacers become a permanent part of the lintel. If you cannot get hold of these spacers, try casting your own (*see* Fig 28).

You may be asked to bend the ends of the rods at 45°, 90° or 180° (Fig 47). If you are using 8 or 10mm mild steel you can do this for yourself on a bending table. This consists of two pieces of 50 × 25mm softwood screwed onto a 19 or 25mm plywood base, which in turn is screwed or clamped onto a firm base — a work table or bench. The two pieces of wood are fixed parallel and about 12mm away from each other (Fig 48). To bend a metal rod, insert the end that is to be bent into the space between the two pieces of wood and, using the remainder of the bar as a lever, simply pull the metal rod till the required angle is reached (Fig 49). This is almost exactly the way it is done on a building

53

**Fig 47** Bent ends of reinforcement bars

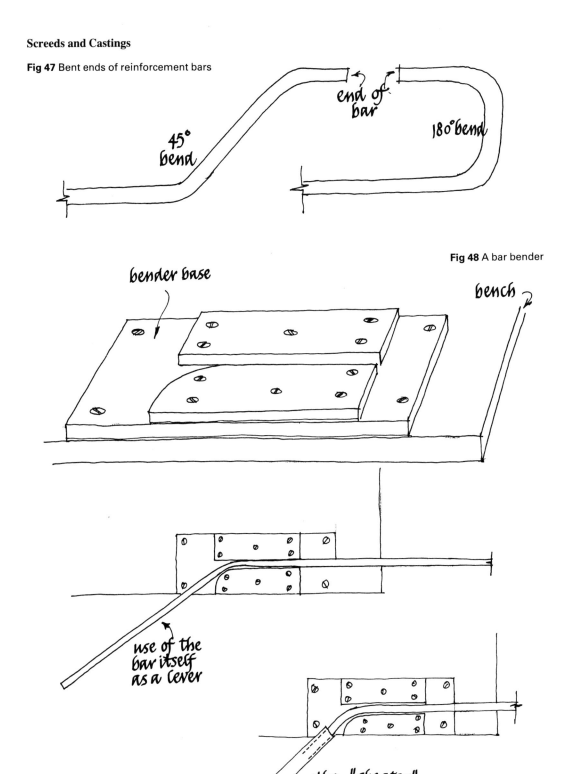

45° bend

end of bar

180° bend

**Fig 48** A bar bender

bender base

bench

use of the bar itself as a lever

the "cheater" ~ a steel tube slipped over end of bar to increase leverage

**Fig 49** Bending reinforcement bars

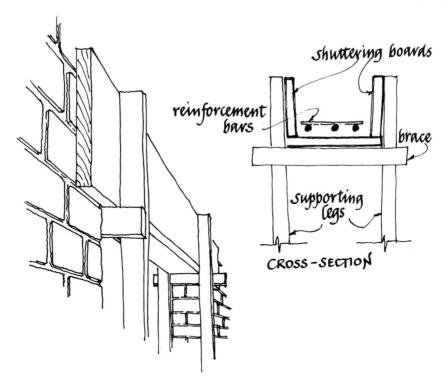

site, except that the bending table would be made of metal, last longer and take thicker rods. (For very thick rods, a power bender will be needed, but this is unlikely to be necessary for ordinary domestic buildings.) The reinforcement rods are cut to length, bent and wired into place as a frame, making sure that the space between the rods is at least 25mm.

Use a coarse concrete (*see* p 11) and prod it into place to make sure that it penetrates all corners of the mould and in between the reinforcement. Fill the mould to the top, and tamp and 'saw' the concrete surface in the usual way. Finish off with a wooden float to get a flat and even surface. Allow the concrete to cure for about 2 weeks, and then break away the mould. The lintel can then be hoisted into place and set on the brickwork on a bed of ordinary mortar (*see* Project 6).

A pre-cast lintel has the advantage that it can be cast well before it is needed, then hoisted into place without interrupting the building of the brickwork. However, pre-cast lintels are limited to fairly small spans. For spans greater than about 1 metre, you will

**Fig 50** Casting a concrete lintel *in situ*

probably have to cast a lintel *in situ*, that is, in the place where it is required — high up in the air! (Fig 50). The method is little different from that used for a pre-cast lintel, but this time the shuttering is built around and up against the brickwork. The joints between the timber shuttering and the brickwork must be thoroughly sealed to stop any cement and water slurry leaking through the gaps and staining the brickwork. A mastic sealant can be used for this job.

The reinforcement is wired together, spacers are fitted below the rods and the assembly is lowered into the mould. The concrete is poured as before, but you may need several people to pass the buckets of wet concrete up to you as you perch on a stage or trestle. The concrete should be prodded into place, as usual, and finished off by tamping, 'sawing' and using a wooden float. Leave the lintel to cure for about 2 weeks before removing the shuttering, but do not continue the brickwork until at least 3 weeks after casting.

# 4 Choosing and Buying Bricks

Bricks have been in use for a long time. We know that the Babylonians used bricks for their ziggurats; and that the captive Jews complained that they could not make bricks without straw. Few Babylonian buildings survive; their bricks are what we would nowadays call 'adobe' — a sun-hardened mixture of cow dung, mud and straw. Adobe bricks are still used in parts of Spain and Mexico; and walls built of adobe can last a hundred or a hundred and fifty years as long as the top of the wall is kept dry, and the wall is replastered with fresh mud from time to time. Much later, the Romans used bricks. Their bricks were properly fired, and many of their brick buildings survive. Roman bricks look rather like tiles; they are about 20mm thick (about ¾in) and about 100 × 200mm on plan (about 4 × 8in). The mortar joints between the bricks are almost as thick as the 'bricks'; Roman brickwork therefore looks very different from modern brickwork.

English brick sizes are based on the concept of the 'module' (Fig 51). The module was 3 × 4½ × 9in to use the old Imperial units; nowadays we talk of 75 × 112 × 225mm. The module consists of the brick plus one mortar

joint on each edge. The brick itself might be of a very odd size, such as 2⅝ × 4⅛ × 8⅝in (67 × 105 × 219mm); the addition of the mortar makes it into a conveniently sized module. The modern English brick has been with us since about 1500; it was one of the very first modular building units available. It is possible simply to look at any building erected since 1500 and, by merely counting the courses, estimate within a few inches the length, height and depth of the building. On the Continent the concept of a brick module never emerged. It is possible to buy dozens of different-sized bricks, although factory production and modern techniques mean that it is becoming more and more difficult to buy other than three or four standard sizes.

To make life even more complicated, the sizes in millimetres mentioned above are the *nominal* sizes, the sizes which are quoted when ordering or otherwise describing the bricks. Three inches (old Imperial measure) comes to 76.2mm and not 75mm. For a while after Britain changed to the metric system, bricks continued to be made 2⅝in thick, course heights were actually 76.2mm high but were referred to as 75mm high. Then the brick manufacturers changed their machines slightly to make bricks which were a fraction

**Fig 51** English brick module

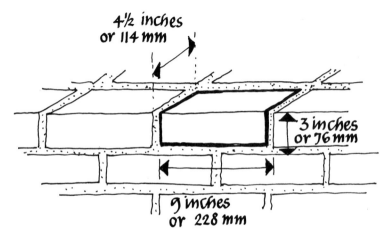

4½ inches or 114 mm

3 inches or 76 mm

9 inches or 228 mm

A typical selection of bricks (*Brick Development Association*)

smaller, and the bricks could be laid at an actual 75mm course. However, when you are trying to mix old and new brickwork (for instance adding an extension to the side of an existing house) you will have to thicken your horizontal joints.

While in England bricks are only available in one standard size, there is nevertheless a wide range of choice as regards finish, texture, hardness and colour. Your local builders' merchant will not, of course, keep all these in his backyard; nor will it necessarily be possible to obtain all of them quickly and easily. However, given time, money and effort, a very wide selection can be obtained. Think about the following factors before making your choice.

(1) *Facing bricks*
Some bricks are designed to be seen — for use on outside walls. Others are intended for inside walls — to be hidden by plaster or other brickwork. Facing bricks can look more attractive either because the brick as a whole is well made or, more usually, because the two sides of the brick which will be seen have been specially coated with coloured sand or decorated with a pattern before the brick is fired. Not all facing bricks are suitable for work below ground or for copings — check this with your supplier.

(2) *Hand-made and machine-made bricks*
Hand-made bricks are made by scooping the clay out of a bin and pressing it into a wooden mould; the bricks are then dried and baked. The resulting brick has a great deal of texture on all six faces, but it is expensive, as is anything made by hand. A machine-made brick will generally be made of a smoother clay. Often the clay is extruded, like a long, square tongue, from a machine and is cut at intervals by a wire. Such a brick is called a 'wire-cut'. They are very accurately made, but lack the rugged texture of a hand-made brick.

(3) *Self-finished and textured bricks*
The wire-cut, machine-made brick generally lacks interest; it has a smooth, absolutely squared-off finish which many peope find

incompatible with their idea of the homely cottage. Bricks can, however, have coloured sand or even a texture pressed into the face before drying and firing. The result is a 'textured' brick. It will not fool anyone who knows about hand-made bricks, but it looks a lot less machine-made than a self-finished wire-cut.

(4) *Engineering and common bricks*
Bricks, besides looking attractive and keeping the rain out, also have to carry loads. If you are building a small garage, this should not concern you a great deal, but if you are putting up a two-storey extension, you might find it necessary to consider the carrying capacity of the bricks.

Engineering bricks — generally a very dark blue — can carry enormous loads. This is unlikely to be necessary in any work you need to do, but they can also resist knocks and corrosion by acids. This makes them very useful in underground work (such as foundations and man-holes) as well as protecting the corners of buildings against damage from passing lorries (the corners of warehouses are often built using engineering bricks).

Semi-engineering bricks are not quite as hard and dense as engineering bricks, and they come in a variety of colours. You may well find yourself using these for work below ground level in some 'difficult' soils if the building inspector insists.

'Commons' are ordinary bricks of no special strength, although their resistance to crushing can vary enormously. If you are building a two-storey extension to your house, you may find yourself occasionally having to satisfy the local building inspector that the brick you have chosen is strong enough.

(5) *Specials*
Bricks can be of different shapes — known as 'specials' — and each brick manufacturer will have a whole catalogue of these. However, they are usually only available as expensive, hand-made bricks, need to be ordered specially and may take many months to be delivered. This is no problem if you are going to order your bricks a year before you start building, but few amateurs really want

to wait that long. Some of the more common specials are shown in Fig 52. Some of these, eg the bull-nose, the half-round and the 45, are attractive and have many uses. Nevertheless, the amateur is best advised to stick to standard bricks.

(6) *Frost resistance*
Frost is one of the main enemies of any stone; if you look at brick buildings more than three or four centuries old, you will see the way the brickwork is eaten away — by frost. The brick gets saturated with water when it rains; should it then freeze, the water expands — enough to burst radiators, car engine blocks and milk bottles. The brick is much tougher, and the amount of water inside the brick much less, but even so, over the years, bricks can get damaged. Frost erosion is kept to a minimum if the brick is reasonably smooth-faced, if the interstices inside the brick are very small, and if the joints between the bricks do not permit the water to lie still (*see* p 66).

**Fig 52** Brick specials

## (7) *Efflorescence*

Efflorescence shows itself as wide white streaks all over the face of a brick building. It usually appears within a couple of years of being built, and may take fifty or so years to disappear. The trouble begins when the brick is made. The clay used may contain too much salt, and the salt remains when the brick is fired. When the brick is built into an external wall it soaks up water in its porous structure whenever it rains. Once thoroughly wet, the water inside the brick will dissolve some of this salt and as the brick dries out, the water evaporates, leaving the salt neatly deposited on the face of the brick. Check with the builders' merchant what sort of guarantee he will give that there will be no efflorescence if the brick is properly used.

Despite the variety of bricks available, you may find that your local builders' merchant only keeps three types in his yard. If so, go along to the Building Centre (in London or Manchester) and look at brick samples, or contact the brick manufacturers (look them up in *Yellow Pages*) who will send brochures; you can end up with hundreds of possibilities.

To help you sort out priorities, start by thinking about prices. Prices are usually quoted per 1,000 standard bricks as a rough guide, but this will vary with the quantity required and delivery distance. Do not forget VAT.

If the price is right, your next concern is delivery. Invariably you will be told that delivery is no problem, but do not believe this; in my experience as a job architect, the only time that delivery is no problem is when the bricks are sitting in your backyard! Ideally, if you have room enough on the site and can afford the cash, it is best to order the bricks the moment you know what type and how many you want. Bricks do not deteriorate if they sit outside waiting to be used. Delivery time can vary from immediate to six or even nine months. The reason for this is that no manufacturer wants to tie up too much capital either in a large enough plant to produce all the bricks needed at peak time or in building up large stocks waiting in his yard for a possible order. Hence you usually order bricks that have not yet been made, unless you choose a brick which is commonly used and of which the builders' merchant has five or ten thousand sitting in his yard. This cuts the choice down considerably. These standard stocks are usually wire-cut, sand-faced, machine-made bricks with little character. Cheap and cheerful — but anything else is two or three times as expensive and difficult to obtain.

One way out is to use second-hand bricks from houses that are being pulled down. The bricks are often broken, covered in old mortar or plaster and have to be sorted and cleaned. The commercial contractor, because of his high labour costs, is reluctant to use second-hand bricks, but you should think of them for the following reasons. They are usually much cheaper to buy than new bricks; you save a lot of hard cash even if it means spending more time sorting them out and cleaning them up. You can get a brick with a lot of real character and one which will integrate better with the brickwork in your area. This can be especially important if you are building a garage or extension to your house in an area of older properties.

Sources of second-hand bricks can be found by touring the area looking for demolition sites or through advertisements in local papers or magazines like *Exchange & Mart*. Local demolitions are better, since the foreman will be only too glad to sell directly. It also means that you keep your transport costs down. Make sure that all the bricks are cleaned off properly; there should be no mortar or plaster left on them. Use a club hammer and bolster chisel to break up resistant mortar. With a bit of luck, a typical demolition may also release some 'specials'!

# 5 The Basics of Brickwork

## Pointing

If you apply for a mortgage for a house that is more than twenty years old, it is quite likely that you will be asked to have the brickwork repointed. This means chiselling out the first 5 or 6mm of the mortar joint and inserting fresh mortar. The surveyor may be quite insistent — why is it all so important?

The brickwork taken as a whole is quite porous. Rain falling onto the brickwork is absorbed and slowly soaks into the surface. When it stops raining, the sun dries off the outer surface, and the water inside the brick slowly evaporates till all the brickwork is dry again. If your house has solid 225mm brickwork you may have some trouble with dampness if:

(1) The wall faces the direction of the wind and there is little protection from this wind.

(2) There are long periods of rain with little sunshine in between.

(3) The house is unheated, or heated by paraffin stoves or open gas fires (these give off a lot of water as they burn their fuel).

A house with cavity walls (with a total thickness of some 275–280mm) will keep much drier, unless for some reason the cavity is bridged.

Alternate wetting and drying out does not harm the brickwork much. The real problem occurs because the water inside the brickwork can freeze; the water expands and breaks up the mortar a little. This happens particularly at night; during the day, the sun warms up the brickwork, causing it to expand a little. At night, the building cools down, and it contracts.

The combination of occasional frost and the contraction-expansion cycle slowly erodes the mortar over the years, especially the outmost 10 or 15mm. This will eventually fall off, leaving the next 10 or 15mm of mortar exposed. And as the mortar gets weaker, it soaks up more water, allowing the frost action to accelerate. In due course, the bricks themselves are attacked and pieces of brick spall off. In this way, the whole wall is weakened, and will ultimately topple. That is why, long before this stage is reached, the wall must be repointed.

Brick repointing is probably one of the first jobs in the wet trades that most DIY people tackle, but it is not one of the easiest. If you learn to repoint you are already halfway to learning how to lay bricks.

Begin by looking at how much has to be done, and how high you have to go. The builder usually works from a ladder, but for the inexperienced a scaffold tower is a lot safer and is not all that expensive to hire. You can stand sand, lime, cement and water on the tower and mix up as you go along, instead of having to climb up and down every hour or so. The tools needed for repointing are: a pointing trowel; a hawk; two or three plastic buckets; a squeezy bottle; a stiff wire brush; a pointing rod; a bolster chisel and club hammer if the old mortar is very hard; and an old screwdriver or two.

The first stage is to rake out the old mortar. If it is very soft, an old screwdriver run along the joints will easily scrape it out; if it is harder, you may have to break it out using a bolster chisel and club hammer (Figs 53 and 54). Make sure that all the old mortar is cleaned out to a depth of 8 or even 10mm.

The new mortar is made up from a mixture of sand, cement, lime and water. The sand used is builder's sand, and the cement ordinary Portland cement; both should be kept dry and clean before use. The lime is needed to make the mortar a little more 'plastic' when it sets, able to take the small settlement movements that occur. You will need what is technically known as hydrated non-hydraulic lime, though if you tell your builders' mer-

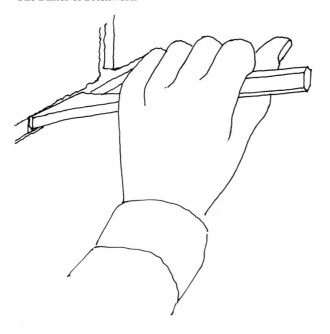

**Fig 53** Chiselling out a mortar joint

chant that you need it for brickwork that will probably be enough. The lime is poured into a plastic bucket half-filled with water and stirred to a creamy consistency. After standing overnight, the excess water will separate from the lime putty, and can be poured off. The putty will keep for weeks if covered with plastic sheeting.

When the time comes to mix the mortar, dip your trowel into the lime mix and serve yourself a generous helping. Add six similar helpings of sand, and finish with a helping of cement. Mix all these together well in a plastic bucket, then add enough water, a little at a time between further mixing, to obtain a plastic mix. It should be 'slurpy' but not wet. When mixing becomes difficult, try chopping the mixture with your trowel, and turning it over and over to make sure that the mix is evenly wetted throughout.

Mix only small amounts at a time; the mortar will not be much good after an hour or an hour and a half. During this period, add a little water (from the squeezy bottle) to keep the mixture plastic. If you are working from tower scaffolding, keep all the materials at the top, and mix as you go along.

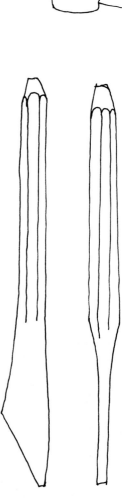

**Fig 54** A plugging chisel

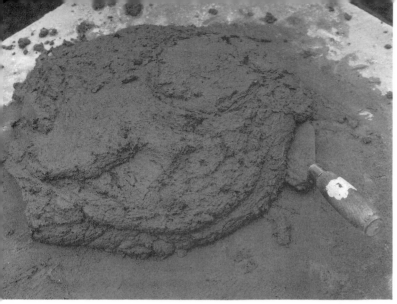

(*above and right*) A good mortar mix giving the right workability

An incorrect mortar mix giving poor workability

Using the underside of the trowel, push the sliver of mortar straight into the waiting joint

Putting in the new mortar requires skill and practice. Take the hawk in your left hand, and put on a trowel's worth of mortar. Chop it and mix it once again on the hawk, then flatten the heap at the far edge so that it is about 7 or 8mm thick. Cut off a sliver that is also about 7 or 8mm wide, using the side of the trowel, and then, tipping the hawk towards you, slide this sliver off and away using the underside of the trowel (Fig 55). Hold the hawk close to the joint you wish to fill, and push the sliver of mortar almost straight into the waiting horizontal joint (Fig 56). Even so you will find at first that the mortar slips off the trowel and misses the joint. Do not despair; you will soon learn to get the mortar into the joint. Once you have the first sliver in, push the blade of the trowel into the joint and 'chop' the mortar further into the crevice. Now apply a second sliver on top of the first. This time use the flat of the

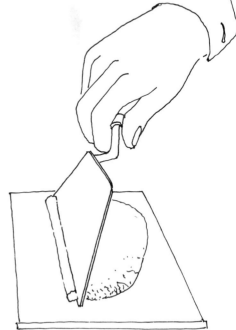

**Fig 55** Slicing off enough mortar mix for a joint using pointing trowel and hawk

**Fig 56** Transferring the mortar to the joint

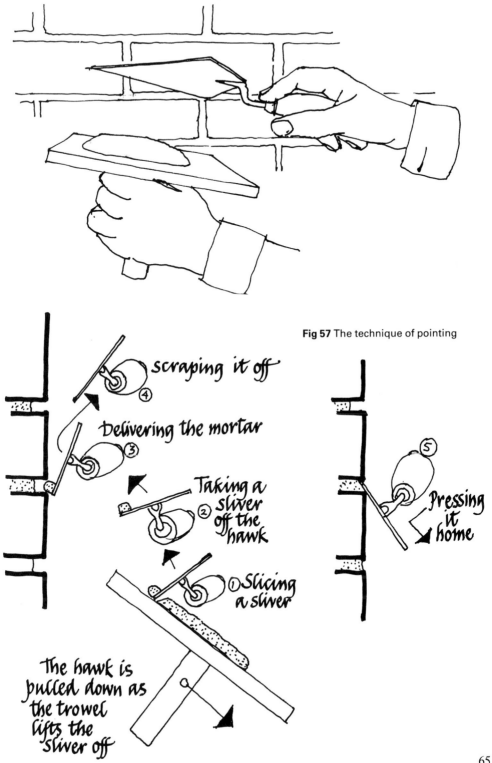

**Fig 57** The technique of pointing

scraping it off ④

Delivering the mortar ③

Taking a sliver off the hawk ②

① Slicing a sliver

⑤ Pressing it home

The hawk is pulled down as the trowel lifts the sliver off

blade to press the mortar home so that the whole crevice is filled (Fig 57). Repeat this exercise a few hundred times and you will gradually fill all the horizontal joints in the brickwork you can reach without moving the platform.

Now start on the vertical (or perpendicular) joints. You will need a slightly stiffer mortar. If you have begun with the horizontal joints your mortar will probably have dried out enough to tackle the perpendicular joints. This time you have to cut off your 8mm square sliver and pick it up on the flat of the trowel before twisting your trowel to push the mortar into the vertical joint — a little trickier perhaps but, having practised on a few hundred horizontal joints, not too difficult.

When you have filled the joints of a square metre or so of brickwork with mortar, the joints should be finished off in one of four ways:

(1) *The flush joint* (Fig 58a)

The mortar is finished flush with the bricks above, below and to each side. The wall as a whole looks flat and uninteresting, and the joints look much thicker than they really are. However, the joint is finished very simply by rubbing an old sack over the face of the

brickwork while the mortar is still soft. Not a very difficult method, and hence often used by amateurs.

(2) *The half-round* (Fig 58b)

A cylindrical tube (*see* p 132) is run along the joints while the mortar is still soft, and impresses a shallow, half-round channel. Straightaway the brickwork looks more interesting and the joints much thinner. As the joint is half-rounded, water cannot lie in the horizontal joint to cause trouble in winter.

(3) *The raked joint* (Fig 58c)

The mortar on the horizontal joints (and sometimes the vertical ones) is raked back about 2 or 3mm using a rectangular tube or bar. This produces quite dramatic effects but does allow water to lie in the horizontal joints. This type of joint is best used indoors if you have 'fair-faced' brickwork instead of plaster.

(4) *The weatherstruck joint* (Fig 58d)

This is not a joint for amateurs, unless you need to repoint a small section of the brickwork to match work done in the past. The mortar is pressed into the joint so that it slopes outwards and downwards; this is done by pressing in the second sliver of mortar while holding the trowel at an angle. The bottom of the mortar is cut off neatly by run-

**Fig 58** Methods of pointing showing (a) flush, (b) half-round, (c) raked and (d) weatherstruck joints

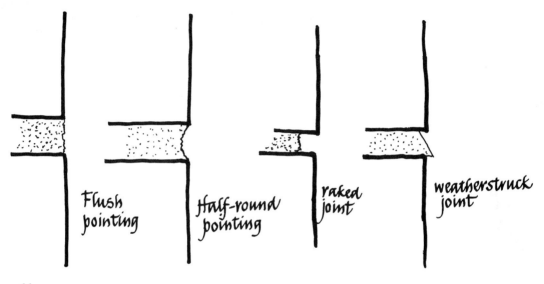

Making a half-round joint

Making a flush joint

A weatherstruck joint

67

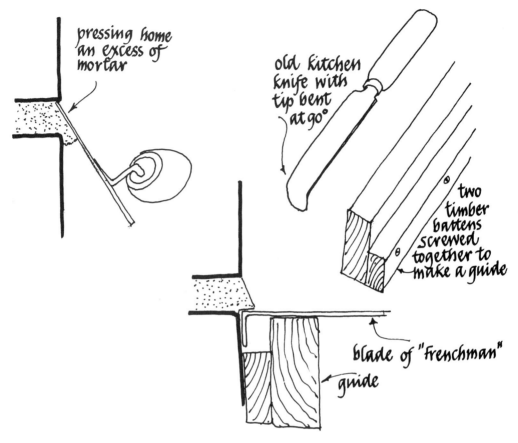

pressing home an excess of mortar

old kitchen knife with tip bent at 90°

two timber battens screwed together to make a guide

blade of "frenchman" guide

**Fig 59** Forming a weatherstruck joint

ning a 'Frenchman' trowel (or an old kitchen knife held horizontally) along a wooden batten (Fig 59). This creates a very impressive joint, and one that throws rainwater away from the face of the building, but is definitely not one for the amateur.

When the joints have been filled and finished, leave the mortar to dry for a day or two, and then remove all surplus cement from the face of the brickwork using a stiff wire brush. Make sure that all cement is removed, since old cement stains can remain on brickwork for years. Repointing the brickwork of your house can save you money and will give you the confidence (and basic skills) to tackle larger projects.

## Brickwork

Laying bricks can be utterly satisfying, and many people — Churchill is a well-known example — have laid bricks not so much to cut the costs of a building project, but simply by way of relaxation. Nevertheless, laying your own brickwork does allow you to build garden sheds, conservatories and garages at a fraction of the cost that a builder would charge.

The beginner, of course, should start with small projects — barbecues, garden walls — and gain a fair amount of experience before tackling larger jobs. In this way, you will acquire a bricklayer's 'feel' for the job. Bricks, as seen by the amateur, all look alike, but they do in fact differ from one another. The experienced bricklayer will almost instinctively lay each brick in such a way as to compensate for this. He will also align perpendicular joints as he goes along. The result is a satisfying piece of brickwork that 'feels' right.

Brickwork is the combination of bricks and

mortar. This may sound obvious, but needs to be stressed in order to understand the choice of bricks and mortar mix. The most important rule is: 'The strength of the mortar should be the same as the strength of the bricks.' Many people knock up a nice strong mortar to 'glue' the bricks together. As the wall or house settles (and all structures settle a little bit in the first year at least, and often later), the brickwork copes with the resultant stresses by cracking slightly. When the mortar is of the same strength as the bricks, the tiny cracks will occur in the mortar, where they can be dealt with by repointing. When the mortar is much stronger than the bricks, the bricks will crack — something that cannot be patched up.

The mortar acts as much like a bedding as anything else. Individual bricks are only approximately flat; if they were simply laid on top of each other as high as a wall, the bottom ones would crack at the point where the brick above bulges or sticks out.

## Bonding

Since the mortar acts only like a weak glue, it is best to arrange the bricks in such a way as to prevent long lines of cleavage. The bricks are therefore laid in a pattern, called a 'bonding', which minimises continuous vertical lines of cleavage.

Many types of bonding have been used in the past, eg English bond, Flemish bond, garden bond. Few of these are used by the professional bricklayer today, since most modern housing is built with a cavity wall (two leaves of brickwork with a space in between for insulation). Since each leaf is only a single brick thick, only one bond can be used, the simple stretcher bond (Fig 60). It is a simple bond, and easy to lay, but it is extremely dull. If you compare modern houses with those built in the past century, the difference will be immediately apparent. Older houses might be built using an English bond (Fig 61) or a Flemish bond (Fig 62), ie a wall that is two bricks thick with no intervening cavity. These houses have a tendency to damp and lose heat more quickly than modern cavity-wall houses.

In practice, you may only need to know the older bonds if you are bricking in an opening in an existing wall built of one of these bonds. Other bonds of interest are the garden wall bond (Fig 63) and the wild or random bond (Fig 64). Random bond is a modern variation of the simple stretcher bond that is used a great deal in Holland. The rules are quite simple: no more than seven headers in a row before a snapped header is used, and no perpendicular immediately above another. This

**Fig 60** Stretcher bond

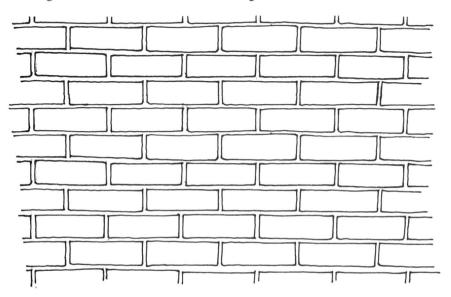

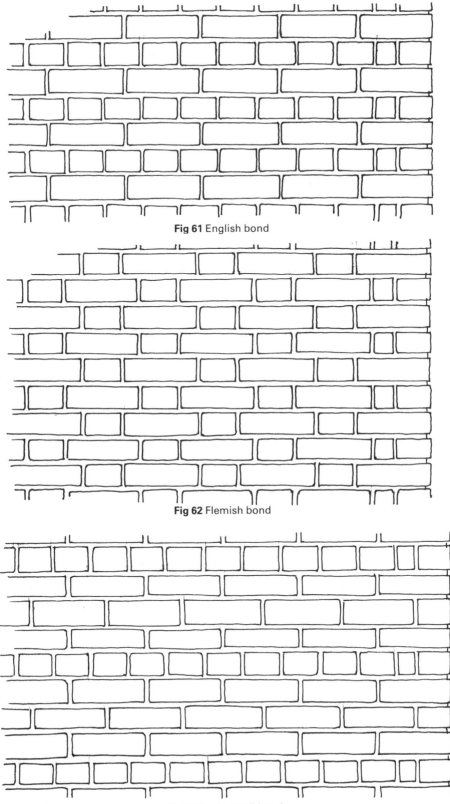

**Fig 61** English bond

**Fig 62** Flemish bond

**Fig 63** Garden wall bond

bond could prove very suitable for the amateur, since there is not quite the same pressure to keep up a regular 'feel' to the brickwork.

If you are building a small structure, such as a barbecue (*see* Project 3) or garden seat (*see* Project 1), it may well be useful (and save time) to design the size of the structure in terms of the brick module and the bond used. Even larger structures can benefit from a little forethought. For instance, you might decide that a garden shed of 3 × 2 metres meets your needs; in practice, if built to exactly that size you would find yourself cutting four bricks to each course. Much better to make it 2.025 × 2.925 metres, and avoid cutting any bricks. Similarly, a window opening is much easier if made 670mm wide rather than an even 700mm.

## Mortar

Mortar is a mixture of cement, sand and water, to which lime can be added. Use Portland cement, which comes in 50kg bags, and ordinary tap water or, if this is not available, the cleanest water you can obtain. The sand should be clean river sand (containing no dirt or salt) known as builder's sand; your builders' merchant will know what this means. The colour of the sand will have an important bearing on the colour of the mortar, but it is difficult to judge the final result before the

**Fig 64** Wild (random) bond

mortar is dry. If the colour is important, eg if you are filling in or extending existing brickwork, put together three or four bricks and let them dry for a week or so to check the colour before ordering your full requirement of sand. It is possible to add special colouring agents to the mortar; judicious use of these can result in a final dry colour that matches the existing mortar. However, you can also try the effect of a variety of sands from different merchants.

Lime is a possible additive; it is a slower-acting binding agent which allows the brickwork to take up small settlement movement without cracking. On small jobs where cracking will not pose a problem, you can omit the lime. Larger projects, such as a garage or house extension, may require the addition of a little lime.

Lime can be bought, again in 50kg bags, from your builders' merchant in a bewildering variety of types: hydrated, hydraulic, non-hydraulic and semi-hydraulic. For a typical mortar use hydrated non-hydraulic (or semi-hydraulic) lime. Tip the lime into water in a clean container, stir to mix the two, and let it all settle down for one or two days. Then remove the excess water and add the lime putty to the other ingredients when you are knocking up some mortar.

71

Depending on the strength of the brick (*see* p 58), you will need to mix the sand, cement and lime in different proportions. The most common proportions and the purposes for which they are used are shown in Figs 65 and 66. The amount of water required will depend on the mix and the amount of water already in the sand or in the lime putty; in other words, you will need to add water by trial and error each time you mix a batch. In general it is important to add as little water as possible. The mixture must be properly mixed, smooth and creamy so as to slip on and off the trowel smoothly and yet stick to the brick tenaciously.

In order to see what this means, start by mixing a batch of mortar. Onto a mixing board (*see* p 11), using a shovel or a large trowel, heap three level measures of sand, one level measure of cement, and stir thoroughly until the mixture is evenly grey with no pockets of cement or sand. Now add a small amount of water, and continue mixing. Gradually add more and more water, and keep on mixing. The mixture will start to become pasty and very hard to stir. You will now have to turn it over and chop it up between turning it over. Eventually the mixture

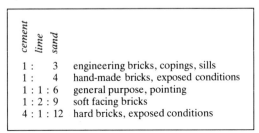

| cement | lime | sand | |
|---|---|---|---|
| 1 : | | 3 | engineering bricks, copings, sills |
| 1 : | | 4 | hand-made bricks, exposed conditions |
| 1 : 1 : 6 | | | general purpose, pointing |
| 1 : 2 : 9 | | | soft facing bricks |
| 4 : 1 : 12 | | | hard bricks, exposed conditions |

**Fig 65** Mortar mixes

| | | |
|---|---|---|
| 1 : 1 : 6 | 1 : 4 | 1 : 3 |
| 1 : 2 : 9 | | 4 : 1 : 12 |

| more sand or lime | more cement |
|---|---|
| ◄──────── | ────────► |
| resists hair-line cracks | resists weathering |
| use for foundations main walls soft bricks | use for copings, sills, hard bricks |

**Fig 66** Purposes for which mortar mixes are used

will be almost the right consistency; this is when you will need to use the squeezy bottle to add a little more water now and then to keep the mixture just wet enough to work easily. As each batch of mortar is used, it dries out, so that you may have to add a little water from time to time.

If you are mixing a cement/lime mortar, then the proportions will be different, and so will the procedure. Start by mixing the sand and the lime putty, adding water as necessary; only add cement after the lime and the sand are mixed (this is called 'coarse stuff'). Again, you should finish up with a smooth plastic material.

## Laying the first brick

Before starting, gather all the tools you need: several plastic buckets; a shovel or medium trowel for mixing; a pointing trowel; a hawk; a spirit level; pegs and string; a mixing board and a spot board (these can be combined); a squeezy bottle; a handbrush and a bowl of water. Put beside the mixing board (for larger jobs) or mixing bucket (for smaller jobs), standing upright, the first bag of cement. Next to it will be your supply of sand and, if required, the bucket(s) of lime putty. Have to hand the various buckets and measuring boxes, as well as the shovel or trowel for mixing. Knock up the mortar mixture as described above; never mix more than you can use in a couple of hours. Now fill a plastic bucket with the mixture and take it to the spot where you are going to lay your first brick. Before we go any further, we need to say a little about this brick.

The brick will have come off the top of a stack of bricks. It should be dry, having been protected from the driving rain, but not too dry. In summer, especially if the weather has been very hot, it may be necessary to moisten the brick, ie run your garden hose over the pile about an hour before starting, and let the

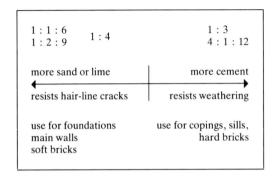

(*top*) Laying the mortar bed

(*below*) Placing the brick and removing surplus mortar with the trowel

bricks absorb a little water. If this is not done the brick will suck up the moisture in the mortar which will get too dry to 'set' properly. The same applies to the surface on which the first brick is to be laid. This will, in most cases, be either concrete or existing brickwork, which will also need wetting. Dip your handbrush into a bowl of water, and flick the brush at the concrete or brickwork to wet it. Now you are ready to lay your first brick.

Tip the contents of the plastic bucket onto the spot board, and use the trowel to mix, chop and virtually knead the mortar into a nice, plastic heap. Help yourself to a good slab of mortar. This is done by cutting off a generous slice, rolling it towards you to form a sort of sausage, and then sliding the trowel underneath. This helping is judiciously transferred to the existing concrete (or brickwork) by turning the trowel 90 degrees while holding it parallel to the length of the brickwork. The mortar will slide off to form a long roll along the length of the brickwork. Lay a series of such rolls to provide the mortar bed for several bricks.

Now take the first brick in your left hand (if you are right-handed) and place it firmly onto this bed. If you have judged the amount of mortar correctly (this will come with practice) you should, in theory, be able to push the brick down exactly level and straight without further ado. This is what the expert

bricklayer will do, but the less experienced will have to resort to tapping the brick gently into place using the end of the handle of the trowel or even the end of the handle of a small club hammer. Gently tap the brick into place till it is level and straight (more about this in Chapter 6).

On the principle that it is better to put down too much mortar on your bed than too little, you will probably find that when the brick is finally in place, mortar will have been squeezed out of the joint. Rescue the surplus mortar with your trowel by moving it upwards from beneath the joint. This mortar can be reused unless it has fallen onto the ground and thus become contaminated.

Now pick up the second brick and 'butter' its header face with a dab of mortar. This means picking up the brick in your left hand (if you are right-handed) and holding it vertically, head upwards, while the trowel in your right hand picks up a medium-sized helping of mortar. Flick the mortar off your trowel onto the header face, and then neaten up the dab using the underside of the trowel. You should finish up with a dab, more or less in the shape of a pyramid, that sticks to the end of the brick. Now push the brick into place, as before, but this time not only push it down to squeeze the mortar bed, but also push it to the side to squeeze the dab of mortar on the brick's side (or head, if you prefer) to the right side onto the first brick.

# 6 Building up Brickwork

Brickwork is not just a matter of piling up bricks and hoping for the best; it has to be tackled methodically. The professional bricklayer at work makes it all seem so easy, but there is nothing haphazard in his approach.

Brickwork should be laid on a clean and level base. Whether it is a foundation that you have poured yourself, or someone else's concrete or brickwork, make sure that the surface is clean; this means brushing (and occasionally chipping) away all loose and unwanted bits of cement. Have to hand all the usual brick-building tools (*see* Chapter 9) as well as a mortar mix (*see* p 61).

To begin with a straight wall without any piers or corners, make a start by placing all the bricks you will need along the length of the wall to the far side of their final position. Space them out with a 10mm gap between bricks. Now take some twine, wind it round and round a brick crossways and place the brick on the ground just beyond what will be one end of the wall (Fig 67). Put two bricks on top to weigh it down, and place a small piece of wood (the thickness of the mortar joint) under the string. Wind the other end of the twine round a second brick which is placed at the other end of the wall, again with a couple of bricks on top. Pull the two bricks apart till the twine is taut, and position the bricks in such a way that the line runs exactly along the outside of the proposed wall. When you lay the first line of bricks, the top of the edge facing you should be touching this string. If the line is more than about 4 metres long, you may need to put a brick halfway along to act as an intermediate support (Fig 68).

Now lay each brick in the right position, using the techniques described in Chapter 5. Go along the line, missing out the centre brick if need be, till you reach the other end. Each brick must be laid square and horizontal; check this with a small spirit level and tap the brick into place using the handle of your trowel. When you come to any intermediate support bricks, simply leave them for later.

**Fig 67** Setting down one end of guide line

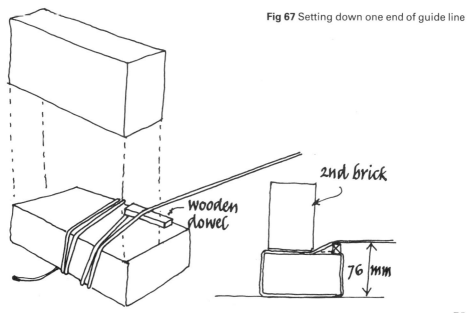

wooden dowel

2nd brick

76 mm

**Fig 68** Setting out first-course guide line

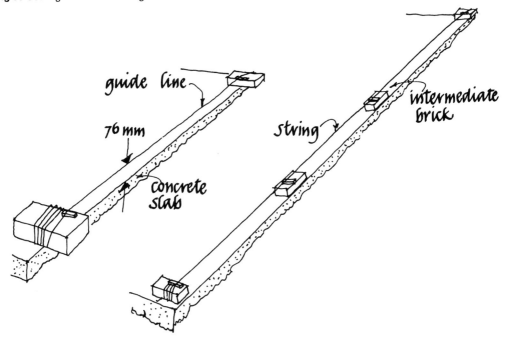

When the first course has been laid, take away the string and lay the intermediate bricks. Make sure, using your spirit level, that all bricks are laid square. If they are not, pull them up, take away the mortar bed and mix it back into the pile on the board. Use a fresh roll of mortar and try laying the brick again.

Next, we need to build up the ends. The method used is to build a little 'half-pyramid' — you have probably seen this being done on building sites. It has a useful purpose: the pyramid is built up using the spirit level extensively to check both that the wall is vertical and that the courses are horizontal. You will also need a gauge rod (*see* p 131), or at least a tape measure, to make sure that each course (brick + mortar) is exactly 75mm.

All this measuring and checking takes time. However, if the bottom course and the ends are built accurately, making extensive use of spirit level and gauge, then the brickwork in between can be built more quickly using just a builder's line (*see* Fig 70).

Whichever brick bond is used, sooner or later we come to the problem of half-bricks (or even one-third bricks). Unless you go in for extremely expensive 'specials', you will

have to learn to cut bricks. Cutting bricks is not the same sort of problem as cutting tiles. There are two methods. The professional will take the brick in his left hand, and the trowel in his right and, using the trowel as an axe, he will chop at the brick exactly halfway along each of its four faces. If the brick is hit with exactly the right amount of force in exactly the right place, it will break in half. This technique, however, can only be developed after spoiling the odd hundred or so bricks! When perfected, though, it means that there are no hold-ups in the brick-laying process.

The second method is more suitable for amateurs; it is also used by professionals if the brick must be cut to an exact length. The brick is rested on some sacking (or a sheet of expanded polystyrene) and the cut marked in pencil. A bolster chisel is placed on this line, and hit — not too hard — with a club hammer. The process is repeated on all four faces; and the object is to score a line with the chisel all round. Then the bolster chisel is used to give one slightly sharper blow, and the brick should snap neatly into two pieces. If the brick is not snapped clean in two, then use the trowel like an axe to 'whittle' away the surplus. Chips will flake away and, with any luck, you will be left with at least one half-brick.

Back to the end pyramid. Begin by laying a half-brick as the first brick on the second course, using the spirit level to check that it is sitting squarely. Put down a full brick next to the half-brick, then position a full brick over the half-brick on the third course, again making sure that it is laid square. Last of all, a half-brick is laid in position on the fourth course (Fig 69).

You cannot yet go any further up, so go along. At each course, a full brick is added; when this is done, you can add a full brick on the end on the fifth course, and a half-brick on the sixth. Continue like this until you have built up about ten or twelve courses. Repeat the process at the other end of the wall, and let the ends dry for at least an hour.

Now you can fill up the space in between. The built-up ends are used to support the twine which marks the top front edge of your new line of brickwork. Each end of the twine is wound around a metal peg which is pushed into the (still-soft) mortar between two

bricks somewhere near the corner (Fig 70). Continue laying the brickwork between the two end pyramids until you reach two courses below the top half-brick. If the wall has to go still higher, build up your pyramids once again for another ten or twelve courses at each end of the wall, and leave the space in between to be filled at the next session.

At the end of each session, clean up the mortar joints between the bricks (*see* p 66 for jointing). Make sure that none of the bricks is stained by cement; it is very difficult to clean off mortar once it has hardened.

You have just completed your first wall — a very basic wall, but perhaps the forerunner of a lot of ambitious projects. There are strict limits to the length and height of such a basic wall because it is only a single brick thick and built without piers or returns — the local building inspector will explain this to you. By and large, a wall only one brick thick has to have some provision in the way of piers or returns if it is over 2.4 metres long. Thicker

**Fig 69** Beginning the pyramid at the corner

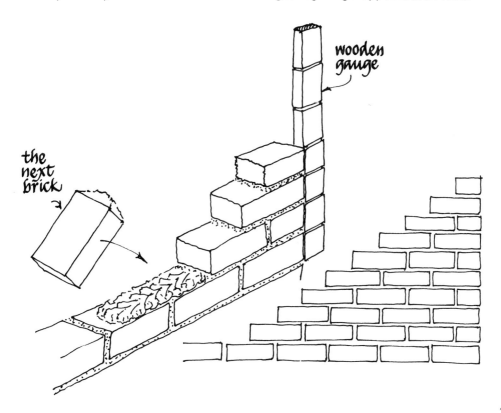

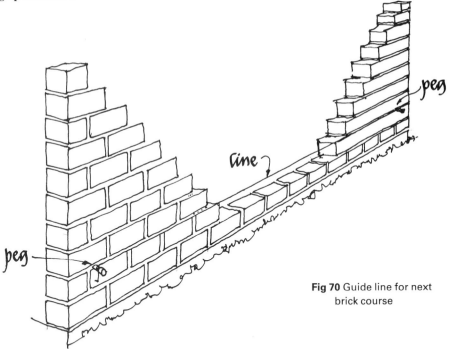

peg

line

peg

**Fig 70** Guide line for next brick course

walls can be much longer and higher, but even these have limits.

If you are building a garden wall, therefore, you can either build it two bricks thick and avoid piers (but use up a lot more bricks) or keep it one brick thick and put piers at about 3 metre intervals. When putting down the first course of bricks directly onto the concrete footing, at chosen intervals along the wall, bond in the bricks that form the base of the pier. On each alternate course, either two bricks are laid at right-angles to the main wall, or one brick is laid parallel to the main wall (Fig 71). As the courses are taken up, the pier is bonded in. On no account should the pier be built with a continuous vertical joint between wall and pier.

The size and position of the pier will depend on the size of the wall and what it is to carry. A garden wall up to 1.5 metres high can have 225mm piers at intervals not more than 3 metres apart. A garage with return walls at each end and long enough to house the average car with some storage at the end (say, 6 metres in all) would probably need either two 225mm piers or one 330mm pier along its length. Discuss this with your local

building inspector (by law, you must discuss a proposed garage with him); it is unlikely that he will want plans, but he likes to be informed and can often give good advice.

If you do not want piers, you may have to build a 225mm thick wall. To set against the major disadvantage of using a great many more bricks, sand and cement, it offers a much more pleasant appearance and a chance to use something other than stretcher bond.

First, choose your bond. If this is the first time you have laid bricks, or a particular bond, it may well be useful to draw out two complete courses to show exactly where the bricks are to go. Use graph paper with a large pattern; it makes drawing each brick to scale much easier.

The first course is laid using more or less the same methods as for the single stretcher course described above. Lay all the bricks for this first course on the foundation on the far side of the proposed wall. Put down the two corner bricks to hold the guide line, and lay the bricks in between — this time to the pattern of the bond. Next, build up the ends of the wall in half-pyramids. Proceed care-

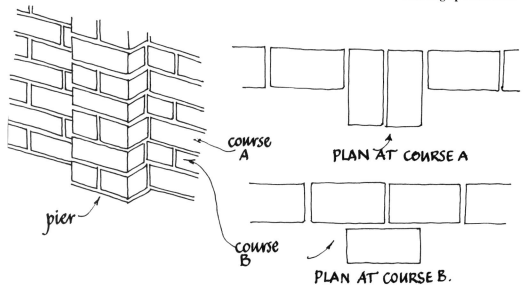

**Fig 71** Bonding in a pier to a single-brick wall

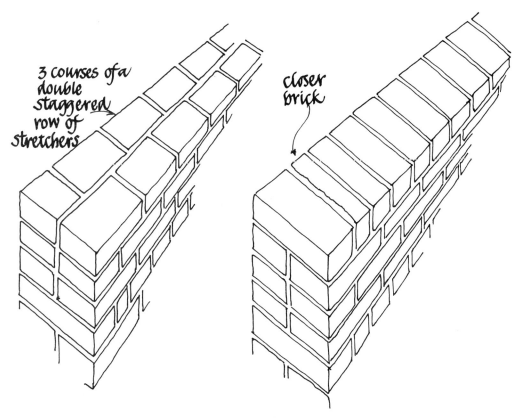

**Fig 72** Two different courses on the same wall: three courses of a double staggered row of stretchers, with a course of headers on top

fully, and consult your sketch of the alternate courses in order to get the bond pattern right. Finish by filling in the courses in between (Fig 72).

The walls so far described have all been straight walls, but most brickwork is used for structures with corners — sheds, garages, extensions etc — so you will need to learn to turn the corner. Turning a corner is largely a matter of correct setting-out. Take your time doing this, and you will have much less trouble later on.

Begin, as before, by wrapping twine around two bricks, and stretching a line along the line of the proposed wall. Place a third brick underneath the string, 1.8 metres in from the corner, as if it were an intermediate support. Do the same for what will be the return wall, but this time place the intermediate brick 2.4 metres away from the corner. Ask someone to help you, and get them to hold the end of the tape measure at the point where the two lines cross — this should mark the external corner of your brickwork. Measure, in turn, to each of the intermediate bricks; the distance to one should be exactly 1.8 metres, and this should be marked with a pencil cross

Fig 73 Turning the corner using garden wall bond

on the brick itself. The other mark should be exactly 2.4 metres from the corner, again marked on the brick. To check that your brickwork is to be built on a right-angle, the diagonal distance between the two pencilled marks should be exactly 3 metres. If it is not, you may have to move the brick on what will be the return wall and so increase or decrease the angle until you have a right-angle at the corner, and a triangle that is exactly $1.8 \times 2.4 \times 3.0$ metres. (If you have not got room for these exact dimensions, any triangle with the proportions 3 : 4 : 5 will do; so, of course, if you happen to have one, would a builder's square.)

Now that you have two lines at right-angles, start laying the first course of bricks along one of the two lines in the normal manner in your chosen bond. When this is finished, lay the first course along the return wall. The corner half-pyramid is built up in the usual manner, making frequent use of a spirit level to check that the bricks are set square.

Turning a corner in 225mm thick brickwork is, of course, more complicated. A sketch of each layer will definitely be helpful; if you are using single Flemish or English bond, you will only need two such sketches,

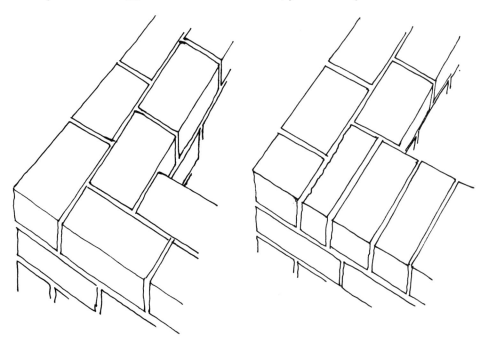

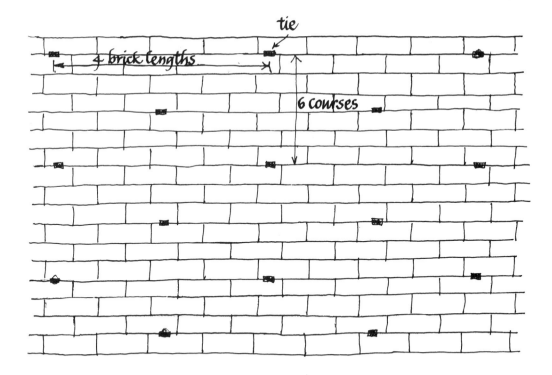

tie

4 brick lengths

6 courses

**Fig 74** Pattern of ties in cavity wall

so it is not much extra work. Turning the corner in 225mm thick brickwork will also involve you in 'queen closers'. These are bricks cut in half lengthwise. As shown in Fig 73, you will need one of these at every course. In the past, when brickworks supplied good, hand-made bricks, queen closers could be bought ready made. Now that the brickworks like to put out millions of standard bricks and no specials, you will have to cut your own. This can cause difficulties. Usually, using bolster chisel and a club hammer, the brick will split both across its length and width. This does not matter: the break across the width will not be seen. Just build in the two quarter bricks: it is the ends which must be clean and square.

The walls considered so far have been suitable for garages, conservatories and garden walls and sheds. But if you are building an extension to your house you will have to consider cavity walls and DPCs which are designed to prevent damp penetrating into the room. A cavity wall is made up of two single-brick walls separated by some 50–60mm of air. Generally speaking, the two

'leaves' are built more or less simultaneously. The professional bricklayer will usually build them both while standing on one side (generally facing the outside) and concentrate on making the outer leaf look good on the assumption that the inner leaf will be covered by plaster. You can, of course, take a little more time, and build each leaf alternately a few courses at a time.

To give stability, the two leaves are tied together at intervals of about six courses vertically and about 900mm horizontally. The ties are usually staggered in a diamond pattern (Fig 74). Butterfly ties, the most common type, are made of mild steel wire twisted into the shape that gives them their name (Fig 75). Each 'wing' of the butterfly is laid into the mortar bed and covered with a little extra mortar before the brick above on the next course is lowered into place.

It is also necessary to keep the cavity reasonably clear of mortar. This can be done by resting a 50 × 50mm softwood batten on the butterflies. Strings tied at each end of the

81

batten enable the batten to be pulled up every six courses or so when the new butter-flies are built in. As it is pulled up it scrapes the inside of the walls clear of surplus mortar (Fig 76).

The DPC is simply a layer of plastic or other proprietary material which is water and damp proof. The material is laid on top of a thin bed of mortar on top of the second course of bricks and is in turn covered with more mortar before the third course is laid. This horizontal joint will end up slightly thicker than normal and in the middle will be the DPC (Fig 77). The junction between the DPM in a solid floor and the DPC some 150 or 225mm higher can create difficulties. Project 5 shows you how to tackle the problem.

It is also necessary to lay a DPC above a concrete lintel if the lintel bridges the cavity. Building in a window (or door) frame thus becomes a little more complicated. Begin by building up the brickwork to the position of the underside of the frame. The frame itself is treated against rot and primed. A small mini-DPC is laid onto the brickwork to minimise damp penetrating into the timber

**Fig 75** Cavity wall ties

Fish tail

Butterfly

**Fig 76** Keeping the cavity free from mortar droppings

82

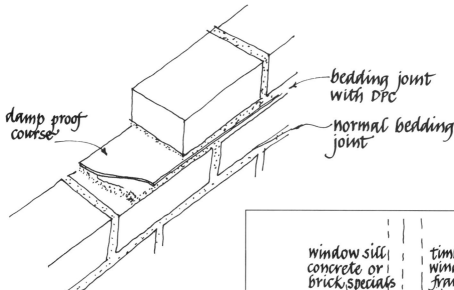

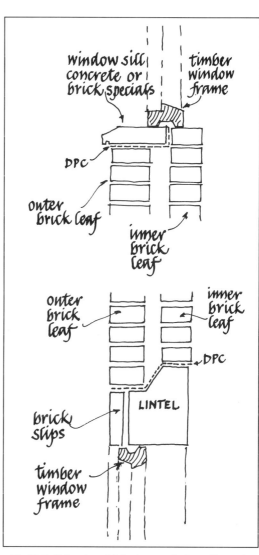

**Fig 77** Damp proof course

sill (Fig 78*a*). The frame is held in place temporarily using a long batten spiked to the floor and to the top of the frame. The brickwork is then built up in the normal way to each side of the frame. Two galvanised steel ties (three for door frames) are screwed to the side of the frame, and built into the brickwork as you go along. When the brickwork has been taken up to the top of the frame, the temporary support can be removed, and a lintel built in over the window (*see* Project 6). When the time comes to build up the brickwork over the lintel, a DPC is again built into the mortar bed immediately above the lintel (Fig 78*b*); the brickwork can then be continued in the usual way.

By now you should see your way to building a garage or small extension. Obviously it is best to practise your bricklaying on smaller items like garden walls or barbecues, but eventually you will build up enough expertise to tackle the bigger jobs. Most of this work will be in cavity-wall or single-leaf brickwork; the more complicated bonds are rarely encountered unless you need to tackle older brickwork in existing houses (*see* Project 6).

**Fig 78** Building in a DPC when a window sill and lintel breach a cavity wall. (*a*) Section through area of the sill; (*b*) section through area of concrete lintel

# 7 Plastering

Plastering is one trade that many people shy away from. DIY buffs will cheerfully tackle plumbing, bricklaying and even the roof of the house, but when it comes to plastering they say 'too difficult', feeling that they cannot possibly achieve the perfectly smooth flat finish that the professional seems to produce so effortlessly over an entire wall. It is not easy to achieve this sort of finish but, if you are prepared to take the time and effort, there is a great deal that you can achieve. When you have gained experience by learning to fill holes and mend cracks in plaster, you can go on to larger jobs such as plastering whole walls.

## Preparation

Plaster adheres best to a slightly damp, rough surface or to a suitable bonding agent, so you will need to prepare the background surface in order to provide the best adhesion. The background may be a brickwork or blockwork wall (with rough or smooth joints or — much more difficult — painted over), a rough or smooth concrete lintel, pillar or beam, or it may be plasterboard. All these different surfaces need different treatment.

An ordinary brick wall, if it is recently built, will still be fairly damp (it can take up to a year before a brick wall is properly dry) and will not absorb the water mixed in the plaster as you apply it. This is important. If the bricks absorb the water in the plaster mixture as it is being applied to the walls, the coating of plaster next to the brickwork will dry out too quickly and fail to 'set' and, eventually, the plaster will come away from the wall.

It is therefore important to wet the wall before you start plastering. Dip a hand brush (the type used for sweeping dust into a dustpan) into a bowl of water and flick it at the wall until the water penetrates into all the crevices and wets the wall thoroughly. An older wall (built more than a year ago and therefore completely dry) will need a more thorough soaking. Use the same brush to flick on water, but do this three or four times during the course of the day (or two) before you start plastering.

It is also important to provide a 'key' for the plaster. Plaster is not all that 'sticky', especially when it is dry, and a rough surface to which it can cling will help adhesion. When you are building a brick wall which you know is to be plastered, it is therefore a good idea to leave the joints raked out (*see* p 66).

Many brick walls are built with smooth joints; at the time of building there was no intention of plastering the wall. If the mortar is soft, it is best to rake out these joints; but if the mortar is very hard, the time and effort required to do this may be prohibitive and you would be better advised to apply a special bonding coat, a sort of glue to which the plaster can cling. This also applies to concrete which has been finished with a smooth surface. Suitable bonding agents come under a variety of brand names; your builders' merchant should be able to advise you if you tell him the surface that needs attention. Usually you will need to apply the bonding agent in two or three coats with a drying time in between: follow the manufacturer's instructions. After the last coat has been applied, wait a day or two before you start plastering.

The most troublesome surface to plaster is the bare brick wall which has been painted over. If it has been painted with emulsion, use a bonding glue and apply the plaster after the glue has dried thoroughly. A whitewashed wall (or distemper) is more difficult because the whitewash tends to come off the wall in flakes; the plaster sticks to the flakes and not to the wall itself. Wash off as much of the whitewash as you can with water, and stick the remainder to the brick wall using a slightly different bonding agent (your builders' mer-

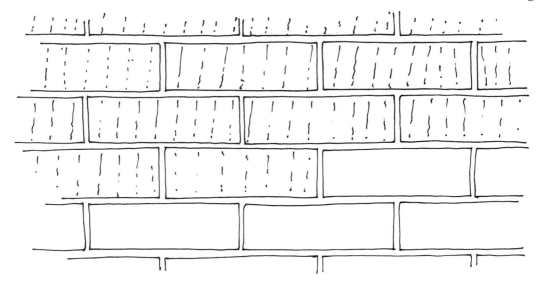

**Fig 79** Plastering key on brickwork covered by oil-based paint

chant can recommend one). The bonding agent should be applied a few days later when the wall has dried out a little.

The most difficult surface to prepare for plastering is the wall coated in oil-based paint, which frequently occurs in the kitchen or scullery in the back extension of Victorian and Edwardian terrace housing. It may be possible just to clear off flaking areas and then paint over with a bonding agent, but I would recommend spending a little more time and effort to try to produce a mechanical 'key' rather than relying solely on the bonding agent.

Use a bolster chisel and hammer to chip off all the layers of paint along the old joints. Then rake out the joints themselves; the mortar is generally soft after eighty or a hundred years. Next, using the bolster chisel, score diagonal lines in the paintwork across the face of the brick (Fig 79). There is no need to score lines in the bricks themselves, but try to penetrate the layers of paint to reveal the brick at the bottom of the score. Then paint the whole surface with a bonding agent in the usual way, before starting to plaster.

### Choice of plaster

Books on the techniques of plastering will talk long and hard about hydrous and anhydrous plasters, classes 1, 2 etc but, in practice, life is much easier: you will need cement and sand for outside work and browning and finishing plaster for inside work. These are plasters which are mixed with a light-weight aggregate ready for you to mix with water and slap on. The browning is used for the first coat, applied directly onto the brickwork, blockwork or concrete. If you need three coats, the browning is also used for the second coat. The finishing plaster is used to achieve a smooth finish. Of course, there are exceptions. When plastering onto metal lathing or Newtonite you may need special plaster. There are also special plasters for external work although, more usually, water-resistant cement/sand mixtures are used.

### Mixing the plaster

Mixing plaster is simplicity itself: simply add water to the powder till you get a paste of the right consistency. The paste must be plastic, ie you should be able to pick it up, slap it on the wall and smooth it out; the paste must also be sturdy enough not to slump off the wall onto the floor. After a few tries, you should know roughly how much water to add.

What is surprising about mixing plaster is how much you need and how quickly you use it up. When you are making good a small hole in the wall this will not be so obvious, but any area over a couple of square metres seems to need two people: one to apply the plaster and one to mix it. For instance, for a 500 × 500mm hole in the existing plasterwork of an old cottage, you may well find you need a full bucket of plaster mix. As you should normally only mix up one-third of a bucket at a time to give you room to mix the materials properly, you can see that even for this small job you are going to spend almost as much time mixing as plastering.

Small batches of plaster can be mixed simply in a plastic bucket, which you can carry to the work site. Larger quantities — for a whole wall or even an entire room — are mixed in a larger container. You could go out and buy one specially, or you could use an old baby bath (try jumble sales) or a plastic 50 litre container used for transporting oils and chemicals; with the top cut off it makes a splendid mixing trough. For outdoor renders — which are mainly cement/sand mixes — you will need a small cement mixer or a mixing board and a large shovel, depending on the area to be rendered.

## Making good a hole in the wall

Most amateur plasterers begin their career by mending bad patches in existing plasterwork. This will teach you quite a lot about handling the various floats, how to apply the material and how to finish off.

If the hole is very small, or is just cracked, it may be easier to apply a plasticised filler; there are dozens of competing brands on the market. However, very often, if you tap the wall immediately around the crack or hole, it will sound hollow. This could be because you are dealing with a hollow wall (a stud wall, see below), so tap a little further around to see if the sound changes. If elsewhere on the wall the sound seems more solid, then you know that in the area around the crack the plaster no longer adheres to the wall. There are two things you can do. You can leave it, and unless someone knocks violently against

that bit of plaster, the chances are that it will stay up for many more years. Or, making a lot of mess and involving yourself in a strange new art, you can remove the defective plaster and replaster.

Begin by clearing plenty of space around the area. Then use a hammer and light steel chisel to break away the loose plaster. Make sure that all loose plaster is removed; the plaster at the edges of the bare patch should adhere firmly to the brickwork. Next, using the light chisel, remove some of the mortar in the joints between adjacent bricks, to a depth of 5 or 7mm. This will provide a key for the new plaster.

Clear up the mess of dust and rubble thoroughly. If you have a plant spray, set it at mist and spray the air to settle any floating dust particles. Nobody would bother to do so on a building site, but it stops you breathing in large quantities of dust, and also helps to cut down the amount of dust settling in the rest of the house.

Gather together the following plastering tools: a trough to mix plaster in (for a small area a large washing-up bowl will do; a steel and a wooden float; a squeezy bottle; a levelling batten (50 × 25mm or 75 × 40mm in section), and long enough to cover the hole; a bowl and brush to flick water onto the wall; a hawk.

You will need to buy two types of plaster. Browning, which is used as undercoat, usually comes in 50kg bags, but a lot of builders' merchants also stock 25kg bags or even smaller quantities. You will also need a finishing plaster. If you are going to need only enough for making good one hole, you could do worse than buy just a large box or bag of filler instead of finishing plaster.

Using the brush dipped in water, flick the bare patch of brickwork with water, making sure that the water penetrates into the crevices and joints between the bricks. Start knocking up the browning plaster for your first layer. Mix it thoroughly, then use the steel float to lift up some of the mixture onto your hawk. Use the back (or top, if you like) of the float, and slide the mixture sideways onto the hawk with a jerking movement (Fig 80). Lift it up again with the back of the float,

Sudden jerk upwards to stop plaster onto hawk

**Fig 80** Picking up plaster (*a*) and transferring it onto hawk (*b*)

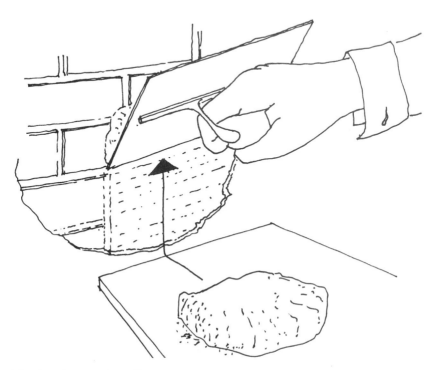

**Fig 81** Applying the plaster to the wall

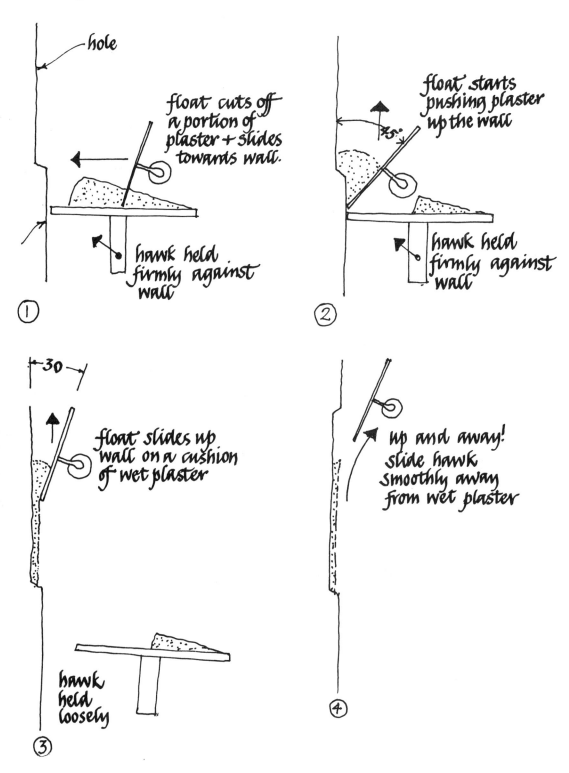

**Fig 82** Laying a stroke of plaster

and slide it down onto the hawk; do this several times to obtain a really plastic mixture.

Hold the hawk against the wall at the foot of the hole and, using the float as a push, slide the plaster onto the wall (Fig 81). The hawk is held at about 90° to the wall, and the float starts at about 45°, and then, with a fluid movement, switches over to about 30° to slide the plaster up and press it against the brickwork (Fig 82). As this is the thick undercoat, your hawk will be empty within two or three pushes. Pick up more, mix it again on the hawk, and continue filling the hole.

This undercoat should be no more than 10mm or so thick. In practice, the thickness of the undercoat is determined by the thickness of the adjacent plasterwork, and the undercoat should finish about 1mm below the surface of the old plasterwork. If you are dealing with a house whose walls have been plastered more than forty years ago, it is likely that the total thickness of plaster will be about 18–20mm, and you will need two undercoats (each about 9mm thick) before you finish 1mm below the surface of the existing plaster. More modern houses will have only about 10–12mm plaster, and you will therefore need only one thick undercoat. Use the batten as a measure; lay the ends on the surface of the old plasterwork, and see how much space is left between the underside of the wood and the new plaster undercoat.

The undercoat should be finished reasonably flat, but not smooth, using the wooden float. It should then be roughened with a scratching float, which is essentially a wooden float with nails sticking out through the bottom.

Leave the first coat to dry for at least a couple of hours. A good idea is to apply the first coat in the morning, and the second one (if needed) after lunch. Again, wet the whole area, and apply a second coat of browning over the first one, using hawk and float as before. This coat must finish roughly flush with the adjacent surface (but never proud of it), and be really flat. This is simple enough. As you apply the second coat, use the long piece of timber batten as a vertical levelling batten. The two ends are placed on the existing (old) plaster, and the batten is slid backing

Using the wooden float for the first coat

wards and forwards in a sawing fashion, and at the same time is slowly slid sideways. Any plaster above the level of the old plasterwork is 'sawn' off and falls to the ground. Any hollows are filled up with more plaster using your float. Eventually the whole area of the patch is filled up with fresh plaster level with the old plaster.

The second coat will now be level, but not smooth. Leave it, in its roughened state, to dry out for a day or so. This coat does not need to be 'keyed' with the nail float; the surface is rough enough as it is.

Using the metal float for a smooth finish on the final coat

The final coat — the finishing coat — needs a little more care. Use a different type of plaster specially formulated for finishing, mix the powder with water as before, and apply using the same steel float and hawk. This time the mix is pushed against the wall, and the steel hawk run up with it to spread the mixture as quickly as possible in a very thin layer over the rough surface of the second coat. Cover the whole surface of the patch with the plaster as quickly as possible, and then start polishing the surface with the flat of the steel float. Start at the bottom left, (if you are right-handed), and sweep the float in an arc, up to the right and then down again. Slide the float off the plaster surface, and start again at the left a little higher up this time. Continue till all the rough surface is smoothed over.

You will be surprised to find that the float does all the work. As long as you put a little more pressure on the left-hand edge of the float (assuming you are right-handed) than the right-hand side, and sweep to the right, you will find that you leave behind smooth surfaces. As the finishing coat of plaster begins to dry out, you may need to dip your float into the basin of water before continuing to sweep.

When the whole area has been swept smooth, hold a light against the wall to one side, so that any hollows or bumps will be revealed. Fill any hollows with a little extra finishing plaster and smooth as before. Flatten bumps by dipping the float into water and pressing down very firmly as you sweep over the offending area.

## Making good corners

Corners are more difficult to deal with because there is no surrounding wall on all sides to make the level across which you can slide your wooden levelling rule. Internal corners are not such a problem — you can always slide your rule across vertically; and,

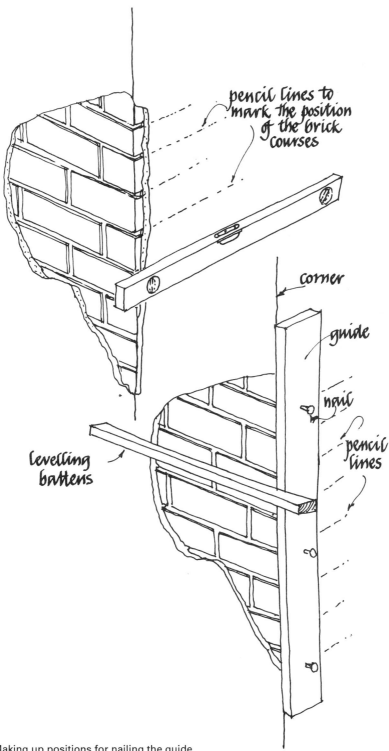

pencil lines to mark the position of the brick courses

corner

guide

nail

pencil lines

levelling battens

**Fig 83** (a) Making up positions for nailing the guide batten; (b) guide batten nailed into position at damaged corner

in any case, internal corners rarely get damaged. External corners can, however, be a problem.

Knock the old plaster away till you reach solid plaster, and clean up the joints between the bricks in the usual way. Run a spirit level along the wall, and mark the position of the mortar joints on the wall around the corner from the wall to be plastered (Fig 83a). Now take a length of 100 × 150mm wide board and nail it to the good wall using masonry nails driven through the wood into the mortar joints (the pencil marks show where these are). The edge of this board should be level with the good plaster on the wall we want to repair (Fig 83b).

Now plaster that section of the wall in the usual way, using as a guide the edge of the timber board on one side and the good plaster on the other. Apply all three coats (and

**Fig 84** Plastering an entire wall using the guide batten method.

let them dry in between) before removing the timber board.

If both walls approaching the corner need plastering, then the second wall cannot be started until the first wall is complete. (This is not the way a professional would tackle the job, but this book is specifically written for those who have not got the time or opportunity to develop professional skills.)

## Plastering a wall

Two methods can be used to plaster an entire wall: the dab method and the batten method. The batten method is the one usually recommended to the amateur. Battens are fixed to the bare brick (or whatever) wall to serve as a guide for the levelling rule (Fig 84). Its great disadvantage, however, is that the battens have to be nailed to the wall and fixing the battens to the brickwork can be quite a problem. Either the masonry nails hit a brick which is too hard to penetrate or the nails hit

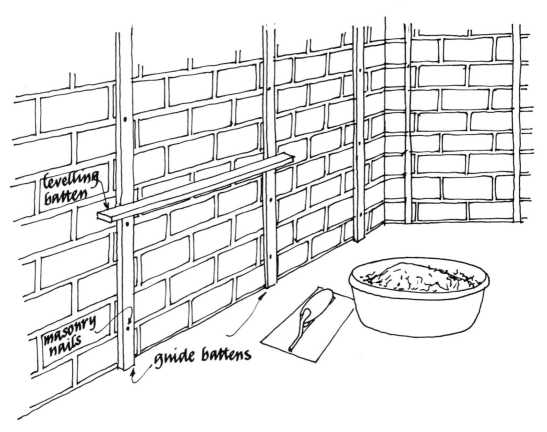

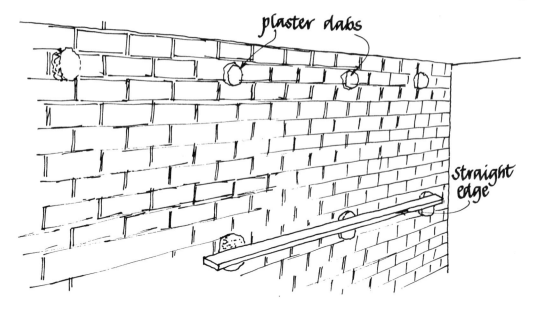

**plaster dabs**

**straight edge**

the mortar joint which is too soft to hold the batten! On top of this, the battens have to be removed at a later stage when the plaster is flush with the top of the batten. For these reasons, I have given up this method and prefer the professional one — the dab method.

Begin by mixing up a small amount of browning plaster, and place a dab (approximately the final thickness of the plaster coat) near the top of the wall at each corner, and in between at intervals of not more than 1.2 metres. Using a straight timber batten about 2.5 metres long, check that the finished thickness of each dab is such that the surfaces of any three dabs are in line (Fig 85). This way you can check that all the dabs on the wall are

**Fig 85** Plastering an entire wall using the dab method

level. If the brickwork has not been built absolutely straight, you may well find that the dabs are of different thicknesses; it is more important that they are level than that they are all of the same thickness (Fig 86).

Place similar dabs at the foot of the wall immediately below the upper dabs. Use the 2.5 metre timber batten and a spirit level to check that the lower dab finishes exactly at the same level as the upper one. Complete all lower dabs, and again check that the surfaces

**Fig 86** Making sure that the dabs are level on a horizontal plane

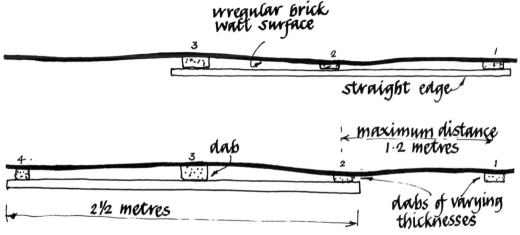

irregular brick wall surface

straight edge

maximum distance 1·2 metres

dab

2½ metres

dabs of varying thicknesses

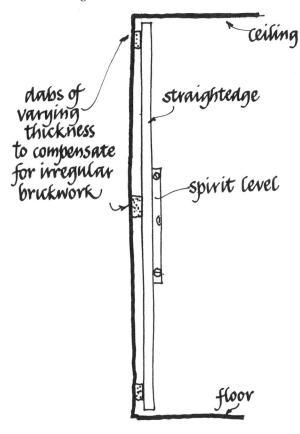

dabs of varying thickness to compensate for irregular brickwork

ceiling

straightedge

spirit level

floor

of any three of them are in line, and that each is vertically below the upper one (Fig 87). These dabs form the framework of your finished wall, so proceed slowly and carefully till they are all exactly level. The size of the dab is not all that important; 100 × 100mm is about right.

Now mix up a much larger batch of plaster and, using the hawk and metal float, lay a vertical strip of plaster, about 200mm wide, starting at the lower dab and working up to the top. Use your 2.5 metre rod, resting each end on the plaster dabs, in a sawing and sliding motion to level off this strip of plaster. Form similar strips connecting each pair of upper and lower dabs. Then let this dry out for a couple of hours (Fig 88).

Now apply the undercoat to the rest of the wall; the vertical strips of partly dried plaster form the guides for the timber levelling batten to slide/saw surplus plaster away and produce a level surface. The area next to the corner is left to the last. When the rest of the wall is reasonably flat, this last section is filled with undercoat, with the levelling batten resting on the main plastered area.

**Fig 87** Setting up dabs on a vertical plane

**Fig 88** Laying the vertical strokes first

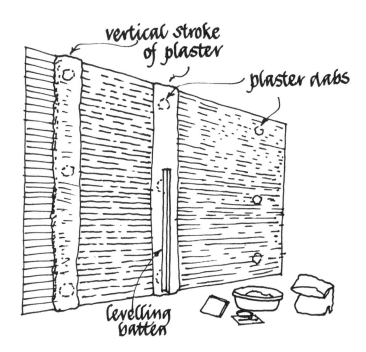

vertical stroke of plaster

plaster dabs

levelling batten

Finish the first undercoat with a wooden float, and then use a scratch float to roughen the surface before it dries. Use the 2.5 metre batten to check that the wall as a whole is reasonably straight and flat. If the wall is not straight enough, you can remedy this when putting on the dabs for a second undercoat.

The second coat is applied in the same way as the first coat, but this time the depth of the plaster dabs is much less (7–10mm). You can also thicken some of the dabs if you feel the wall should be straightened out. The second coat is also finished with a wooden float, but this time is not roughened. You should now have a wall with a reasonably thick (but not too thick) coat of plaster that is flat and straight, and ready to receive the finishing coat.

This one is the most difficult of all. However, if the second coat has been finished reasonably straight and level, and smoothed over with a wooden float, then the third coat can be applied with a steel float and stand a reasonable chance of being finished flat and smooth. Apply only a thin coat — just enough to cover the second coat — and smooth it using the steel float in broad sweeping strokes of the arm.

If this is your first wall, do not expect too much of it. If you can manage to finish flat and smooth enough to receive a thick wallpaper then you have done well. Plastering such a surface completely accurately demands more experience than you are likely to build up dealing only with odd jobs around the house.

## Corner beading

If you are plastering entire walls, you will occasionally have to deal with external corners. These can be dealt with using the same method used to repair the odd corner, but this takes a lot of time, and in any case it might be advisable to strengthen the corner first.

Use a metal corner for this; these are long strips of metal cut to suit, with an expanded metal flap to each side, which are bent over in the middle to form a bead (Fig 89). The two flaps are nailed to the brickwork using

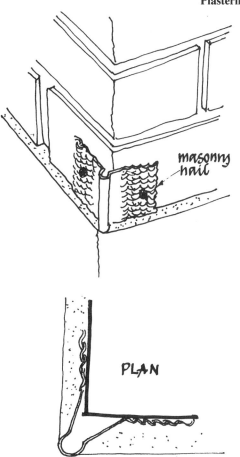

**Fig 89** Reinforcing a corner

masonry nails. The strip should be positioned accurately so that the bead (that is the rounded metal corner sticking out) is exactly at the corner of your two walls.

You can now use this bead as the guide to the left (or right) of the wall you are plastering. Eventually the new plaster is taken right up to the bead; after paint or wallpaper is applied, the bead will not show and yet it will prevent chips being knocked out of this vulnerable corner.

## Patching plaster-and-lath

Older houses have ceilings which show distressing tendencies to crack or even come down at times, such as the time when I flushed an old lavatory hard and brought the bathroom ceiling down.

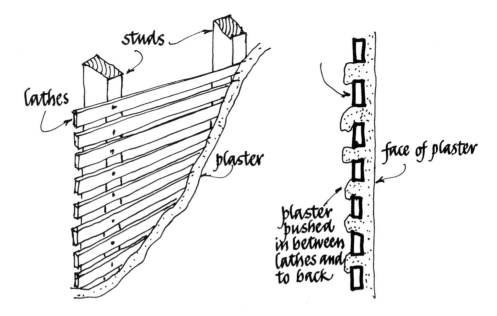

**Fig 90** Plaster-on-lath stud partition

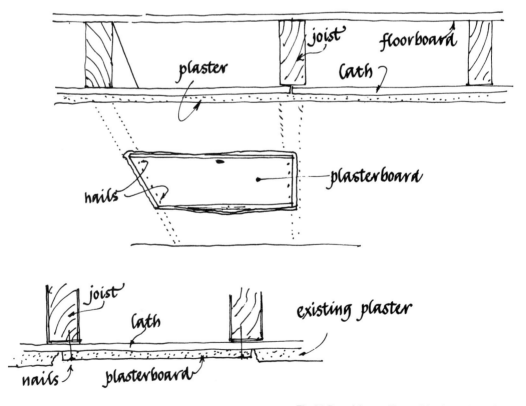

**Fig 91** Repairing ceiling with plasterboard

The plaster used in these older houses was usually a mixture of plaster of Paris and goat (or ox) hair, pushed onto a lathing made of irregularly split strips of wood nailed to the ceiling joists (Fig 90). The laths are generally so thin that they are flexible; over the years, as furniture is moved, the joists move, the laths move and the plaster tries to move. Being plaster, it cannot, and so it cracks instead.

Generally, when an old house is being renovated, the contractor prefers to remove the old ceiling completely and replace it with modern plasterboard. Bearing in mind the cost of labour, this is the cheaper alternative to making good all the cracks and renewing the plaster in one or two areas. However, renewing a plaster ceiling makes an incredible mess, and your labour charges as a DIY man (or woman) are minimal, so there is no real reason why you should not learn to repair the old type of ceiling. And anyway, mending a ceiling is not all that different from mending a wall.

There are two main methods used to mend a small(ish) area of ceiling. Both involve you in cleaning up the area thoroughly, and removing the crumbling plaster at the edges. The first method uses plasterboard which is nailed to the joists, leaving the laths in place and skimming over the plasterboard to leave a flat ceiling. Usually this means enlarging the hole along the direction of the laths till you reach the joists; it also helps if the hole produced is rectangular (Fig 91). The plasterboard is nailed into place using flat-headed plasterboard nails (felting nails will do if you cannot get hold of the proper nails) which are driven home till the heads are flush with the plasterboard (Fig 92).

Using bonding, roughly fill up the gaps between the existing plaster and the plasterboard. Now comes the difficult bit; we need to finish off neatly to leave a perfectly flat ceiling.

Make sure that the floor below the patch is adequately covered with plastic, as you are going to make an awful mess — even a professional would, so do not feel ashamed about it. Mix up a slightly stiffish finishing plaster, slop the mess on your hawk as usual,

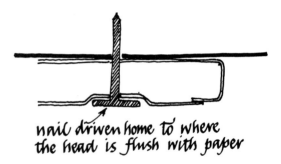

*nail driven home to where the head is flush with paper*

**Fig 92** Punching in nail head so that it is flush with the plasterboard

and use your steel float to transfer a small amount directly onto the plasterboard. Spread it out, but do not try to smooth it. Continue to transfer small amounts of plaster over the whole area till enough plaster adheres to the ceiling to make up the amount needed for finishing off.

Now you can use the levelling batten to saw the area flat; you may have to add a little more plaster in places. You may be tempted to hold a bucket under the levelling batten, hoping to catch some of the plaster before it drops, but you will fail to catch it, and your other hand is better employed holding the float to prevent whole areas of plaster being rolled off where they have not adhered properly to the ceiling. Once fairly level, the area is now floated smooth in the normal way, and then left to dry.

The plasterboard method is the one usually recommended to amateurs, but it has one or two disadvantages. First, the hole has to be made much bigger, thus increasing the chances that further bad patches will come loose and have to be repaired; before you know it, the whole ceiling has to come down. Secondly, knocking in the nails to hold the plasterboard can disturb the laths to such an extent that adjacent areas of plaster come down.

To avoid this, why not simply replaster the hole in the old-fashioned way? As with the plasterboard method, clear the area of loose and crumbly plaster, but there is no need to enlarge the hole. Instead, knock up a large quantity of slightly stiffish browning. If you can get hold of plastering hair (some old-fashioned builders' merchants still stock it) or can unravel sisal string, mix it in with the plaster to act as reinforcement. Now pick up this messy mixture from the hawk, dexterously swivel it up and simply push it against the lathing. Hold your hawk beneath to catch the mess as it slops down. Try again, picking up a good load and pressing it firmly. This time, some of the plaster will squeeze through the laths and the mess will stay in place.

Make no attempt to flatten the plaster at this stage, but simply try to get plaster to stay in place over the whole area. Once this is done, you can use the wooden float to flatten the worst of the bumps. Check with the levelling batten that none of the bumps comes below the general level of the ceiling. Leave it all to dry for an hour or two.

Now apply a second coat of browning; this time the plaster will adhere easily. Concentrate on getting this coat flat, using the levelling batten to 'saw' the area. Again, the coat should be left to dry for several hours. The last coat will be finishing plaster; flatten it and then float it in the normal way.

So much for making good holes in the ceiling. Other problems may arise when you have to deal with mouldings and coves. There are no real short cuts; you will have to try to replace damaged parts with new plaster using merely a good eye and a steady hand.

The stud walls found in so many old houses can be repaired in exactly the same way as the plaster-and-lath ceiling, using either method. This operation will be much less difficult since you (usually) work at a much lower level, and you work on a vertical plane instead of horizontal but upside-down.

## Replacing a whole ceiling

Replacing a complete ceiling means that the old ceiling must be taken down. This is an extremely messy job — wear a breathing filter and goggles and allow a full day for the work. When all the old plaster and laths have been removed, check the joists for nails. These must be removed or hammered in. Now gather the plasterboard, large quantities of plasterboard nails and a large box (or even bag) of filler.

Manoeuvring large sheets of plasterboard can be quite difficult. It is easiest when there are three of you, two to hold the board up while the third one nails it into place. Begin by making some props. Fig 93 shows more or less what is required. Use 50 × 25mm softwood nailed together. Old timber is perfectly good enough, but make sure there are no nails or splinters to damage your hands.

The length of the plasterboard sheets

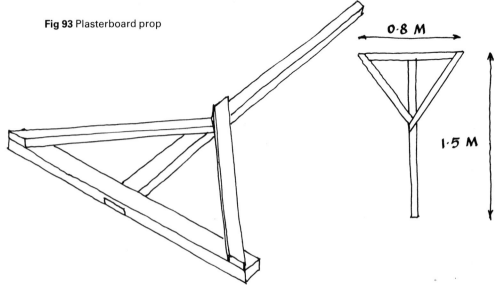

**Fig 93** Plasterboard prop

0·8 M

1·5 M

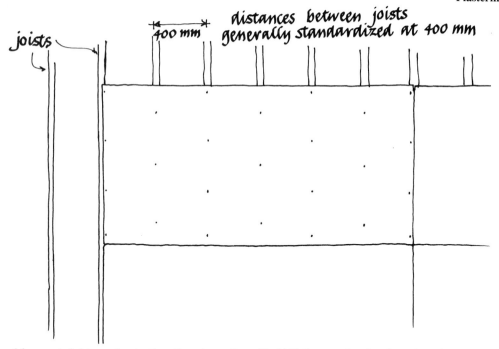

joists

400 mm

*distances between joists generally standardized at 400 mm*

**Fig 94** Nail patterning for plasterboard

should run at right-angles to the direction of the joists. Plasterboard has two slightly different sides:

### (1) *The 'good' side*
This is usually white with no paper seams or bits of paper folded over. Use this side when the plasterboard is not to be skimmed over with finishing plaster.

### (2) *The rough side*
This is often slightly grey and will have the paper of the 'good' side folded over and stuck down. This side will take a plaster skim coat much better.

Decide, before starting to nail the plasterboard into place, whether you will finish the surface by patching over the nail holes, or whether it will be skimmed (which I would be inclined to have done by a professional).

The ends of the plasterboard should finish at the halfway point of the thickness of the joist; this may mean that you have to cut the plasterboard. This is done by pushing the point of a reasonably sharp Stanley knife into the plasterboard and running it along a steel rule. The knife need only cut through the paper backing and a few millimetres of the plaster core. Turn the plasterboard over, and

fold along the line; then slit the other paper backing with a sharp kitchen knife.

To put the plasterboard up in place, one person holds one end and climbs up a stepladder while a second person stays on the ground holding the other end. A third person stands in between and pushes up with his prop to hold the plasterboard against the joists. Now the second person can use the second prop to push against the far end while the first person nails the plasterboard to the ceiling joists.

Once one end is nailed into place, the two people with props can move along a little, and the other end is then nailed into place. Now it becomes fairly easy to hammer in nails through the plasterboard into the intermediate joists (Fig 94). Use four or five nails on every other joist and three or four nails on the joist in between. The nails should be punched in so that the head of the nail is level with the surface of the plasterboard (*see* Fig 92).

When all the plasterboard is up, fill in the joints between adjacent sheets. The method of making good the joint depends on how the ceiling is to be finished, as follows:

### (1) *Professionally skimmed*

A very thin layer of finishing plaster is applied over the entire ceiling. Before applying the skim coat, the joint and the area around the joint are filled with board finish plaster into which cotton scrim (which looks like bandage gauze) is pressed to act as reinforcement.

### (2) *Self-finished plasterboard*

Use old-fashioned brown-paper gummed tape to cover the cracks between adjoining sheets of board. Cover over the tape and the nail heads with a filler paste (such as Polyfilla) using a palette knife. If you have taken care to drive the nails in properly, and the boards are accurately nailed to the joists, the resulting ceiling will not need any further treatment. The ceiling can be finished using thick lining paper or wood chip paper.

The junction between ceiling and wall can be left plain, but most rooms look more attractive if a cove is fitted. Coves used to be made of plaster and required skill and craftsmanship to construct. Nowadays ready-moulded polystyrene coves can be bought which can be cut to size and stuck into place.

You might also, if you like a roughly textured surface, experiment with decorative ceiling finishes. These are pastes halfway between plaster and paint, which can be mixed and applied with an old sponge or brush to leave a textured ceiling. Such a finish can cover up a lot of sins!

# 8 Tiling and Paving

Tiles go back to very ancient times, to ancient Egypt and even Babylon. The Romans used them to decorate their villas. They were used throughout the Middle East, and even today you can see whole mosques clad in ceramic tiles of gorgeous colours: blues, greens, purples and even gold.

Because ceramic tiles have such an ancient history, there are now many various types of tiles of differing design and construction. Traditionally, tiles were made by hand and the crude firing process, coupled with incon-sistencies in the clay, resulted in tiles that could differ in size by 1 or 2mm in length, width and even thickness. These differences were accommodated by varying the thickness of the mortar bed in which they were laid, and by varying the width of the joints be-tween the tiles. Fixing tiles was therefore a craft needing great skills and a true eye.

Modern tiles come in more exact sizes, and will often have spacer lugs so that the joints will be of uniform size throughout. They are designed to be fixed using special glues, which are thinner than traditional mortar, and therefore do not allow you to accommo-date variations in tile thickness.

In countries like Spain and Italy tiles are used on walls and floors throughout the house. Obviously they help to promote a feeling of coolness during the long hot Mediterranean summer, but in winter they are cold surfaces. It is therefore best to avoid tiles in bedrooms and living rooms unless you have underfloor heating or are prepared to cover the tiles with mats or carpets in winter.

In Britain, tiles are used in moderate quan-tities in the kitchen and bathroom, generally

Kitchen walls and worktops tiled with matching plain and patterned mosaic tiles (*Langley London Ltd*)

Bathroom floor, walls and surrounds tiled with matching plain and patterned tiles (*Langley London Ltd*)

as splashbacks; occasionally, a shower area has tiled walls, but usually that is the limit. Yet tiles can be used with great effect throughout the house and, although tiles can be expensive, if you are laying them yourself, the cost need not be all that great.

Tiles provide a hard, durable, waterproof and decorative finish. They can 'iron out' uneven floors and walls, and hide the ugliness of the bare concrete or brickwork wall or floor. They are easy to clean, maintain their fresh look over many years, and wear only very slowly. No wonder they have retained their popularity over the centuries.

## Choice of tiles

There are two main divisions in the world of tiles: floor tiles and wall tiles. Floor tiles are generally larger, stronger, thicker and heavier. They need to be wear-resistant and tough enough to take the weight of human beings and furniture without cracking or chipping. Some floor tiles are so decorative that one is tempted to use them as wall tiles; in such a case, the wall that takes them must be solid and strong: plasterboard on studs is not ideal.

Wall tiles are generally thinner, lighter and smaller. They are meant to be decorative only, although they also form the waterproof surface that is so useful near sinks, basins, baths and showers. Most British wall tiles seem to be machine-made, and form perfect (or almost perfect) squares of 100 × 100mm or 150 × 150mm (4in or 6in square) with little nibs protruding to give an automatically spaced joint to the next tile (Fig 95). There are specials for use at corners and edges where the nibs are left off, and the side(s) of the tile are glazed. This type of tile is very thin, can be easily glued to the wall, and is very easy to cut and work. They are very practical and are used in bathrooms in Britain by the million — though they are perhaps a little dull.

A second way of classifying tiles is by the method of applying them to the chosen surface. From the start you will need to know whether the tile you want can be fixed using glue (a fairly simple and quick method) or

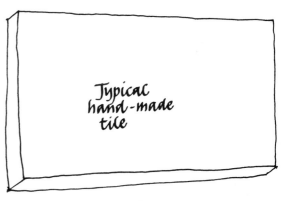

**Fig 95** Machine-made and hand-made tiles

needs the old-fashioned mortar bed (a more complicated procedure). Thin wall tiles are easily applied using glue, but thicker floor tiles will need mortar; so also the fancy imported tiles with curved or interlocking patterns which are often irregular in size and need to be accommodated in mortar.

While in the past most British builders' merchants would stock half a dozen plain square tiles in British Standard colours, and perhaps two or three specials with a pattern printed on the background before firing, nowadays there is a much greater choice. Most large builders' merchants have a tile department and there are now specialist tile shops in Britain where there is an incredible range of different tiles: in a variety of colours, motifs, sizes, thicknesses, smooth or rough, sculptured or flat. You will be entranced by the possibilities and shocked by the prices.

Vitrified glazed mosaic tiles on kitchen walls and
worktops (*Langley London Ltd*)

The choice is probably even greater on the Continent. In Holland I have seen a warehouse with two or three thousand different tiles to choose from, but most of these tiles are imported and can be found in Britain, given enough time, patience and money.

The choice can therefore be bewildering, so think carefully before you make your decision. The plain or print-decorated wall tiles stocked by most builders' merchants may appear less interesting but they are fairly cheap and are readily obtainable. If you later discover you need more tiles, it should be possible to obtain more of the same. The more unusual tiles from the specialist tile shop may look more interesting, but they also have more drawbacks. First, many of these tiles are hand-made and are therefore both more expensive and less accurate than their machine-made cousins; this can make laying them much more difficult (*see* p 114). Secondly, delivery may be a problem. The tile you want may have a three- or six-month delivery time as it slowly winds its way from Italy (or wherever), a prey to strikes, careless company employees and difficult customs officials. Thirdly, always buy all the tiles you need at one go, since it is more than likely that you will never be able to buy a further matching supply. Do not believe the promises the salesman makes. After all, he will not

suffer if he turns out to be wrong, but you will.

Leaving aside the machine-made British wall tile, there are four basic types:

(1) *A thick and heavy tile that can be used for both floor and wall.* This is usually made by hand and fired under less than perfect conditions: each tile is an individual. Sizes vary enormously; there are as many square as longitudinal tiles, and unlike the British tiles, there are no standard sizes. On the whole these thick tiles should be used on solid floors and walls only: do not use them on timber floors or stud partition walls.

(2) *A thinner tile that can be used for all types of floor and wall.* This more closely approaches the British machine-made tile. Thicknesses are typically between 5 and 10mm; sizes vary greatly, but 100 × 200mm will be a typical size.

(3) *A mini-tile.* This is usually sold in mats of half a square metre stuck to a coarse open-weave fabric; the tiles are invariably square and vary in size between 20 and 50mm each side. The tiles are generally all the same colour with variations in the glaze itself making

**Fig 96** Quarry tile 'specials'

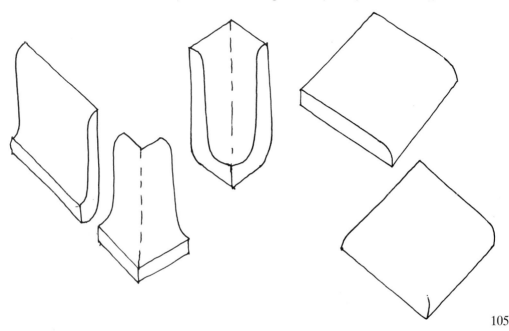

for interest. Some types of mat have an occasional and deliberate differently coloured interloper.

(4) *The quarry tile*. The name comes from the French word '*carree*', meaning square, and the tiles are indeed square in shape, and very accurate in their dimensions. They are used mostly for flooring and are usually about 10–15mm thick and either 100 or 150mm to a side. Their colouring varies from light biscuit to deep reddish-brown, and is the colour of the clay seen through the transparent glaze. They are intended for floors, and a whole range of special shapes allows them to follow the form of the floor, walls and coves (Fig 96). They are extremely strong, acid-resistant and waterproof and are therefore ideal for industrial premises involving water, acids and dirt. They also make a hard-wearing surface around the house.

Standard British tiles are square (either $100 \times 100$ or $150 \times 150$mm), but foreign and hand-made tiles come in all sorts of shapes. Probably everyone has seen the multi-curved Spanish floor tiles that fit so cunningly into

one another. Other possibilities are complementary sets, made up of large and small tiles which can be fitted together to form interesting patterns (Fig 97). Yet another frequently used system is to design the tile pattern in such a way that combinations of tiles produce 'super-patterns'. Some such patterns use four tiles, others eight or sometimes even more. It all makes for variety.

On occasion you may want to lay tiles outside the house (*see* Project 1). Some tiles are deliberately designed to be 'frost-proof' whereas others will simply disintegrate with time.

## Laying tiles

The method of laying the tile depends on two factors: the type of tile and the underlying surface. Machine-made tiles can generally be glued into place. The strength of the bond depends very much on the thickness of the glue — the thinner the stronger. A hand-made tile could mean that the glue would be 1 or 2mm thick in places. Glue can be used for smooth vertical or horizontal surfaces, but a rough floor that will need to take the weight of human beings and furniture needs

**Fig 97** Interlocking tiles

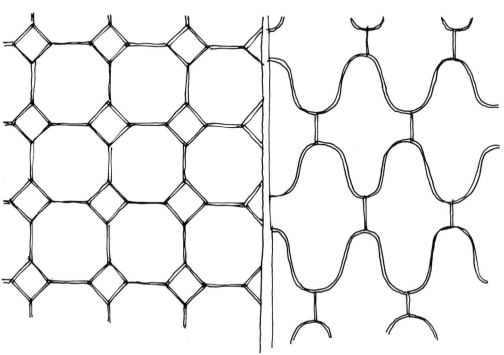

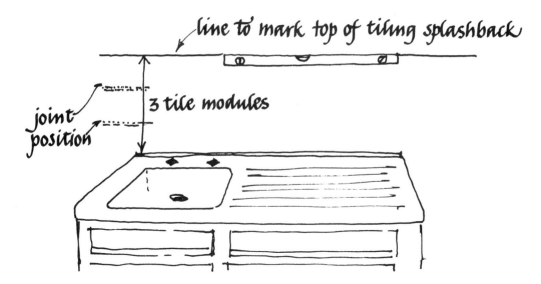

*line to mark top of tiling splashback*

*joint position*

*3 tile modules*

a thick bedding for tiles, usually a weak sand/cement mixture.

## The glue method

For the glue method you will need: the tiles; a large pot of glue; a comb to spread the glue; battens and a spirit level to check that the tiles are laid straight; tiling separators if the tiles have no nibs and are to be laid vertically; and, most important, a flat, clean surface. A plaster wall, plasterboard or a thick blockboard timber surface are all suitable. An old unplastered or rough-plastered brick wall will not do, nor will a roughly finished concrete wall. The adhesion of the tile to the underlying surface depends on a fairly thin film of glue holding the two together over the whole surface of the tile. A rough or undulating surface means the use of great quantities of (fairly expensive) glue, an uneven tiled surface and the strong possibility that tiles will be coming down over the next few years.

The surface must also be clean. If you are tiling in the kitchen, the chances are strong that a thin film of grease will have built up over the years. This must be removed, along with all wallpaper and flaky paint, especially whitewash or distemper. If you are tiling over old distemper or whitewash, remove as much as possible, and then seal the wall with a bonding agent, as for plastering.

**Fig 98** Marking top of tile splashback

Let us assume the simplest situation: a splashback over a kitchen sink or bath. This usually involves fixing two or three rows of tiles over the full width of the kitchen sink or bath and a little bit extra to each side.

Begin by marking off the top edge of the splashback (Fig 98). This top edge will be determined by the tile module and the height of the sink or bath in most cases. Obviously, you do not want to cut tiles unnecessarily, so that if you make this top line exactly two or three or four times the height of the tile (plus an allowance for the thickness of the joint) then life will be a lot easier. Occasionally the top edge will be determined by a window or other feature. Try to come to a sensible decision as to whether the cut tile will be at the top or the bottom course. Alternatively, you could use a different, and perhaps contrasting, tile that happens to fit. Try to use your imagination and common sense.

The top edge should be horizontal but, again, be sensible. If your kitchen sink (or bath or floor of the room) is a little out of true, make the top line parallel with the sink (or bath or floor) rather than have to 'nibble' 2 or 3mm off the bottom of twenty or thirty tiles.

Give some thought to the position of the vertical joints. The professional tiler, for example, tries to set his tiles in such a way that they are symmetrical about either a central tile or a central joint. If you are going to tile between two particular features — such as between two corners or between a corner and window frame — then you should try to finish up with a cut tile at each end of the row. This cut tile should be not less than half a tile (otherwise cutting becomes difficult).

Have a look at the following examples, taking a tile module (ie tile plus joint) of 150mm and considering the length of the tiled surface as:

(1) *2.4 metres:* No cutting is involved. Sixteen tiles are needed, and the centre line of the row is a joint (Fig 99).

(2) *2.25 metres:* Again, no cutting is involved. Fifteen tiles are needed, but the centre line of the row is the middle of a tile (Fig 100).

(3) *2.18 metres:* This will mean cutting tiles. One way is to use fourteen whole tiles (making 2.10 metres) and use one cut tile of 80mm width. This could be in the middle of the row (Fig 101), but that means that the 'odd' tile becomes rather noticeable, and the

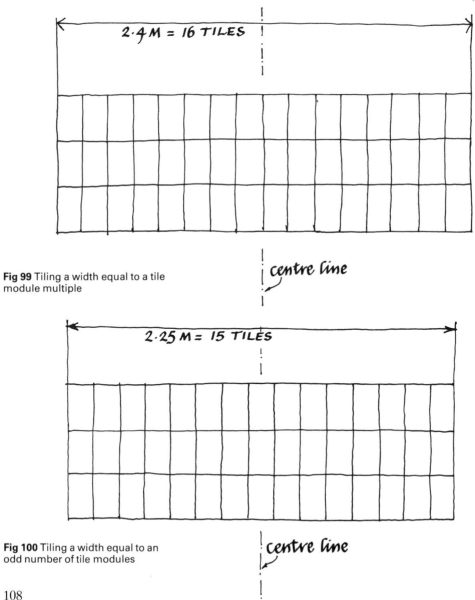

**Fig 99** Tiling a width equal to a tile module multiple

**Fig 100** Tiling a width equal to an odd number of tile modules

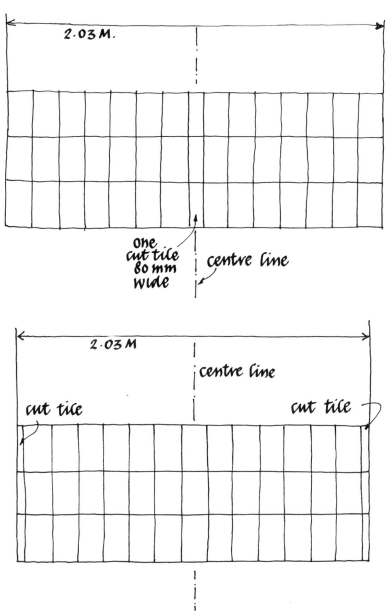

2·03 M.

one cut tile 80 mm wide

centre line

2·03 M

centre line

cut tile

cut tile

**Fig 101** Tiling a width unequal to a whole number of tiles

**Fig 102** Using two narrow cut tiles at end of row

eye quickly sees the ragged cut edge. You could put the cut tile to one end, but then you get an asymmetric tiled surface, and the eye is disturbed. What about fourteen whole tiles and two cut tiles? This is already a more satisfactory solution, even if it means more work because two tiles have to be cut, the two near the end. These would have to be 40mm each, or less than half a tile (Fig 102). Unless you have a mechanical tile cutter, this can be very difficult. Hence, finally, we come to the standard solution of using thirteen tiles, and cut-

109

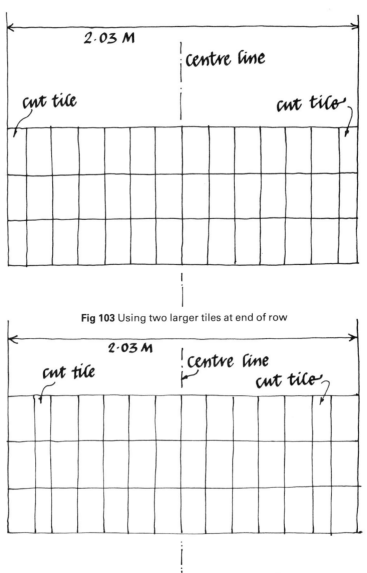

**Fig 103** Using two larger tiles at end of row

**Fig 104** Alternative solution with two cut tiles

ting two tiles of 115mm wide each. These could be at the end of the row (Fig 103), or one pleasing little trick is to place a whole tile in the corner, and the cut tile immediately next to it. Thus the two vertical rows of odd-shaped tiles come at a position a little way in from the corner (Fig 104).

(4) *1.86 metres:* Using the same ideas as for the 2.03 metre wall, we finish up with 11 whole tiles and two cut tiles of 105mm each (Fig 105).

Having decided the number of tiles and their position, it remains to mark up the vertical course nearest the middle of the row (Fig 106). This should be marked using a spirit level but, again, there is no need for it to be 100 per cent vertical.

If there is no horizontal course of cut tiles, then the first course can be laid starting directly at the bottom. However, if the lowest course consists of cut tiles, mark the position of the lowest horizontal joint and nail a timber batten along the whole length to support the first row of whole tiles. The bottom row (cut tiles) is not laid until after the glue holding all the other tiles has had a chance to dry (Fig 107).

Start spreading glue on the part of the wall

110

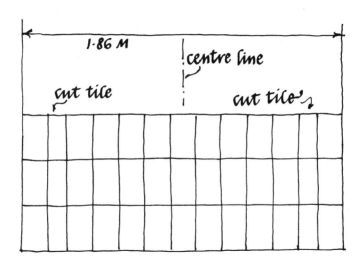

**Fig 105** Solution with an odd number of tiles

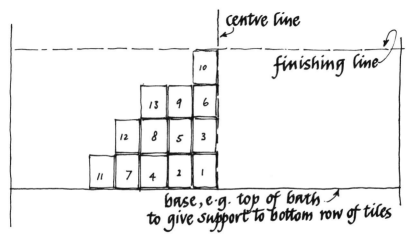

**Fig 106** Order of laying tiles, starting from centre line

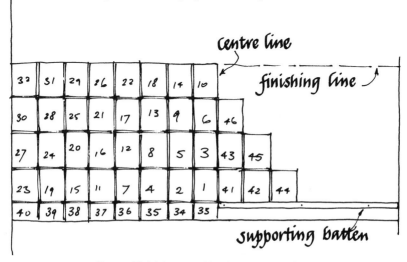

**Fig 107** Finishing up with a bottom row of cut tiles

nearest the corner formed by the bottom line (or the supporting batten) and the centre vertical line. Use the comb provided (or bought) with the glue and spread the glue so that the tip of the comb scrapes the wall; you should leave little ridges of glue. Position the first tile at the junction of the two lines, and make sure it sits absolutely square.

Now lay the next tile to the left and the tile above. If the tile has no spacer lugs, use either the special plastic lugs sold in good tile shops, or use broken-off matchsticks to ensure that the horizontal joint between the two tiles is kept open (Fig 108). Continue to lay tiles above and to the left of each tile already laid; you should advance on a diagonal front. If you work fairly quickly, you should be able to move the tiles already

**Fig 108** Spacing lugless tiles with spacer lug, matchsticks or slips of card/paper

laid just a little if you find, as you go along, that the first tile is not absolutely square. Continue along the wall till you come to the position of the cut tile.

Cutting a tile is one of the less pleasant parts of the job. Depending on the type of tile, there are three main methods:

(1) *On thin machine-made tiles*, use a glass cutter on the glazed surface and, after scoring deeply, crack the tile as you would for glass. This means putting the tile on a flat, felt-covered surface, putting a thin slat or tile off-cut more or less underneath the cut, and then pressing hard on the two edges of the tile. This should snap clean along the scored line. The method is described in all the text books, but seems to require a fair amount of dexterity and practice (Fig 109).

(2) *On most reasonably thin tiles*, a tile-cutter device seems to work better. These are

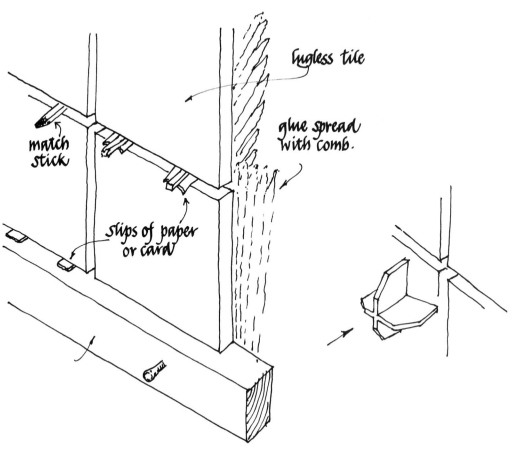

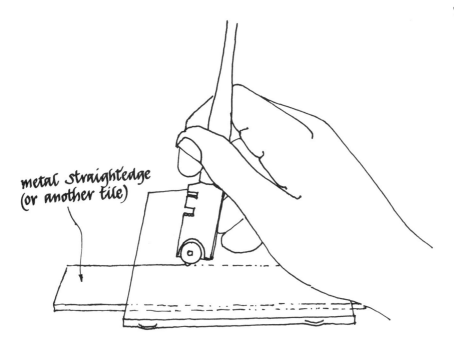

metal straightedge
(or another tile)

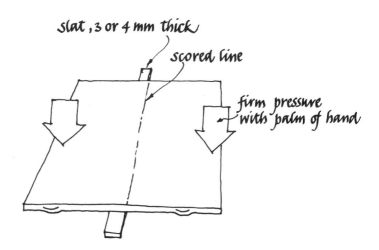

slat, 3 or 4 mm thick

scored line

firm pressure
with palm of hand

Fig 109 Scoring and breaking a tile

tools costing between £5 and £15; instructions vary with each type. The principle seems similar to the glass-cutter method, but you are more likely to achieve a satisfactory result.

The trouble with both methods 1 and 2 is that it is difficult to take 10 or 20mm off the edge of a tile; this occurs quite frequently, and so the third method is the one I much prefer.

(3) *Using a tile saw*. At the most basic level, this can be a thin hard disc attached to the home electric drill; if you are doing a lot of tiling, you might prefer to hire a large machine which can cut thin and thick tiles, and even tackle paving stones! The types made for home drills allow you to cut tiles up to 10 or 12mm thick, to cut out corners (amost impossible with the glass-cutter) or even make a fairly clean wavy cut. They are very noisy, dusty and somewhat slow; the disc tends to wear out fast, especially the

113

variety suitable for the small drill, but this method does really work, even for the unpractised hand.

Now lay the cut tiles and finish gluing the tiles to the surface on the other side of the centre line, proceeding diagonally to the right. If there is a horizontal course of cut tiles, leave these to be finished a day or two later — do not remove the supporting batten until then. Grouting has to wait a further day or two, so meanwhile you can read about laying thicker or uneven tiles on floors and uneven walls.

## Mortar bedding

The mortar bedding is a cement/sand mixture. For walls, this should be a 1 : 4 mix of cement and builder's sand to provide a firm adhesion so that the tiles will not drop off. For floors, the mix should be much leaner: mixes of 1 : 10 or even 1 : 12 are best. As the tiles will not drop off or come up away from the floor, the cement does not have to grip the tiles but the sand/cement mix must support the tile evenly throughout, otherwise the tile would crack as weight is put on one side or the other.

The wall or floor should be clean, free from dust, grease or flakes. A bonding agent spread on the brickwork or concrete is a good idea. You can lay tiles onto a suspended timber floor, but I would advise using the thinner machine-made tiles, glued onto a 12mm thick blockboard base laid over the timber floor.

Tiles are usually fixed using a thick mortar

**Fig 110** Levelling tiles laid in a mortar bed

bed because the supporting wall or floor is irregular, or because the tiles themselves are irregular. This means that additional measures must be taken to ensure that the tiles will be laid accurately so as to form a flat and level surface.

The method generally used on walls is to find battens of the same thickness as the tile plus the bed and nail them to the wall or floor above and below the area to be tiled. A third batten can now be held at right-angles against these first two battens, and used as a levelling batten to check that each tile is laid level (Fig 110). Using a thick cement also means that you cannot possibly see a pencil line marked on the wall itself. You can mark both horizontal guide battens with pencil marks to show the position of the vertical joints, and use the levelling batten as a rule.

If you are tiling a wall, spread enough mortar to take two or three tiles, and wet the back of each tile thoroughly before placing it onto the bed. The bed should be 'ridged' using the point of the trowel so that when the tile is pressed into place, the mortar will have somewhere to go underneath the tile, and not have to be squeezed out at the edges.

Hand-made tiles, of course, do not have the nibs of the machine-made tiles. Nor are they as accurately made. This means that you must decide on the width of your horizontal joint. The general rule is that the top of each tile should line up accurately with the other tiles in that course, but that the bottom will come where it happens to finish (Fig 111). The trick used by tilers is to use slips of hardboard or cardboard between the tiles so that the weight of the tile above is taken by the tile below, and the joint stays open.

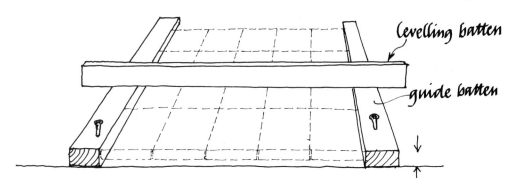

An almost completely tiled bathroom (*Langley London Ltd*)

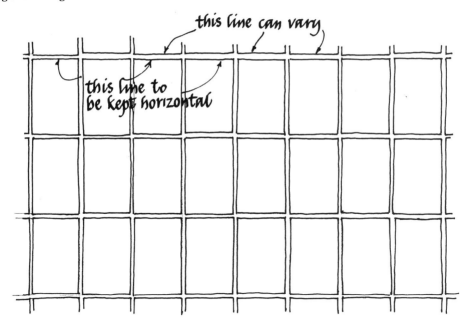

Fig 111 Lining up the tops of hand-made tiles

Begin at the first course above the bottom guide batten, and work upwards. Use spacers between each tile and the one above, so that each tile supports the weight of the tile above until the mortar has set. As each tile is placed on its little mortar bed, check not only that it is square on, but also whether it is level with the face of the finished tile surface. Use the levelling batten on each and every tile.

When all the tiles above the batten have been bedded in, leave the tiles to dry for a day or two. Finally, tile the bottom row after removing the supporting batten.

Unless you have had years and years of practice, you will be unlikely to be able to lay a perfectly smooth tiled wall using a cement bed. However, do not worry — part of the charm lies in the fact that the tiles are hand-made and hand-laid.

## Floor tiles

Floor tiles are laid in a similar fashion to wall tiles. Again, start by working out the total pattern, and aim to finish up with cut tiles (if necessary) near or at the edges. If you can use a different size tile as a border and avoid cutting tiles it will save you a lot of work, but that

is not to everyone's taste.

Having worked out the pattern, mark the two joints at right-angles to each other in the centre of the room. This sounds easy, but no room is ever really square, and so merely marking a line exactly parallel to a wall will not really work. Begin by deciding which line will be most obvious to the eye. Generally this will be the line along the length of the room, but other possibilities are a line at right-angles centring on the fireplace, or a line centring on two doors on opposite walls.

If you choose to centre along the length of the room, measure each of the short walls, and mark the centre point of each wall. Connect the two centre points using a taut line; this gives you your major axis. The first joint-line will be either on this axis or one half-tile's width to the left or right.

Using the 3 : 4 : 5 method, draw a line at right-angles to this first line. Again, this line will mark either the middle joint of the room, or the middle joint will come one half-tile to the left or right (Fig 112).

Use guide battens nailed to the floor to mark the first quadrant. The top of the battens should be the level of the finished tile floor. Now you can start laying tiles, using the same laying sequence as for walls (*see* p 111).

Patterned and mosaic tiles give completely different effects in these bathrooms (*Langley London Ltd*)

Check each tile as it is laid to see that it is square, flush and level. Take your time, and do not expect to finish the job in a few hours.

Floor tiles also need to be laid with a gap at each joint. Matchsticks are often used but, if the tile is a hand-made one, check every three rows or so that the tiles march parallel to the centre guide batten. Some people will spend time and do this by accurately measuring the distance; others prefer to do so by eye on the theory that it is the eye that must be satisfied, and that the eye is often more accurate than the ruler.

Working from the centre of the room towards the edges in each of the four quadrants, you will sooner or later need to cut tiles at the edges and borders. This should be left till last; to find out where to cut, hold the tile against the wall and upside down over the last whole tile (Fig 113). Make two marks where the cut tile crosses the edge of the whole tile, and draw a line between these two marks to show where the tile must be cut. If the cut is to be very irregular (such as near a door post), use a pair of pliers to 'nibble' the tile roughly to shape, and a very rough file to finish off the job.

When all is dry (this applies both to wall and to floor tiles, whether glued or bedded in mortar) finish the job by grouting in the joints. This means mixing up a very watery paste of cement and filler (it is usually sold ready-mixed) and adding colour and water. The mixture is then applied with a rag or sponge and 'washed' over the tiles so as to seal the joints. The grout is left to dry, but

**Fig 112** Deciding the centre of the room

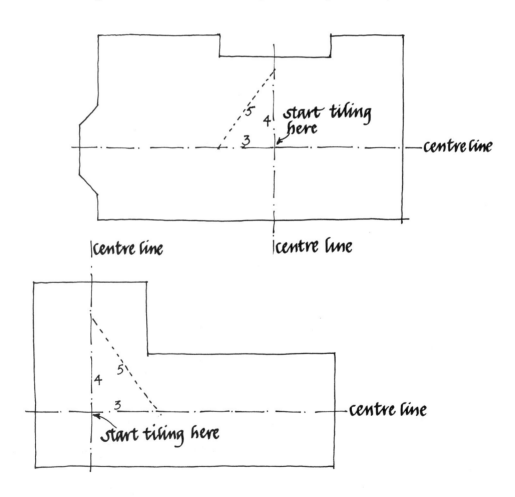

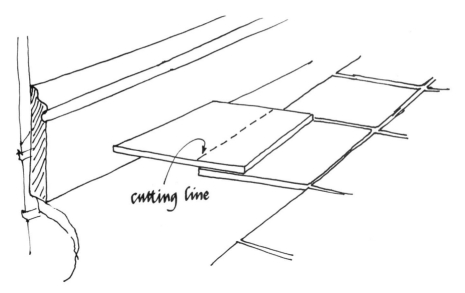

cutting line

**Fig 113** Marking the cutting line

before it is perfectly dry the whole tiled surface is rubbed clean with a dry rag. Finally, a day or two later, clean off the whole surface with a wet sponge or rag to leave a perfectly tiled surface — something to admire.

### Replacing tiles

Cracked or unwanted tiles can be broken away using a flat steel chisel. Remove old backing mortar or glue and replace with new tiles as described.

### Paving

Paving stones can come in all sorts of sizes, especially if you cast your own but generally they are made a standard 600 × 900mm in Britain, which weighs about 60kg or so, a fairly hefty weight to carry and lay down flat. Take care, therefore, that at no time do you lift one of these stones with your arms more than about 15° from the vertical, and that you avoid lifting them with a bent back whenever possible.

Begin by preparing the surface to be paved. Clear the ground of top soil to a depth of 150mm and remove all tree roots likely to disturb the paving. If the soil is soft, a layer of hardcore is a good idea, but make sure it is well compacted.

The paving stones need to rest on sharp sand; a layer of about 40–60mm is sufficient. This sand must be levelled and smoothed before laying the paving stones. This can best be done using guide battens as for concrete. The guide battens are nailed to softwood pegs hammered into the ground at the edges of the proposed paved area. For very large areas, more than about 3 metres along their shortest section, it might be as well to put down intermediate guides. Use a spirit level to check that the top of the guide batten is level throughout its length and at the same level as all other battens, and use a levelling batten to 'saw' and slide the sand bedding in much the same way as for concrete (Fig 114).

Once the sand bed is level and smooth, lay the first paving stone and use a large rubber-faced mallet to tap the paving stone gently down into place; check the stone is laid horizontally with a spirit level. Then lay the second stone adjacent to the first and against the guide batten, using small wooden pegs to separate the two stones and to make sure that the joint is kept open at a regular distance. These wooden pegs are withdrawn as soon as the second paving stone is found to be level. Then lay the third paving stone to the other side of the first one. Gradually, a diagonal laying pattern is developed. As with floor tiles, it is important to check that each course

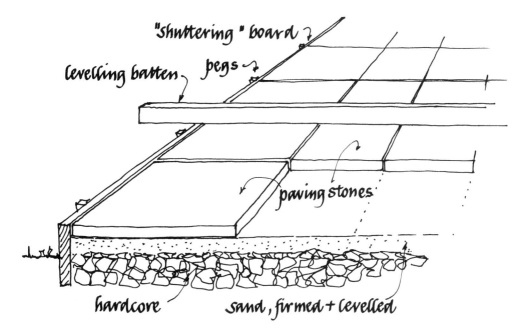

"shuttering" board

levelling batten    pegs

paving stones

hardcore    sand, firmed + levelled

**Fig 114** Laying paving stones on sand

(*left*) Levelling the sand with a roller and using a guide batten to lay the slabs

appears regular to the eye. It is not sufficient to trust to the small wooden pegs, since the paving stones themselves will be very slightly irregular. When all the paving stones have been laid, take away the guide batten, and brush sand over the paved area to fill the open joints.

Besides paving stones, bricks can make an extremely attractive paving and are much used in Holland for minor roads as well as footpaths. Again, the bricks are laid on levelled and smoothed sand, and can be laid in a variety of patterns other than the straightforward rectangular grid pattern. Possibilities are the herring-bone pattern and a radial layout. The bricks should be laid with a small gap all round into which sharp sand can be brushed once the whole area has been bricked over.

# 9 Tools

Tools are only a means to an end, though we tend to forget this when we wander into an ironmonger's shop and see rows of shiny tools hanging neatly on a rack. For some people, the end may really mean the joy derived from using, and being able to use, the best tools available. For other people, and I am one, the end means the completed project, ready for use and made without too much blood, sweat and tears.

Most books recommend the use of the best tools that money can buy, on the assumption that people will use them carefully, skilfully and lovingly. If you are planning to spend most of your weekends and holidays laying foundations, building brickwork and plastering, then learn to use tools properly and spend all the money you have on first-class equipment. Your first project could be the erection of a tool shed in which to keep all those tools! The rest of us, however, will just muddle along using whatever comes to hand in order to get the job done.

Some equipment is best hired: it would be ridiculous to spend hundreds of pounds on a concrete mixer when you will only need it for two or three weekends. Other tools are best borrowed: there is always the neighbour who will lend a wheelbarrow and shovel on the understanding that they are returned clean and in one piece together with a promise to lend him your car jack. And a whole range of equipment can be made at home, which is no worse (and certainly a lot cheaper) than if bought.

Regrettably, there will be tools that must be bought. Of course, you can go out and buy the best available, but bear the following in mind. Do you know enough about them to be able to use them without ruining them? Where will you store them so that they will not rust, get lost or be damaged? And will the tool costing two or three times as much get the job done two or three times better or faster?

Generally speaking, the cheaper tools will handle the two or three jobs for which they are required perfectly adequately. This does not mean, though, that you should buy the cheapest tool available, and most definitely does not mean you should buy the 'wonder tool' that does seven jobs. Nevertheless, you will find yourself offered the choice between two differently priced tools and the shop assistant will be unable to tell you why one is better than the other except that one brand is better known. Simply ask yourself whether the tool can do the job that you want done to the standard which satisfies you.

Also look out for second-hand tools at market stalls and junk shops. These are often of very good quality, and since little can go really wrong with the tools used in the wet trades, they will generally be perfectly serviceable. If they are broken or useless, that can usually be seen directly.

To sum up, there is no need to be fanatic about tools; borrow, hire or buy second-hand tools as the opportunity arises, and only buy first-class tools when you really know how to use them to their full capacity. By that time you will not be an amateur any more, and you will not really need this sort of advice.

The range of tools and equipment necessary for the wet trades can be grouped together by trade (concreting, bricklaying, plastering or tiling) as shown in the first table opposite.

Tools can also usefully be grouped by method of acquisition, whether hired, bought or made at home, as in the second table. As you will see from the first list, many of the tools needed for one trade are also necessary for another, although they may be used a little differently. The professional will have the equipment intended for a specific job only, but we can mix them quite easily.

In the following pages the main tools required are listed, with a brief description of what each one looks like and how it is used.

| Concrete | Brickwork | Plaster | Tiles |
|---|---|---|---|
| Spirit level | Spirit level | Spirit level | Spirit level |
| Medium trowel | Large trowel | Wooden float | Medium trowel |
| Wooden float | Medium trowel | Steel float | Claw hammer |
| Steel float | Pointing trowel | Scratch float | Levelling batten |
| Claw hammer | Bolster chisel | Claw hammer | Tile-cutter |
| Club hammer | Club hammer | Squeezy bottle | Glue comb |
| Wooden mallet | Brush | Brush | |
| Saw | Buckets | Buckets | |
| Squeezy bottle | Pegs and line | Hawk | |
| Brush | Gauge rod | Levelling batten | |
| Buckets | Builder's square | | |
| Pegs and line | Set square | | |
| Builder's square | Jointing rod | | |
| Tamping beam | Hawk | | |
| Levelling batten | Shovel | | |
| Shovel | | | |
| Fork | | | |
| Concrete mixer | | | |
| Rammer | | | |

| Available in the home or home-made | Bought | Hired or borrowed |
|---|---|---|
| Scratch float | Spirit level | Shovel |
| Paving mallet | Large trowel | Fork |
| Squeezy bottle | Medium trowel | Concrete mixer |
| Brush | Pointing trowel | Wheelbarrow |
| Buckets | Wooden float | Tile-cutter |
| Pegs and line | Steel float | |
| Gauge rod | Bolster chisel | |
| Builder's square | Claw hammer | |
| Jointing rod | Club hammer | |
| Hawk | Wooden mallet | |
| Tamping beam | Saw | |
| Levelling batten | Glue comb | |
| Rammer | | |

Later on in the book, when dealing with a specific project, more detailed instructions are given to describe a particular technique.

## The spirit level

The spirit level (Fig 115) is used for checking that a surface is perfectly level (or horizontal) or perfectly vertical. Buy one which is at least 600mm long with bubbles that indicate both horizontal and vertical planes. Nowadays spirit levels are usually made of aluminium and should not break or dent, but the bubbles will be made of glass and will smash if anything is dropped on them. This is one of the few instances where it is worth while spending a little more money to buy the type in which the bubbles can be replaced.

## Trowels

Trowels (Fig 116) come in a variety of sizes.

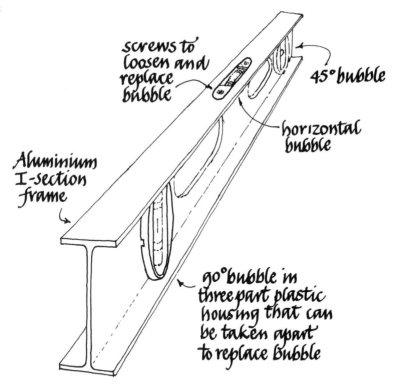

screws to loosen and replace bubble

45° bubble

horizontal bubble

Aluminium I-section frame

90° bubble in three part plastic housing that can be taken apart to replace bubble

**Fig 115** Typical spirit level

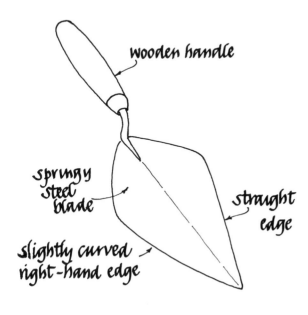

wooden handle

springy steel blade

straight edge

slightly curved right-hand edge

**Fig 116** Right-handed trowel

The larger ones are intended for use when laying bricks, the medium ones for filling in odd gaps in concrete or brickwork, and the smallest ones for pointing brickwork. The largest are best left to the professional bricklayer who can pick up a brick in the left hand and enough mortar in one scoop of the right hand to butter the brick's head. This is quick and efficient but needs two or three months of practice; the amateur would do better to use a medium-sized trowel and butter the brick in two or three movements.

Thus a medium-sized trowel and a small pointing trowel are enough for most projects. If you are buying second-hand, make sure that the blade is still straight and that the handle is not too chipped or split: rough handles are uncomfortable. Rust and old cement can be cleaned off, but if anything (either handle or blade) feels loose, reject the trowel.

Try not to let the mortar harden during (and after) a job — once you have had to clean off hardened mortar you will know why! Before putting a trowel away, rub a little oil over it.

**Fig 117** Timber float

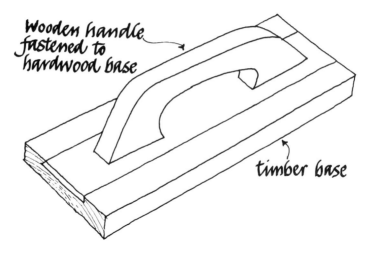

Wooden handle fastened to hardwood base

timber base

**Fig 118** Metal float

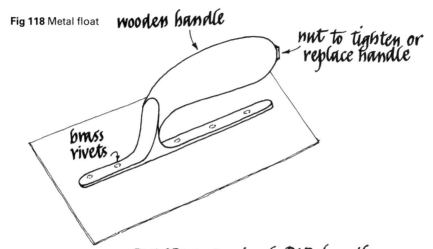

wooden handle

nut to tighten or replace handle

brass rivets

50 × 25mm nominal PAR handle

**Fig 119** Home-made scratch float

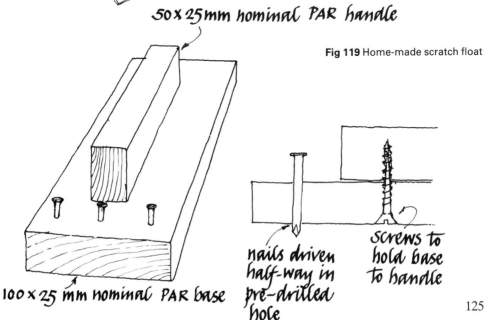

100 × 25 mm nominal PAR base

nails driven half-way in pre-drilled hole

screws to hold base to handle

*Floats*

These are the tools used to level off, both vertically and horizontally, the concrete and plaster finish to walls and floors. They all have a rectangular blade made of wood or steel, and a handle parallel to the blade. You will need both types, wood for the rough preliminary levelling, and metal for the smooth final finish (Figs 117 and 118). Only use the steel float for the final smoothing on the finishing coat, since the steel float tends to bring up the binding element (ie the cement or the plaster) resulting in crazed plaster and dusty concrete floors.

The blade must always be flat; check that a wooden float has not pulled into a curve, and check metal floats for accidental damage: a steel blade cannot really be straightened out once bent, if you want a perfect finish to plasterwork. Again, the handle should not be chipped or split, and above all, it must feel firm: a loose handle will make it very difficult to achieve a flat finish. Again, keep everything clean during and after the job.

A scratch float is used to roughen the surface of wet plaster so that it will more easily hold a subsequent coat. You could hammer nails through a spare wooden float; as an alternative, make one up yourself. Screw a piece of 50 × 25mm softwood batten to a 100 × 25mm softwood plank about 200–

250mm long; then drive nails through the plank so that the points stick out about 8–10mm on the underside (Fig 119). When run over a freshly plastered surface, this will provide all the roughness required.

*Bolster chisel*

This is a cold chisel (one made entirely of steel); the blade is very wide, often as much as 100mm wide (Fig 120). It is used to cut bricks, to roughen up brick walls before plastering and to clean out or deepen the joints between bricks before pointing.

To break bricks in half, lay the brick on sand or earth (to cushion the shock) and rest the blade of the bolster chisel on the brick. A smart blow with the club hammer will score the brick, but will rarely succeed in breaking it. Therefore turn the brick on its side and repeat the blow. Usually by the time the brick has been scored on three or four sides it snaps easily and evenly into two halves (Fig 121).

If the break is not reasonably square, use the medium trowel as an axe and, holding the brick in one hand, bang the side of the trowel smartly against the bits that have still to be removed. Small bits can thus be removed; if necessary you can chip, little by little, 20 or 30mm off the end of the brick. It needs patience and a little practice — you may have

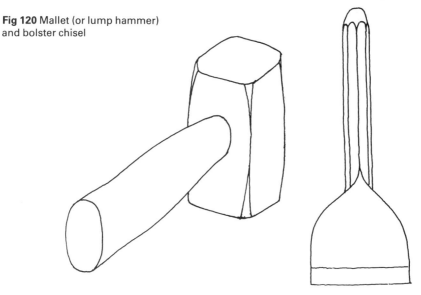

**Fig 120** Mallet (or lump hammer) and bolster chisel

to waste two or three bricks till you get the exact size.

The bolster chisel is also used to score the surface of older brickwork to make it easier for new plaster to adhere. Place the bolster chisel on the face of a brick with the blade held vertically, and bang the chisel smartly with the club hammer. Do the same again some 50mm to the left (or right) till the whole brick course is scored. Then move up a course and repeat. It sounds easy when described, but is in fact back-breaking labour; take it easy and do it in easy stages of an hour or two at the most each day.

## Hammers

To build shuttering, fix battens and nail metal lathing to walls you will need a claw hammer (Fig 122). The claw is used for pulling out nails that have gone in wrong. Regrettably, the claw wears out after pulling out the first two or three hundred nails (and often sooner). The part that bangs in the nails also becomes rounded with much use, after which the nails tend to bend and be pounded sideways into the wood. This part can be ground flat if you have a grindstone, but it is easier and quicker (though not cheaper) to buy a new hammer.

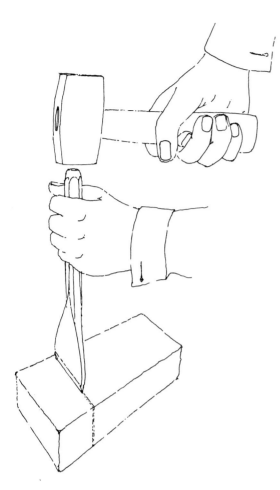

Fig 121 Breaking a brick using mallet and chisel

Fig 122 Claw hammer and wooden mallet

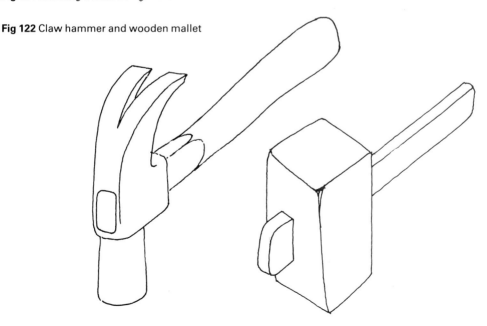

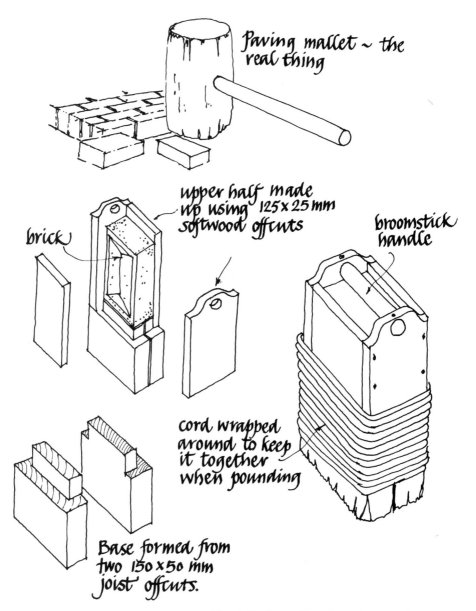

Paving mallet ~ the real thing

upper half made up using 125 x 25 mm softwood offcuts

brick

broomstick handle

cord wrapped around to keep it together when pounding

Base formed from two 150 x 50 mm joist offcuts.

**Fig 123** Paving mallets: the real thing and the home-made alternative

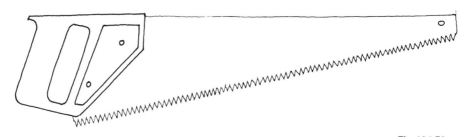

**Fig 124** Rip saw

The hammer is held by the handle somewhere near the end away from the head (it is only held near the head when starting a nail), and swung so as to hit the nail with the handle parallel to the wooden surface.

You will also need a club hammer — a hammer with a heavier head and a much shorter handle — for use with chisels to make holes in brickwork or to split bricks (*see* Fig 121). Since you will be pounding quite a heavy weight onto a chisel held by the other hand, a miss-swing will be extremely painful. Miss-swings happen more often when you are tired, so use the club hammer in five-minute spells with ten minutes of rest in between. That way you can keep the actual work going very much longer.

A wooden mallet (Fig 122) — if you have one — is useful for driving wooden pegs into the ground to keep the shuttering in place when pouring concrete for foundations and floors, but a club hammer will also do the job. A club hammer will tend to split the head of a wooden peg but this does not matter all that much unless you want to use the pegs for many future jobs, in which case hold a tough block of wood between hammer and peg.

If you are laying paving stones a very large wooden or rubber mallet is necessary. These can be extremely difficult to get hold of, and you might find it necessary to make one. Since basically all you need it for is to pound paving stones gently into place, it should be possible to make up something. Fig 123 shows one possible solution: basically a brick wrapped in wood to which a handle is screwed.

## Saw

You will need a saw for cutting boards when building the shuttering for mass concrete. The ideal type is what is called a cross-cut saw, ie one with a long blade (about 500–600mm) and large rough teeth. A similar saw (with even bigger teeth) is called a rip saw, which should give you some idea of how it works (Fig 124). Try to avoid buying a multipurpose saw with interchangeable blades; usually all the blades become bent or blunt within a short time. The best type to buy is a saw with high-tensile steel teeth sharpened and toughened in the factory. It cannot be resharpened except in the factory, but will stay really sharp for the one or two major jobs for which you will need it.

## Squeezy bottle

An empty bottle that once held washing-up liquid is extremely useful for squirting water into the nooks and crannies of the brickwork before applying cement or plaster. It is also handy if you want to add small amounts of water to mortar or plaster on a hawk; in very hot weather the mix dries out before being used up and needs a little extra water from time to time.

## Brush

The brush will be of the type normally used to sweep the dust off the floor into the dustpan. Soft brushes are useful for flicking water onto a wall to wet it properly before plastering. Stiff brushes allow you to clean the mortar off brickwork before it sets on the face of the bricks. A steel brush can be used on the bricks if the mortar is too hard for an ordinary brush (Fig 125).

## Buckets

Buckets are used for carrying materials such as sand or cement to the mixing board, for measuring materials to be mixed and for bringing the mixed materials to the work area. You can even use them to 'knock up' small quantities of mortar or plaster. You will need at least three or four buckets, since life is a lot easier if there is no need to clean out the cement bucket thoroughly before carrying the sand.

Reasonably strong plastic buckets are best; they do not weigh much, can be cleaned out easily even of dried mortar by flexing their sides, and are cheap. Throw-away buckets that have held paint, glue, soap powder or whatever can often be obtained for nothing, but make sure they are really clean before using them, since mortar and concrete can be weakened if foreign elements are added to the mix.

129

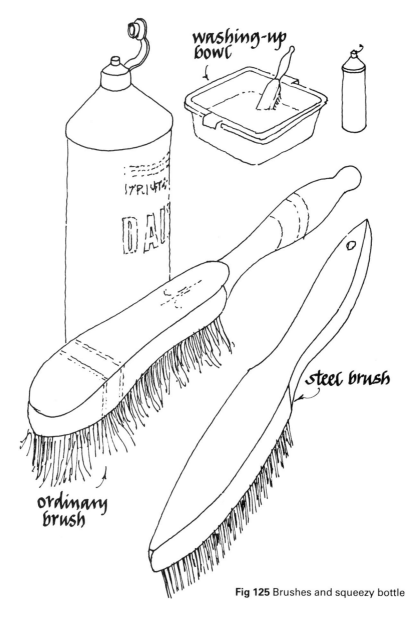

washing-up
bowl

steel brush

ordinary
brush

**Fig 125** Brushes and squeezy bottle

*Pegs and line*

Pegs and lines are used to provide guidelines to which you can work when building brickwork, digging foundations or setting out formwork before pouring concrete.

For brickwork, the pegs need to be metal, with a flat blade and a round shaft (Fig 126). The flat blade slips into the horizontal joint between two bricks, and the surplus string is wound round and round the shaft. You can make such a peg from a 100–120mm length of

15mm copper pipe by flattening one end with a club hammer. Timber pegs can be whittled from off-cuts of wood; try using old broom-handles.

Pegs for setting out foundations and formwork are usually made from 40 × 40mm softwood (50 × 25mm will also do), pointed at one end; a small axe will do the job quickly. The line used should be a non-stretching twine.

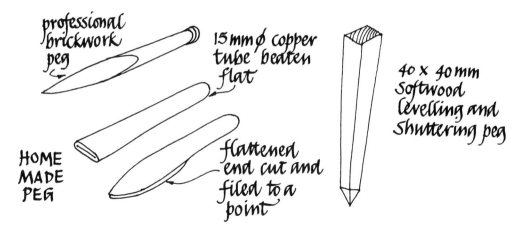

**Fig 126** Pegs for brickwork and shuttering

**Fig 127** Gauge rod

### Gauge rod

Rather than measure each course of brick-work to make sure that the top of each course is always a multiple of 76mm above the base, use a gauge rod instead (Fig 127). This is simply a piece of 50 × 25mm softwood batten (or whatever is handy) with intervals of 76mm marked along its length and then sawn in to a depth of 2 or 3mm on all four sides. The marks should be sawn rather than just marked, since pencil or felt-tip pen marks are easily obscured by mortar.

### Builder's square

A builder's square is similar to the set square used at school for geometric exercises, except that the sides will be 700 or 900mm long instead of 70 or 90mm. A builder's square can be made by taking two pieces of 50 × 25mm softwood, of which one will be about 600mm long and the other 900mm (Fig 128). One end of each is cut to form a half-house joint and the two pieces joined at right-angles using glue and two nails. Before the glue has set, a third piece of 50 × 25mm

131

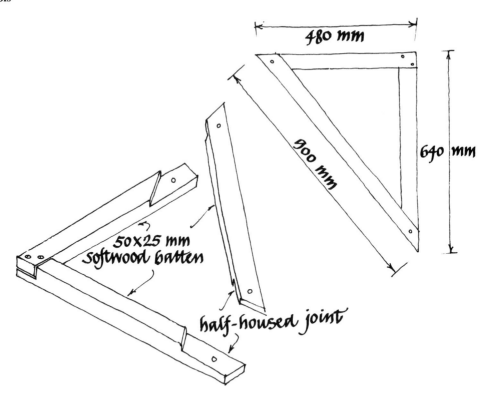

**Fig 128** Builder's square

softwood is glued and screwed to the other ends to form the hypotenuse; the exact position is checked using a smaller try-square before driving the screws home.

The builder's square is used to check that walls are at right-angles to each other.

*Jointing rod*

You may well be able to buy this tool, but most bricklayers make their own out of a 300mm length of 10mm diameter reinforcement rod bent into the shape shown in Fig 129. If you do not have the sort of vice that can handle this job, you can either wander onto a small building site where concrete shuttering is being put up and ask the foreman to help, or you can try to find a helpful blacksmith. As a last resort, bend some 8mm copper water pipe using a bending spring; this is softer but will certainly last you through one or two small jobs.

The rod is used for making the shallow half-round depression in a mortar joint between two bricks, and is drawn through the wet mortar after the bricks have been laid. Use it about an hour after a course has been laid, to form an attractive weather-resistant joint.

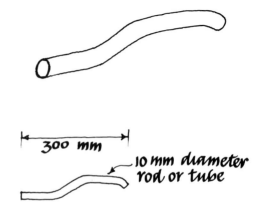

**Fig 129** Jointing rod

## Hawk

You can go into an ironmonger's shop and buy a purpose-made hardwood or aluminium hawk. Or you can saw a piece of 19mm thick marine-quality plywood (or buy an off-cut) about 250mm square or so and nail it to a 200mm length of broom handle (Fig 130). The choice is yours.

When pointing bricks, pick up the mortar with your trowel, slop it onto the hawk held in your left hand (if you are right-handed) and use it as a tray from which to pick up the small amounts you actually need as you go along. Not only can the hawk provide an instant supply of small amounts of mortar, it can also be used as a surface against which to push your trowel for making small 'rolls' of material to push into the joint between two bricks.

In plastering, the hawk holds the supply of plaster that you are about to push onto the wall with your float. The hawk is held against the wall and the float simply slides the plaster direct from hawk to wall without really picking up the plaster.

**Fig 130** Hawk

## Tamping beam

The accurate flat surfaces of concrete floors and drives are made with a tamping board or beam. This is essentially a piece of wood some 150 × 50mm in section and of a length equal to the width of the floor or drive with 50 or 70mm to spare at each end.

After concrete has been poured, the tamping beam is held at each end (you will need two people for this), lifted 50 or 100mm and then dropped onto the wet concrete. The formwork (*see* p 134) at the sides of the bay prevents the tamping beam from going too far down. The beam is picked up again and dropped about 30mm to the right (or left); this action is repeated till the whole surface of the drive has been tamped.

The purpose of this exercise is to make sure that the concrete has been pushed into all the little nooks and crannies, and also to make sure that there are no air bubbles left. As you lift and drop across the surface, you will find pockets with too little concrete; these must be filled up with a little extra concrete. Other areas will have too much concrete; as you lift and drop the tamping beam you push this surplus sideways to fill up the

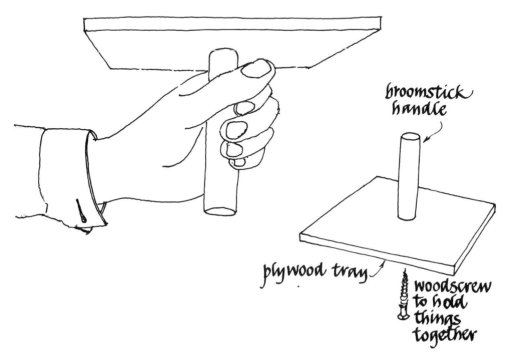

broomstick handle

plywood tray

woodscrew to hold things together

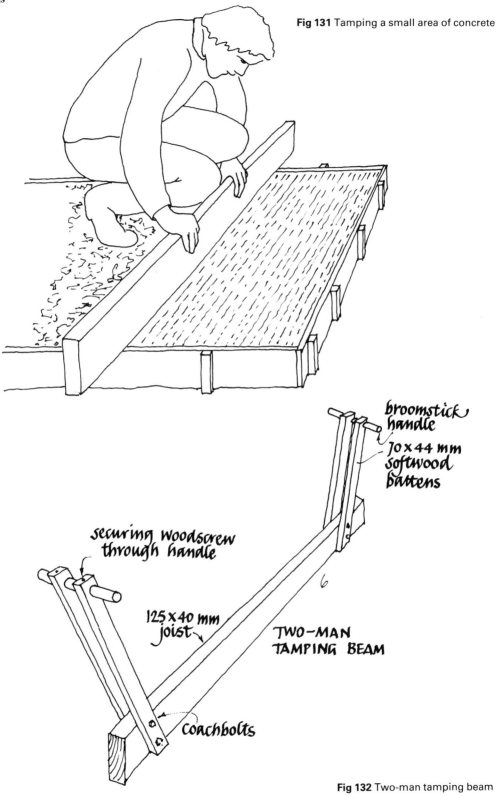

**Fig 131** Tamping a small area of concrete

broomstick
handle

70 x 44 mm
softwood
battens

securing woodscrew
through handle

125 x 40 mm
joist

TWO-MAN
TAMPING BEAM

Coachbolts

**Fig 132** Two-man tamping beam

pockets. The tamping beam is actually lifted and dropped with a slight sideways 'sawing' motion to help distribute the concrete.

The tamping action leaves the concrete surface with little ridges, which give a fine grip for your car's tyres if you are making a drive. It is not so good for kitchen floors, where the final smoothing is done with wooden or steel floats.

If you do not mind kneeling in the muck, a straightforward floor joist makes a perfectly good tamping beam, especially for smaller lengths (Fig 131). However, if you want to do things properly or prefer to do your tamping standing up then make a professional tamping beam; it is not very difficult.

The beam is made from a 150 × 50mm softwood joist with holes bored at each end to which handles are bolted. The handles are knocked up from 75 × 40mm softwood and screwed together with galvanised or even brass screws (Fig 132). You use a Surform (rough rasp) to smooth the parts you grip.

## Levelling batten

This has a similar function to the tamping beam, but is much smaller in both section and length. Typically you might use something like a 1.5 metre length of 75 × 40mm softwood batten.

Whereas the tamping beam is designed to compact the concrete to drive out unfilled pockets as well as level the surface, the levelling batten is used simply to level the surface of plasterwork and cement screeds (Fig 133).

In use the levelling batten is placed across (and at right-angles to) two guiding battens and pushed simultaneously down, across and sideways in a 'sawing' movement that scrapes away surplus plaster or mortar to leave a level and flat surface, ready for smoothing with a float.

**Fig 133** Levelling batten in use

## Shovel, spade and fork

A shovel is used to pick up loose sand, cement, plaster or aggregate into a mixer or onto a mixer board. It is not used for digging the soil for foundations; that requires the use of a spade, which has a much smaller and stronger blade.

The shovel should be kept clean; if cement or concrete dries out on the blade you will have to spend an hour or more banging and scraping it off. In use, hold the handle at one end and use the other hand to hold the shaft fairly near the blade. Swing the whole body forward when picking up the load, and use the inevitable back-swing (as your body recovers from the forward lunge) to straighten your body and pick up the load. Only then do you turn around and swivel the blade to let the load drop into a wheelbarrow or wherever. If you keep it all going in a smooth rhythmic flow you will find that you can shovel more and for longer without feeling tired or having all your muscles ache at the end of the day.

To clear the site before laying down hardcore, use a fork to break up the soil and associated tree roots, and then a spade (not the shovel) to pick up the clods, lumps and stones to deposit them elsewhere.

That is the proper way of doing things; in practice, the shovel and spade can be interchanged, though neither is really efficient at doing the other's job. The spade picks up much less material than the shovel, and the shovel is not stiff enough to push easily into the earth.

## Concrete mixer

The strength of concrete comes through proper mixing. The more evenly the constituents are mixed and the less water is used, the stronger the concrete. Such a mix is laborious to achieve by hand, since you are dealing with very heavy materials in large quantities. Therefore, unless you only need extremely small amounts, it is better and easier to use a concrete mixer.

Almost every small town has a hire shop, and almost every hire shop will have a concrete mixer, if not several. They come in different sizes, and can be hand-powered, electrically driven or supplied with a small (and very noisy) petrol or diesel motor. One hand-powered type is a combined wheelbarrow and mixer; the ingredients are shovelled in and the machine is trundled to the work area, mixing as it rolls along.

Generally, the diesel-powered mixers are of a larger capacity than is necessary for the sort of jobs described in this book. The motors can be, and often are, hard to start and noisy and the machines are far too big to be transported in the back of an estate car.

Electrically powered mixers use either three-phase high-voltage (380 volts) electricity (not normally available in the average house) or ordinary two-phase 240 volt domestic power. They are almost silent, and can often be carried in the boot of an ordinary car if the boot lid is tied up and out of the way. Their capacity is not great, but adequate to cope with the sort of jobs described here. Should you need very large quantities (over 4 cubic metres, say) it becomes cheaper to buy ready-mix concrete.

If you are hiring a mixer, make sure it is reasonably clean before taking delivery and, of course, when returning it. Never leave concrete (or mortar) in the machine for more than about half an hour without either mixing the next batch or cleaning the machine out, first with water and then with stones before a final rinse with water.

For bigger and longer jobs it might be worth buying either a small hand-powered machine (check in *Consumer Magazine* for types available) or a second-hand electric machine (try *Exchange & Mart* or small ads in local newspapers) which can be sold again when the job is done.

When assessing a second-hand machine, check the drum for cleanliness and the electric motor for sparking, especially when it is under load. Too much sparking can indicate a burned-out armature, an expensive item to replace. In any case, do not buy a second-hand machine unless you are already fairly handy at repairing machines; they are not difficult to repair, but there are no handbooks and very few shops with spare parts.

*Rammer*

If the ground on which concrete is to be poured is too soft or too water-logged to take concrete directly, it is good standard practice to spread a 50 or 60mm thick layer of hardcore first. The hardcore can be composed of bits of old brick, lumps of concrete and even large stones if they happen to be handy.

The hardcore should be well compacted, and to do the job properly (rather than merely trampling all over the area in your work boots), use a rammer. You can make one yourself quite easily by sawing off a half-metre length of tree trunk or railway sleeper and drilling a hole into one end into which a broom handle is let and fixed using wedges and glue (Fig 134). The rammer is picked up by the handle, using both hands, and let drop a distance of 300 mm or so; the effect is to ram the hardcore down into place.

**Fig 134** Cast-iron and home-made wooden rammers

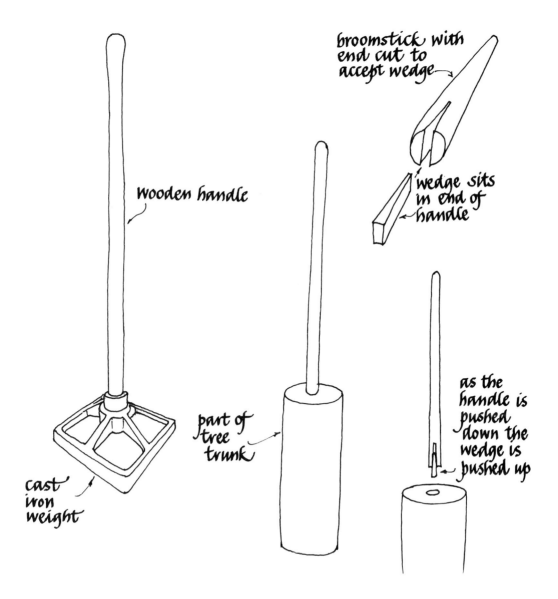

wooden handle

cast iron weight

broomstick with end cut to accept wedge

wedge sits in end of handle

part of tree trunk

as the handle is pushed down the wedge is pushed up

## Clothes

Common sense will tell you to wear old clothes on the job; I tend to buy second-hand overalls and throw them away after the job is done. Some people wear old tennis shoes which do not stop their feet getting wet but allow them to jump nimbly out of the way when they drop a hammer; others wear industrial boots which are expensive, take time to put on and take off, but do prevent old nails and dropped hammers damaging their feet. Other people wear Wellingtons, only to end up with sweaty cold feet.

A pair of stout rubber gloves can be useful when handling concrete, especially for gripping large chunks of timber, wheelbarrows and stones; however, you will have much less 'feel' for many items, so don't use them for brickwork or plastering. Use a barrier cream instead, and make sure your hands are protected before starting the job.

## Other items

Of course, other tools you have may prove to be useful, but with the tools I have described and no more you could, in theory, build a whole house ready for finishing with timber floors, windows and doors, and ready to receive plumbing and electrical services. Other items, such as scaffolding, ladders and Acrow props, are common to all trades and have not been specially mentioned here. And I am assuming that everyone will have that most useful of items — the tape measure!

# 10 Buying and Storing Materials

Materials used in the wet trades fall into three major categories:

(1) Heavy materials that are usually sold loose and in bulk, eg sand and ballast. These are cheap materials, but you will need to buy quite a lot.

(2) Heavy materials that are sold in units, such as bags of cement, bricks or paving stones. These are not quite so cheap as the loose bulk materials, but you will not need quite so much.

(3) Lighter items sold in units, such as tiles, glues and additives. These can be very expensive, especially the tiles.

If you are going to tackle your own building projects, you will need to buy some or all of these. You can, of course, go and buy a 7kg bag of plaster or pre-mixed sand-and-cement and bring it back using public transport. This may well be the best method if you want to brick up a small hole, repoint a few bricks or repair the plaster in your living room, but most of the projects in this book will involve you in more than just a few bags of pre-mix. Building a small garden shed may require 5 or 6 tons of materials, and although the cost of these (in relation to their weight) is much less than those used in many other DIY crafts, it is not entirely negligible.

So, for most of our projects you will need to buy from a builders' merchant of which there are two types. The first type usually sets up shop somewhere on the High Street or in a large warehouse where car-parking is easy. These places advertise extensively in the local papers and are often open on a Sunday morning. There will be a huge display area, many items on the shelves, incredible discounts, helpful assistants and everything under one roof. Beware of them — their prices are not really much cheaper than the local hardware shop, and it is you, the customer, who has to pay for the advertise-

ments, the convenience of having everything under one roof, the facility to choose what you want rather than have to betray your ignorance by having to ask. You also pay for expensive packaging; who has not had to pay 50p for ten pre-packed no 8 50mm wood-screws when the same screws cost £3.85 per box of 144 or 3p each if bought separately?

You will do better with the second type of builders' merchant. These rarely sport an impressive front — usually they can only be reached through a driveway off a back street. In the morning you can see dozens of shabby 1.5 ton vans driving in to pick up sand and other materials. These places do not really cater for DIY people picking up just one bag of sand, but they are just what you need if you are building anything larger than a bird bath.

Once you have found such a place (or maybe several), the next step is to sort out delivery. The four main possibilities are:

(1) If you have a tow hook and own or can borrow or hire a trailer, you can fetch everything yourself.

(2) You can borrow or hire a van and arrange your own transport.

(3) Perhaps you can get a builder to pick it up for you and share the transport costs.

(4) You can have it delivered by the builders' merchant.

Each method has its advantages. Methods 1 and 2 mean that everything is under your control; if you need help with unloading you can arrange times when friends, neighbours or relatives can help. You get the materials (assuming that they are in stock) when you need them, and not when the builders' merchant gets around to delivering them. However, not everyone has a tow-hook and trailer (though if you are going to indulge in this type of DIY I would strongly recommend such an investment).

**Fig 135** A cubic metre of tipped sand

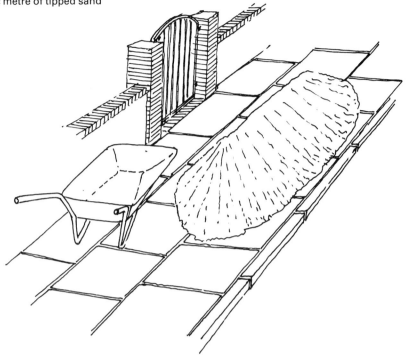

Methods 3 and 4 mean that you are dependent on other people and their ideas of time and place. However, you can save a lot of money; if you are needing items like sand, ballast, cement or plaster (all of which are usually available any time) this method could work out perfectly all right.

Make a list of what you need and start ringing around for prices. Remember that VAT must be paid on everything, and that many quotes over the phone are often given without VAT. So ask for the price (at the quantity you need), whether it includes VAT and what transport is going to cost. Ask if there is a trade discount.

Many builders' merchants will give a discount to a company though not to an individual. Registering yourself (with Company House or its equivalent overseas) costs very little if you are not going to be a 'limited' company, and entitles you to have an order book printed at a local printers. The rest is easy — just wave your order book, and the resultant discounts will amaze you. Some builders' merchants may then ask you to open an account, and will want trade refer-

ences; forget these awkward companies, they are unlikely to be really competitive about prices.

If you are arranging for delivery, remember that most deliveries are made by a single driver; it is assumed that there will be a number of brawny men at the building site who can help unload. Nor can you expect deliveries on Saturday. The best arrangement is to have it delivered first thing in the morning — before 9 o'clock — and hope that coming in an hour late for work will not cost you your job.

Sand and ballast (or aggregate) are usually delivered in a tipper lorry, which means you end up with a large mound on the pavement. Use a shovel to pick it up and a wheelbarrow to transport it to where you want to store it — do not wait for it to rain or for 'helpful' neighbours to borrow the odd bucket!

If you are having sand delivered, check that you are getting the right amount. Often the driver will be delivering two or three small amounts (by his standards) to two or three different addresses. He may tip off what he tells you is about one cubic metre, and hope that you will not know any better. As a guide, one cubic metre of reasonably dry sand, when tipped out on the pavement, is about 3 × 1m on plan and about 0.75m high (Fig 135).

If you are collecting your own sand, get a supply of large, stout plastic bags. Usually you have to pay at the office first, and are then shown a place in the yard and told to shovel it in. Do not feel shy about *filling* the bags!

Cement and plaster come in 50kg bags — only a little less than the weight of a fully grown adult. The bags are also fragile, being made of paper — double-thickness heavy-duty paper, but paper none the less. So stand the bags upright on the back of the lorry, and tip them towards you over your shoulder so that they balance. Then walk to your storage area (of which more later) and tip them forward once again to stand on the floor, upright.

If you are collecting them yourself, remember that the average estate car or small van can rarely carry more than about 450–500kg, including the driver's weight, which means carrying no more than about 7 or 8 bags at a time.

Bricks can be bought loose, as self-stack or on pallets. If they are loose, form a human chain from lorry to storage area, and hand them along the line. A pair of leather gardening gloves is a good idea when handling bricks. Self-stack bricks mean that the delivering lorry has a little crane with a very special grip at the end; the grip clamps the bricks together and hoists them over the side to land neatly, still in a stack, on the pavement. Pallets require a fork lift truck to unload neatly; so if you do not have one to hand you will have to unload them just as if they had been stacked loose.

A selection of concrete bricks and blocks

Again, if you are collecting your own bricks, remember that they are heavy — about 2.5–3kg each! A load of about 150 bricks is usually the maximum you can carry in an estate or light van. That is not very many if you are building a 10 metre long garden wall: if the wall is 1.5m high and 225mm thick you will need about 1,800 bricks or twelve journeys to the builders' yard.

Paving stones come loose or wire-bound. You will need a trolley to transport them from the delivery van to your storage area. Again, they are extremely heavy — a 600 × 600mm paving stone weighs about 35–40kg. Wear heavy-duty gloves when picking them up. Never lift them up at arm's length over the sill of a car; get someone to help you otherwise you are quite likely to injure your back.

Lastly, ceramic tiles come in cardboard boxes, rarely more than about 10kg in weight. You can collect them in the back of the car (unless you are tiling a swimming pool) and carry them in at your leisure.

## Storage

Storing the materials requires a little organisation and a suitable storage area. Since most of the materials used in the wet trades set when mixed with water, it means that items such as sand, cement and plaster must be stored dry. This does not just mean that they must be kept out of the driving rain; they must not be stored directly on a damp floor, nor in a humid atmosphere (such as a kitchen or bathroom), and if possible all partly used bags must be wrapped in polythene or plastic to keep them as dry as possible.

Before buying cement or plaster, then, make sure you have a dry storage space. If you are using a garage or shed, put dry boards down on the floor on which the sacks are to stand and cover the sacks with a polythene sheet.

Properly stored cement, on a raised floor and covered with a waterproof sheet

Try not to buy more material than will be used in the next month or so and use the bags of cement or plaster in strict rotation. Mark each bag (using a thick felt pen) with the date of purchase and use the older bags first. In very old bags the cement may be partly in lumps; it can still be used in places where strength is not all that important, but avoid using lumpy cement in anything else. It should really be thrown away, but I find it difficult to throw anything away that I have paid cash for.

Bricks can be stored much more easily, though they should not be permanently wet, so do not store them directly on the ground unless you are sure you will be using them within a week or so. Standing them on old timber boarding and covering them with polythene sheeting (weighed down with a few old or broken bricks) keeps them clean and dry.

Paving stones must be handled carefully. Because of their weight there is a tendency to chip off corners during handling. They are best stored upright, leaning the first against a suitable wall and then forming a long row.

Sand does not react when wetted but it becomes much heavier to handle and the absorbed water can change the proportions of your concrete mixture, so avoid letting it get too wet. More important is to make sure that it does not get dirty. Good concrete requires clean materials — no bits of twigs, fallen leaves or paper rubbish should contaminate the mixture. It is also a good idea to keep children away from your sand heap and — even more importantly — cats and dogs!

If you have a yard with a fairly smooth and clean surface (concrete or paving stones) then the sand or ballast can simply be dumped onto this surface and, if necessary, covered with a tarpaulin. Other possibilities include:

(1) Carefully shovel all the sand or ballast into large, stout plastic bags. This is a lot of work but does mean you can store loose bulk materials and keep them reasonably clean.

(2) Lay down a large sheet of hardboard on the ground against a wall (or better still in the corner where two walls meet) and dump the

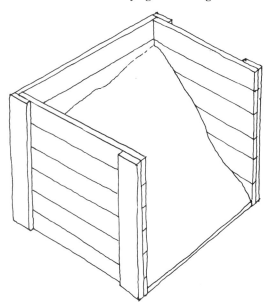

**Fig 136** Home-made bunker for the storage of sand

bulk materials onto this sheet. It makes shovelling the material into a wheelbarrow much easier.

(3) Build a bunker out of old floor boards (Fig 136). A 3.0 × 1.5 × 1.5m bunker needs about a 65–75 metre run of floor boards (which can always be re-used later) and a morning's work to knock it together using hammer, saw and nails. *Exchange & Mart* usually includes advertisements for second-hand floor boards. Also check the price of second-hand concrete shuttering boards — it might be even cheaper.

## Second-hand timber

A lot of the projects described in this book require large quantities of timber for shuttering, supports or guides. Obviously there is nothing to stop you going out and buying nice new shiny PAR (Planed All Round) softwood. It is not cheap, but who knows, perhaps you have money to burn! But most people, wishing to keep expenditure to a reasonable minimum, would be well advised to try to buy second-hand wood. Second-hand floor boards make ideal shuttering, even if they have woodworm holes (but be careful not to let them into the house if your own house has not been treated).

143

Most parts of Britain will have a dealer who can supply second-hand timber. Since he must pick up the material himself, he usually has a large lorry and can be persuaded, for a small favour, to deliver a 50 or 100 metre run of boards.

However, if you can (and are allowed) to pick out what you want and can manage to carry it home on your roof-rack, you will get better bits. The average roof-rack is designed to take about 60kg which will allow you to carry a 30–35 metre run of 150 × 25mm nominal softwood timber boards.

Once home, the boards must be checked for old nails. If you are simply using the board for shuttering, pull out or hammer in all the old nails.

Floor boards can come in 125, 150 and 175 × 25mm softwood sections. Avoid tongued and grooved boards since these are difficult to push together to get a close seal. Try also to pick up 40 × 40mm and 75 × 40mm battening. The timber should be stored off the ground, covered with a tarpaulin (or heavy plastic) and air should be allowed to circulate freely.

# Projects

# Project 1: Flowerbin and Bench

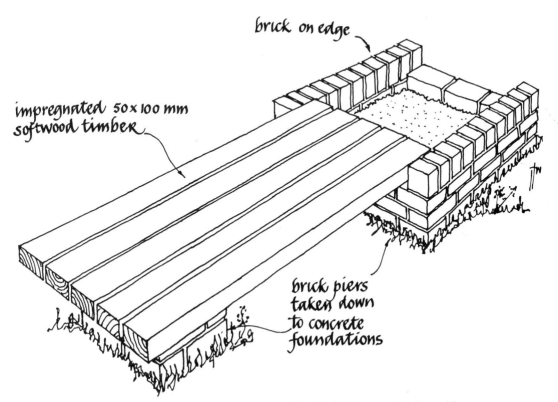

brick on edge

impregnated 50 × 100 mm softwood timber

brick piers taken down to concrete foundations

A flowerbin (Fig 137) may not sound quite as exciting as an extension to your house, but it is a first step. It will give you a good chance to practise the skills so far described in this book.

The basic flowerbin, combined with changes in level and paving stones, can transform a plain flat suburban garden into something much more exciting. Many gardeners buy exotic flowers and plants in an attempt at making their gardens look a little more interesting, but the use of concrete and stone, other than in artificial-looking rock gardens, seems to be avoided. Could this be because concrete and bricks are considered too difficult?

Begin by making an accurate drawing of the design — accurate in so far as it is necessary to show each and every brick (Fig 138). The purpose of the drawing is to make sure that there is no need to cut any bricks.

**Fig 137** Garden seat with flowerbin

There are two reasons for this. First, cutting bricks is a difficult task — there should be no need to make trouble for yourself if it can be avoided by thinking ahead. Secondly, designing the project in such a way that no bricks need to be cut leads to a better, more integrated design.

Clear away the top soil to a depth of about 150mm. The area to be cleared will be the size of the combined bench and flowerbin, plus about 150mm extra all around. Keep this top soil; you may want to return it once the bench has been built.

Dig down a further 250mm to allow the mass concrete foundation to set deep enough to avoid the movement of soil due to frost action, and also to allow the grass (or plants) around the bin to grow right up to the brickwork (Fig 139).

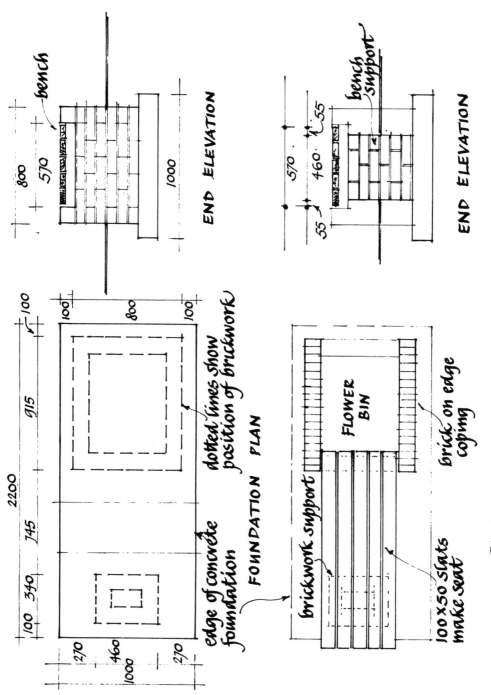

bench

800
570

END ELEVATION

1000

bench
support

570
460 · ↑ 55
55

END ELEVATION

100
100
800
100

2200

915

745

340

100

270
460
1000
270

2200

edge of concrete
foundation

dotted lines show
position of brickwork

FOUNDATION PLAN

brickwork support

FLOWER
BIN

brick on edge
coping

100×50 slats
make seat

PLAN

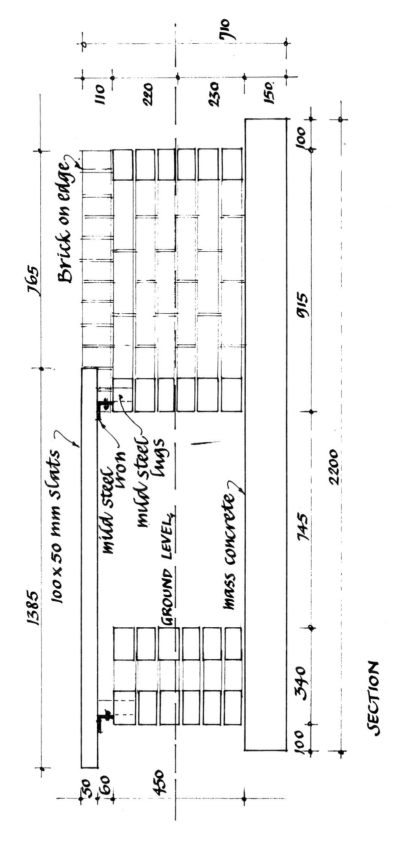

**Fig 138** Accurate drawings of foundation plan, end and side elevations of garden seat with flowerbin

Brick on edge

100 × 50 mm slats

mild steel iron

mild steel lugs

GROUND LEVEL

MASS CONCRETE

SECTION

110   220   230   150

710

765

1385

1965

915

745

2200

340

450

50
60

100   100   100

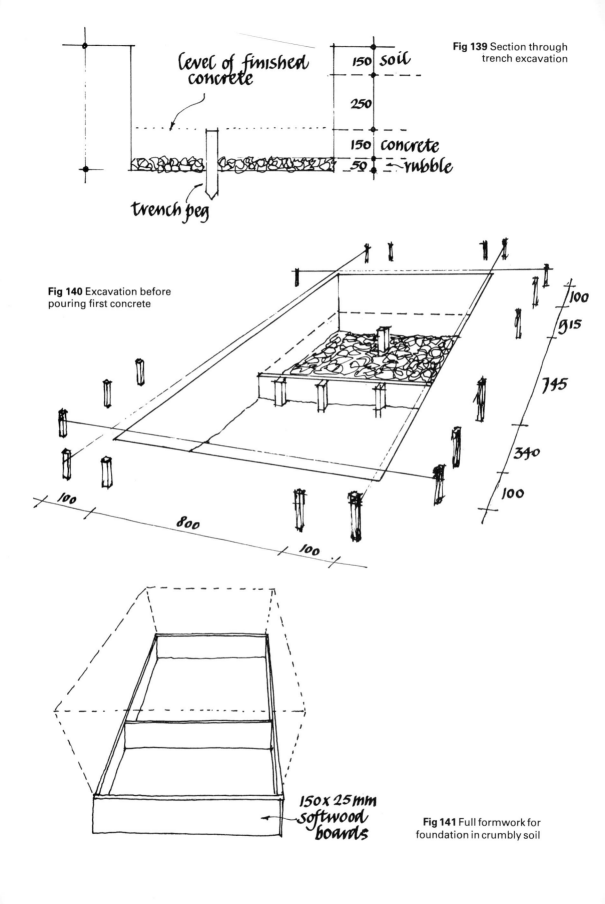

**Fig 139** Section through trench excavation

level of finished concrete

150 | soil

250

150 | concrete

50 | rubble

trench peg

**Fig 140** Excavation before pouring first concrete

100

315

145

340

100

100

800

100

150 x 25 mm softwood boards

**Fig 141** Full formwork for foundation in crumbly soil

If the soil is reasonably dry but not crumbly, then your formwork will consist of a 150 × 25mm softwood plank placed upright across the trench (Fig 140) and held in place by softwood pegs hammered into the ground. If the soil crumbles a lot, it may be necessary to make a slightly more elaborate formwork. A four-sided frame is made from 125 × 25mm softwood planks (old floor boards will do nicely); the ends of the boards are butt-jointed and the sides held in place by more pegs (Fig 141).

Very soft or wet soils will need a layer of hardcore put down first. Hardcore is made up of bits of brick, lumps of concrete and even large stones; make absolutely sure that no old plaster clings to the bricks. The hardcore is thrown into the hole and spread in a layer about 50–60mm thick. Then the layer is compacted — if you do not have size 10 boots, try banging it into place with a rammer.

You are now ready to pour the concrete foundations. On a mixing board, empty two buckets of coarse aggregate, one bucket of sand and about half a bucket of cement. Turn the pile over a number of times until you achieve a greyish well-mixed mass. Heap it all together and make a crater in the middle. Pour water into this crater, and turn the heap over several times. Add more water, and gradually the mass will turn into a plastic (but not too plastic) mess of concrete.

Shovel the concrete into buckets and carry it to your foundation hole, and pour it into the enclosure made by the formwork board(s). Continue making concrete and pouring it in until the two foundation areas are full.

Take a 75 × 40mm softwood batten and use it as a tamping board to push the concrete down into all the nooks and crannies. Then, use the same batten to 'saw' off the surplus concrete so that the top of the concrete is level; use a spirit level from time to time to check that it is really horizontal.

When the concrete has been tamped and 'sawed' flat, use a wooden float to smooth the concrete surface. Cover the concrete with polythene sheeting and insulation, if necessary. Leave for a week or so. Next weekend you will be ready to start bricklaying.

Begin the bricklaying process by pegging in lines to mark the outer edge of brickwork running along the length of the hole. The lines should run about 75mm above the level of the concrete; use long pegs pushed into the ground just beyond the edge of the concrete, and wind the string around these till the line is taut.

The first course of bricks is laid, using a 1 : 3 cement : sand mix and, if possible, semi-engineering bricks. These bricks will not show and they do resist acid corrosion in the soil. If you are unsure how to lay bricks, refer to Chapters 5 and 6.

Use a builder's square to check that the first course of bricks laid across the trench is

Fig 142 Metalwork to connect timber seat to brickwork

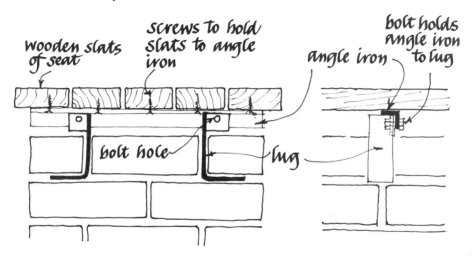

151

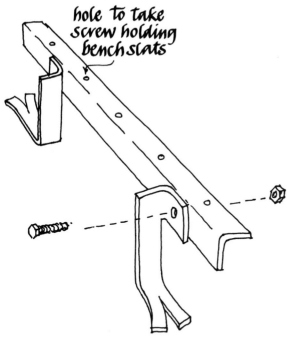

hole to take
screw holding
bench slats

**Fig 143** Combined lugs and angle support of wooden bench slats

**Fig 144** Integrating the flowerbin and bench into a garden path and steps

really at right-angles to the bricks laid along the length. Use a spirit level to make sure they are laid flat.

Once the first course is in place, further courses are added till the brickwork is taken a course or two above ground level. Use your spirit level and builder's square frequently in order to check that you are building fair and square.

At this stage, you will probably have done enough for the day (or even the weekend). Let it all rest for about a week, and then fill up the hole with the soil you laboriously dug out in the first place. Compact the soil (*see* p 137) every 150mm, and continue till the whole area is nicely filled. Be prepared for further settlement in the coming six months or even a year.

The brickwork can now be completed. The design calls for mild steel lugs to be built into the brickwork to connect the timber seat (Fig 142). If you are handy with metal, you can make these lugs yourself (Fig 143); alternatively, you will have to find a blacksmith. The two upright lugs are built into the top of the brickwork. The cross-member is bolted to the top end of the lugs after the wooden slats

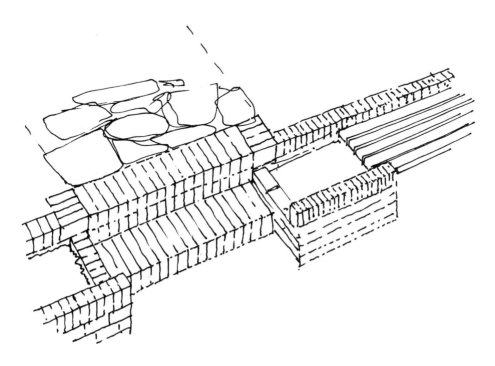

are fixed to the cross-member using wood screws driven into the slats through holes in the cross-member.

The coping of the bin is finished 'brick on edge'. This is a satisfying finish because it looks deliberate, rather than as if you stopped there because it was high enough and you needed a rest!

The bench is made of 75 × 40mm battens in whatever wood you fancy and can afford. Softwood will be cheap, but needs replacing every few years; other woods can be quite expensive but will last that much longer.

Whatever you choose, make sure the wood is treated with a preservative before being built in.

The area around the bench can be finished using either paving stones or bricks laid to a sand base (*see* p 119). Alternatively, if your soil is reasonably well drained, you could allow grass to grow right up to and under the bench.

The flowerbin and bench can be changed in shape and size, combined with steps (Fig 144), integrated with walls or even be built into the conservatory described in Project 7.

# Project 2: A Garden Wall

This second project uses concrete and bricks in larger quantities to make a garden wall. It involves measuring, setting out, digging, some formwork, pouring concrete, laying bricks and pointing them.

Let us assume that the final wall will be built in a full-brick thickness (ie 225mm) in the shape of an L, with one leg about 3.40m and the other about 5.85m (Fig 145). The long leg starts at the side of a house, and the short leg finishes at what will be the gate to a driveway. The wall is to be 1.8m high to give some privacy (Fig 146).

The first step is to work out the materials needed, and to do that we have to 'design' the wall. If you refer to p 16 you will see that the foundation should be set at a depth of at least 700mm below ground level to avoid all soil movement; but the foundation for a simple garden wall need not go that deep — 400–450mm is quite sufficient. As the wall is going to be 225mm wide, the foundation will have to be at least this thickness. Its width will have to be 'wall-thickness + 2 × foundation thickness' which all comes to a total width of 675mm.

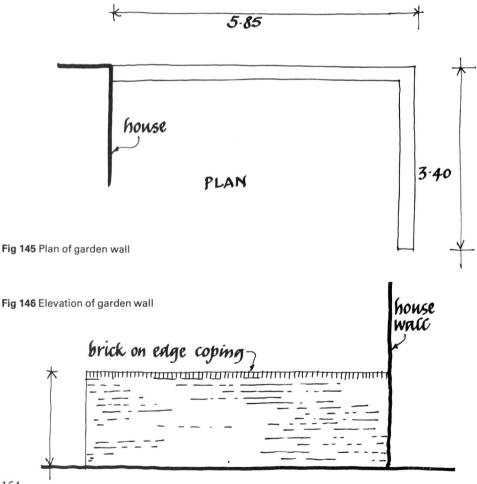

**Fig 145** Plan of garden wall

**Fig 146** Elevation of garden wall

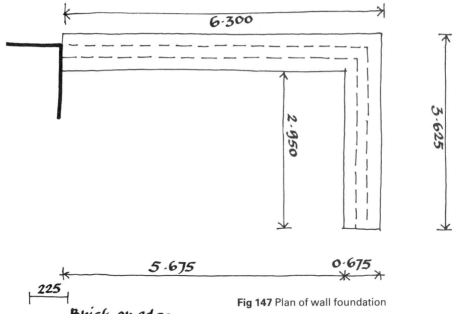

**Fig 147** Plan of wall foundation

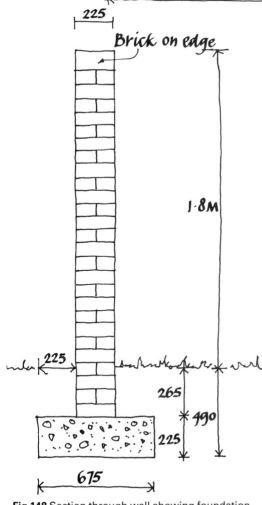

**Fig 148** Section through wall showing foundation

Make a small sketch (Fig 147); a little careful arithmetic will give you the total area of the foundation at about 6.24 square metres. Multiplying this by the thickness of the foundation gives a total volume of 1.4 cubic metres (Fig 148).

Use a strong concrete mix; looking at the table on p. 10 you will need either:

(1) 8 bags of cement and 1.25 cubic metres of all-in aggregate; or

(2) 8 bags of cement, 0.75 cubic metres of sharp sand and 1 cubic metre of coarse aggregate.

You will also need strong (50 × 50mm) softwood pegs to hold up the shuttering to one side of the trench, as well as pegs to set the level of the foundation. Allow one peg for each 800mm length of shuttering, as well as pegs at 2 metre lengths along the foundation itself, which comes to about 20 pegs of, say, 450mm each, or a total of about 9 metres. Finally, you will need some shuttering along the inside of the foundation (Fig 149). Adding the two legs comes to 8.6 metres; as our foundation is to be 225mm thick we will need either 8.6 metres run of 225 × 25mm softwood or, if you are using second-hand floor boards, 17.2 metres run of 125 (or 150) × 25mm.

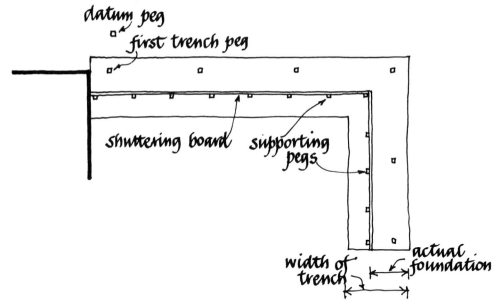

datum peg
first trench peg
shuttering board
supporting pegs
width of trench
actual foundation

**Fig 149** Shuttering and pegs required for wall foundation

For the brickwork you will need about 2,000 bricks (2,200 if you want some spare, just in case); you will also need 3 more bags of cement, 3 bags of hydrated non-hydraulic lime and about 0.75 cubic metres of builder's sand.

For tools, you will need the following:

(1) To set out, you will need hammer and saw (to make the pegs, squares and posts) as well as tape measure and pencil. A spirit level is almost essential. Of course, you will need a lot of string.

(2) To dig the foundations you will need a spade at least and a fork; a pick-axe (on occasion) might well be useful. A wheelbarrow to take the soil away comes in very handy.

(3) Mixing the concrete, depending on the method used, will take at least a shovel, mixing board and various buckets. For this quantity I would recommend a small mixer hired for a day or so when you are pouring the concrete for the foundation.

(4) The brickwork will require large and pointing trowels, brickwork pegs and a jointing rod. You will also need a hawk and a gauge rod.

The rest is simply hard work. If you are not used to a lot of hard physical work, take it easy. In your enthusiasm and desire to get the job done, it is easy to try to do too much before it gets dark. Resist this, take it in easy stages and you will be able to keep it up.

Start off by driving the marker peg into the ground. The top of this peg should be level with one of the horizontal mortar joints of the main house, especially if the brickwork of the garden wall is to butt up to or be built into the brickwork of the main house.

The next step is to set out the position of the walls (Fig 150). Bear in mind the relationship between the new garden wall and the existing house wall. You should finish up with a double set of lines to mark the position of the walls. The width of the foundation is now set out, and again strings are stretched between pegs or between profile boards.

The strings showing the position of the walls are taken down (but not the pegs that held these strings) and you are now ready to start digging. Use a fork to loosen the soil (and, if need be, a pick-axe) and a shovel to remove the loosened soil. Although the foundation is to be only 675mm wide, in practice it becomes quite impossible to dig down in such a narrow trench. Standard practice is to dig a trench of about 750mm wide till you come to the bottom. Officially this extra

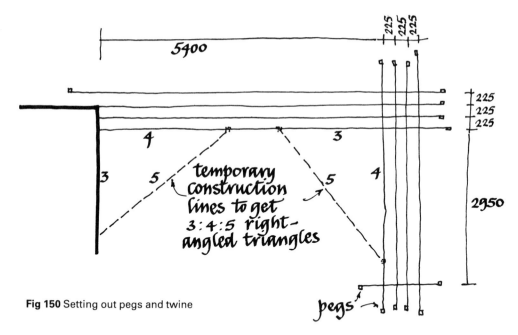

Fig 150 Setting out pegs and twine

width should be dug on what will become the outside of the wall; this is not important with garden walls (where there is no outside) but can be very important when building a shed or garage. In this case, it saves a little work if the extra is dug on the inside of the L-shape (Fig 151).

When you reach the required depth, level the ground by digging — not filling if you can avoid it. The ground under the foundation should be as firm as possible. If the ground is very soft, you may decide to put down a layer of hardcore (see p 29).

The next step is to set out the pegs that will mark the top of the concrete. A softwood peg is driven into the soil at the bottom of the trench. One end of a long plank or batten rests on the marker peg while the other end is

Fig 151 Section through trench

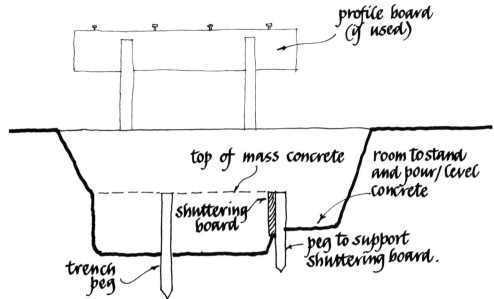

157

suspended over the foundation peg; use the spirit level to check that this plank is held perfectly horizontal. You can now measure the vertical distance between the top of the foundation peg and the top of the marker peg. You may have to hammer in this first foundation peg further before the top is exactly at the level you want, ie the top of your foundation (or bottom of your wall). Alternatively, you can saw off the surplus.

Using batten and spirit level to check the levels, drive in further battens at 1.5m intervals starting at the first peg, and continuing along the trench. In this case, you will need a further three pegs along the short length, and four along the longer one.

When the tops of all the pegs are level, start setting out the shuttering. Put the shuttering board down as a ruler, and drive in softwood pegs at about 800mm intervals (maximum) which comes to a total of 6 on the shorter and 8 on the longer leg. Once the pegs are in, you can nail the shuttering board(s) to the pegs. The top of the shuttering board should be level with the top of the marker pegs. Check with a spirit level as you go along.

**Fig 152** Setting out the line marking the first brick course

It will be sensible to use a small electric mixer to mix the cement, sand and aggregate. Add water, mix thoroughly and pour into the foundation. Use a stick to poke the concrete into all the nooks and crannies, and make enough concrete to fill a length of about 2 metres — from one marker peg to the next. Now use a tamping board laid from one peg to the next to level the concrete along the length of the foundation, and use a shorter batten to span across the foundation, using the top of the shuttering plank as a guide.

You should finish with a roughly level foundation strip. Use a wooden float to level off the concrete, and start pouring more concrete into the next 2 metre stretch. Continue until the whole trench is finished. Make sure that you pull out the levelling pegs as soon as each stretch of foundation is finished; pour a little extra cement into the hole and level it off with your float.

Cover the concrete with polythene (in hot weather) or old sacks (cold weather) and leave this base to cure for a week or so. If the weather is very hot, sprinkle the top of the concrete with a little water — not too much — at the end of every other day. After two days remove the shuttering and all the pegs holding it in place.

When you are ready to start the brickwork,

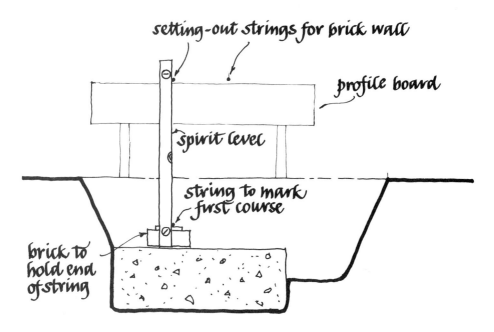

setting-out strings for brick wall

profile board

spirit level

string to mark first course

brick to hold end of string

stretch lines between the pegs in the ground (or the nails on the profile boards) that mark the position of the wall. These lines will be about 600mm above the surface of the concrete footing and are therefore of little help in placing the first course of bricks.

Stand in the trench at the start of the wall and hold the spirit level vertically, with its top touching the building line and its foot resting on the concrete. Mark the concrete with a carpenter's pencil — the mark should be directly under the building line. Repeat this procedure at the other end of the trench. You can now stretch a secondary line to show the position of the first brick course (Fig 152).

Put a piece of wood of the exact thickness of the mortar bed on the concrete footing immediately next to the pencil mark. Place a brick on top of the piece of wood. The top of this brick should then be exactly 76mm above the surface of the concrete. Do the same at the other end of the footing.

Wind some string three or four times around the width of a third brick, and place this brick on top of the first brick. The other end of the string is wound around yet another brick, and placed at the other end of the foundation. Place a brick on top of each pile to hold it in place, and make sure the string is taut.

Move the brick piles to one side or another till the string between passes directly over the pencil marks. Use the spirit level once more to check that the string between the two loose bricks is exactly beneath the string marking out the position of the wall.

Now you can lay your first course of bricks (*see* p 75). As the brickwork will be a bond suitable for a solid 225mm thick wall, we can expect that this course will include both headers and stretchers. Turning the corner will involve us in cutting 'queen closers' (*see* p 81); to cut these you will need a bolster chisel and mallet.

Although this part of the wall will be below ground and therefore not visible, it is still a good idea to try to make the brickwork as good-looking and accurate as you can — simply by way of practice. By the time you get to the part of the wall that can be seen, you will know how to lay bricks properly.

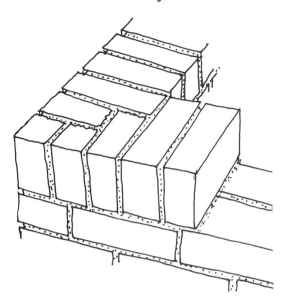

Fig 153 Brick on edge coping at the corner of wall

Once you have laid the first course, build up the corners and ends of the wall in the usual half-pyramids (*see* p 77). Use the spirit level and gauge rod extensively to make sure that the bricks are laid level and in the right position. When the pyramids are finished, fill in the space between, laying the bricks to lines stretched between pegs stuck into the joints of the newly built pyramids.

Finish the wall with a coping of brick on edge. This is not particularly difficult and looks extremely nice (Fig 153). It is worth while using 1 : 2.5 cement : sand mix to help the mortar resist weathering.

The end of the wall against the house calls for a little attention. There are two possible ways of tackling the problem. The garden wall can simply butt up against the house wall, in which case cavity wall ties should be built into the gap at six-course intervals (Fig 154). Alternatively, the garden wall can be built into the house wall using techniques similar to those involved in blocking up an opening (*see* Project 6). Alternate courses of the brickwork of the wall of the house have to have bricks taken out, and alternate courses of the garden wall's brickwork have to be built in (Fig 155). Quite a ticklish job, but well worth doing if you can find the matching bricks.

## Project 2: A Garden Wall

Once the whole wall is built, pointed and cleaned off, the soil from the trench can be returned. It should be filled in layers, and each 150mm or so should be well compacted. Even so, you will find that the soil will tend to sink over the next six months or so, so delay the sowing of a perfect lawn for a little while.

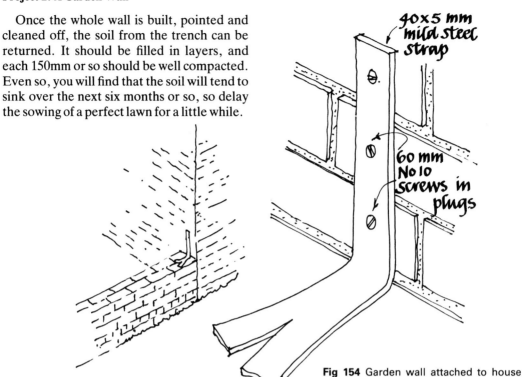

Fig 154 Garden wall attached to house by metal strap

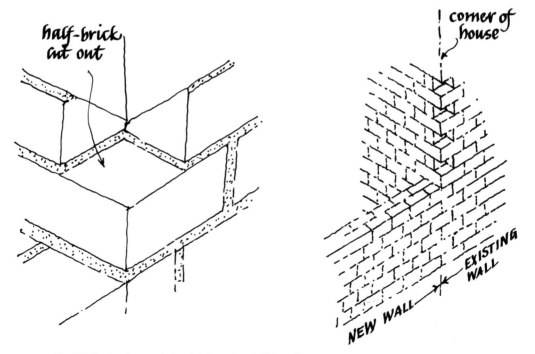

Fig 155 Cutting into existing brickwork to build wall into corner of house

160

# Project 3: A Barbecue

Spending a hot summer evening around a smoky fire eating burned sausages and raw chops can be great fun, I am told. I have also been reliably informed that an old foot-scraper over a couple of bricks will do the trick.

However, if you want to do things in style, you should build a proper barbecue. After all, if you are building it yourself it will only cost the price of a few bricks, a heap of sand and a couple of bags of cement. Not much more, in fact, than the price of a de luxe pressed steel folding twin-burner barbecue set which rusts after a few years and whose connecting toggle gets lost in the first summer.

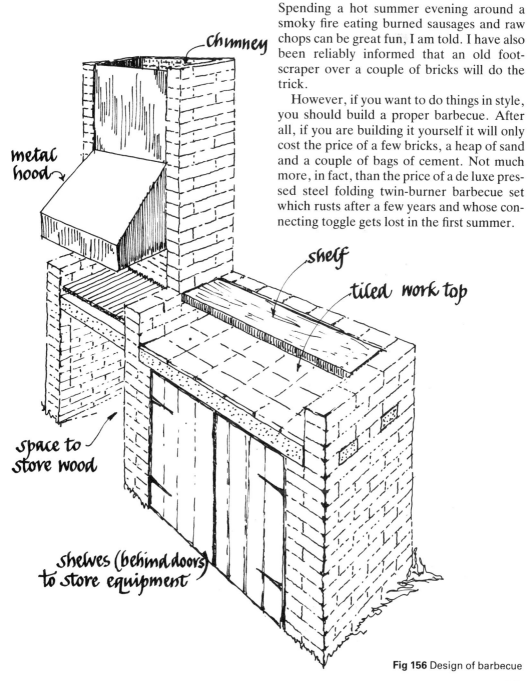

**Fig 156** Design of barbecue

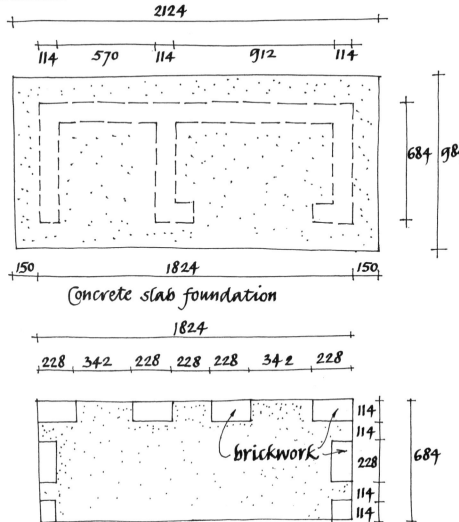

**Fig 157** Plans of concrete slab foundation and combined work top and fire support

There are three things wrong with the usual home-made primitive barbecue:

(1) You have to kneel while tending the fire — not very comfortable.

(2) There is no clean level surface to put down the uncooked meat, the clean plates, the sauces and cooking utensils.

(3) There is no room to store the charcoal (or wood), the grill and all the special equipment.

Our barbecue will therefore need to be built at a level that makes it possible to work while standing up, and it must have storage space as well as a reasonably large work top.

The design shown here (Fig 156) is only one possibility. It may not suit you because it is too big, too long or the design accent falls in the wrong place. Feel free to re-design, but remember it makes life a lot easier if you choose dimensions which allow you to keep to whole-brick modules.

The hearth of the barbecue is, of course, the most important part. Its width and depth can be adjusted to suit any grill which you already have — thus avoiding the need to get one specially made. My experience is that newly bought steel foot-scrapers make very good grills, and are much cheaper than the

162

purpose-made article. Working and storage area sizes are entirely up to you. You will probably need room for at least four plates on your work top, plus room for half a dozen sauce and salad bowls. A small cupboard to store cushions for sitting on hard surfaces such as the bench in Project 1 can make life easier.

Having decided on the design, and made plans of the foundation (Fig 157) sketches to show where the bricks go at each course (Fig 158), the work can begin, using most of the basic concreting and bricklaying tools: shovel, spade and fork; pegs and twine, spirit level and tape measure; wooden and steel floats and trowel; mixing board(s) and hawk; three or four plastic buckets; and a builder's square.

You will also need both builder's and sharp sand, some coarse ballast, bags of ordinary Portland cement and a lot of bricks. Make sure all the materials are kept clean and separate.

Begin, as usual, by clearing away the top soil over the whole area plus an extra 150mm all round. Next, set out the exact position of the base, using pegs driven into the ground between which builder's lines are run. Check that the lines are at right-angles to each other using the builder's square.

The foundation slab (Fig 157) might be taken to some 500mm below ground level, although you can go down another 300mm if you want to avoid all soil movement. It is extra work (and material) and is not all that important for something as simple as a barbecue.

If the soil is a wet clay or is very soft and crumbly, put down a 50–60mm layer of hardcore (broken bricks and pieces of concrete) at the bottom of the hole. Compact the hardcore using either your own weight or a rammer (a home-made one is shown on p. 137) lifted up and allowed to fall on the hardcore.

Place a 150 × 25mm softwood board (an old floor board) across the hole, somewhere in the middle. Hammer in a wooden peg at the far end so that the top of the peg is level (use a spirit level to check) with the top edge of the board.

Make enough mass concrete, using a 1 : 2 : 4 cement : sharp sand : ballast mix, to fill the first half of the hole. You can stand in the other half while filling and levelling the first half. Tamp the concrete down using a small tamping board and check that it is level by running the tamping board over both the retaining softwood plank and the top of the peg. Finish off by using a wooden float to achieve a reasonably flat surface.

The next day the concrete will be strong enough to take your weight if you lay down a square of thick plywood first to spread the load. Take away the retaining plank, mix up another batch of concrete and pour it into the other half. Again, tamp the concrete flat and finish off with a wooden float. Cover both areas with polythene to slow down evaporation, water the concrete once every two days in hot weather and cover with straw (or old blankets) in cold(ish) weather.

The following weekend you will be able to take the brickwork up. Use lines between pegs driven into the ground to mark the position of the brickwork base (see p 76). Mix up a 1 : 3 cement : sand mortar using builder's sand and start laying your first course (see p 75 for details).

The base is taken up to at least 150mm above ground level all round, and to about 760mm above ground level on the two short ends, ie at the level where they will support the concrete base to the hearth. Leave out a couple of bricks near the edges to take the support of the concrete formwork (Fig 159). Probably you have done enough for the weekend; in any case, the brickwork should be left a week or ten days to cure and build up some strength for the next stage.

Do not neglect to clean down and point the brickwork as you go; if either of these tasks is left till the whole structure is finished, you may well have a big job on your hands.

Once the brickwork and the concrete are strong enough to take the strain, shovel back the earth (and rubble) removed to make room for the foundations. Compact the fill every 150 or 200mm.

To make the formwork for the concrete work top and fire support, cut two pieces of 100 × 50mm softwood to a length of 2.2m each. These are slid through the holes left in

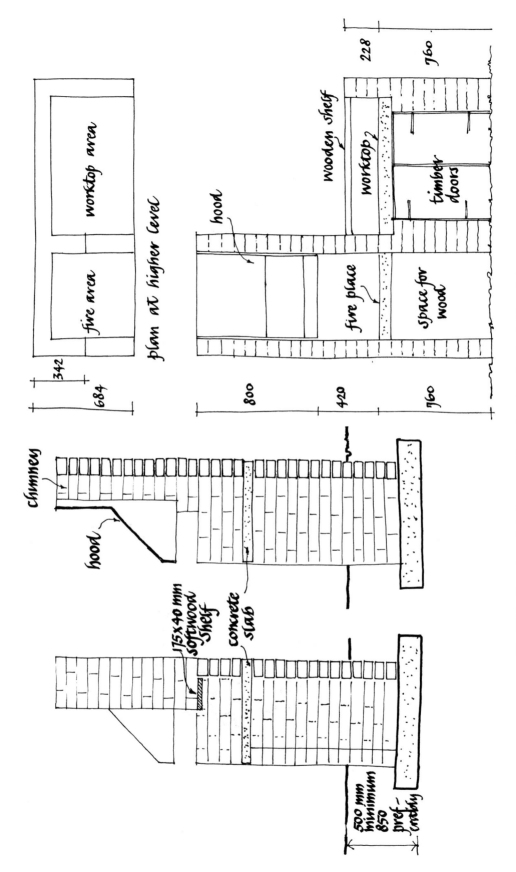

**Fig 158** Sections through barbecue and front elevation, showing brickwork courses

Labels within the figure:

*plan at higher level*

worktop area

fire area

342

684

wooden shelf

worktop

timber doors

hood

fire place

space for wood

228

760

800

420

760

chimney

hood

175×40 mm softwood shelf

concrete slab

500 mm minimum 850

pref-erably

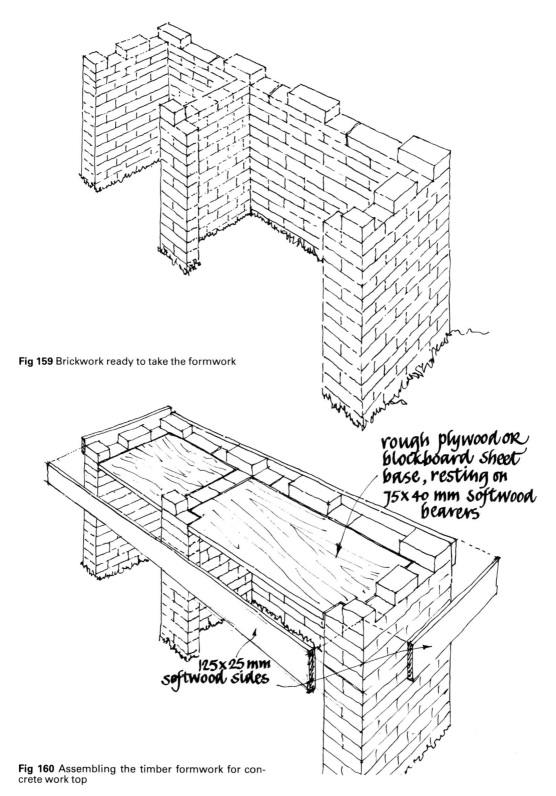

**Fig 159** Brickwork ready to take the formwork

rough plywood or
blockboard sheet
base, resting on
75 × 40 mm softwood
bearers

125 × 25 mm
softwood sides

**Fig 160** Assembling the timber formwork for concrete work top

**Project 3: A Barbecue**

the brickwork base (Fig 159). On top of these bearers sit shorter pieces of wood laid at right-angles to the main bearers. Blockboard or plywood cut to shape (Fig 160) rests on these cross-bearers and makes up the base of the formwork. The sides are made up using 75 × 25mm softwood nailed together at the corners. The whole should form a large shallow tray.

The tray is filled with the same coarse mix used for the foundation to a depth of some 20mm. Heavy-duty chicken wire is laid directly onto this layer, and then the rest of the concrete is added. The wire mesh prevents cracking at a later stage. Use a wooden slat to tamp the concrete level.

The concrete slab is finished with a steel float, taking care not to use it too much (*see* p 37). The slab is then left to cure in the normal way for a week or so before the rest of the brickwork is taken up. Leave the

timber formwork in place for about three weeks. The brickwork for the sides and back of the grill can now be finished in the normal way. The dimensions of the grill hood are given in Fig 161.

The barbecue hood is made from sheet steel. If you are making it yourself you must buy a sheet of steel not less than 1,050 × 817mm; the thickness depends a little on how strong you are, and what is available. The cutting is done using tin-snips; you can cut through quite sturdy sheet steel if you are prepared to take your time. I suggest the use of thick gardening gloves, both to prevent sharp steel edges cutting into your hand, and also to prevent the formation of blisters.

You might like to cut the figure out first using card or paper, and see how it folds to form a hood as shown on Fig 156. The folding is done by laying the sheet on top of an old table, or a sheet of thick plywood or blockboard supported by a table, with the fold line exactly along the edge. Use a ham-

**Fig 161** Barbecue hood cut from sheet steel

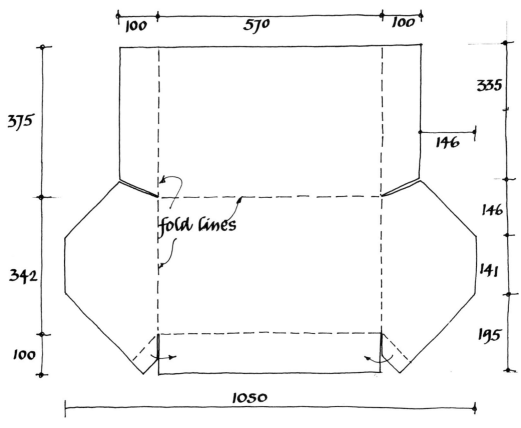

mer to beat down the side to be folded, and eventually work the hammer along the edge of the table (or sheet of plywood) to get a sharp fold.

The hood is secured to the brickwork using Rawlplugs and dome-headed galvanised screws. Paint the hood with a lead primer (or its equivalent if you feel strongly about the use of lead) and finish with a coat of gloss paint.

If you wish to make the space under the work top into cupboards, you will need to make small doors. Fig 156 shows one type of door which might suit you. Why not finish the doors by running a blowlamp over the surface to produce a thin layer of charred wood which can be brushed away using a steel brush to produce an interesting and hard-wearing surface?

The hinges can present a bit of a problem: either use standard butt hinges on a wooden frame (a bit fussy-looking) or build special hinges into the brickwork beforehand.

You might consider tiling some of the work and storage areas. A tough tile suitable for floors will be more hard wearing than the more delicate wall tiles, and should be bedded in a 1 : 5 sand : cement base; even the best of glues would be unlikely to stand up to more than five years of real weather.

The final design might be combined with a brick/timber seat based on the design of Project 1. If the vagaries of the English climate put you off spending time and money on such an elaborate barbecue, why not build it half in and half out of the conservatory that forms a later project (Project 7) in this book?

# Project 4: A Raft Foundation

When you are building a simple garden wall, in most cases you will be using a concrete footing taken to a depth of some 700–800mm below ground level. The reason for this is to have the weight of the brick wall taken by a part of the ground that is not directly affected by frost action.

Most older houses in Britain have suspended timber floors. Timber floor joists rest on brick walls whose footings are built well below ground level. A suspended ground floor seemed at that time to be the best way of avoiding damp rooms at ground floor level (Fig 162).

Over the past fifty years or so the building industry has developed really efficient damp proofing and it is now perfectly possible to build solid concrete floors without any risk of damp ground floor rooms.

As the ground floor no longer needed to rest on the brick walls around it, the load on these walls was lessened. In fact, it became possible to treat the ground floor slab as a huge raft on which the brick walls could rest (Fig 163).

The raft, being fairly large, could ride out any movements in the soil. It meant that although the concrete had to be reinforced with mild steel reinforcement bars, the deep trenches, which seemed to start off every traditional structure, could be dispensed with.

A raft foundation is extremely suitable for smaller structures such as conservatories, garages and single-storey home extensions. It saves a lot of work digging foundations and at the same time reduces the amount of brickwork needed. If restricted to single-storey buildings, the amount and type of reinforcement required is well within the scope of the amateur.

As usual, it is first necessary to visit the building inspector. He will probably tell you what sort of thickness and mix of concrete he requires, and what reinforcement will be needed. He may need more detailed drawings or calculations than you can supply, in which case he may be able to recommend someone looking for a small job; alternatively, look in the local papers or the *Yellow Pages* of your telephone directory for 'building technicians'.

**Fig 162** Suspended timber ground floor

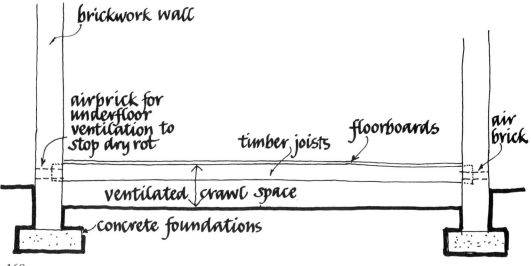

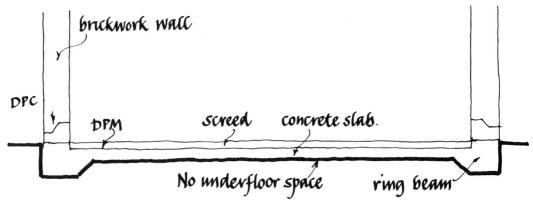

**Fig 163** Solid ground floor

Most likely you will need a slab about 120mm thick increasing to some 200mm at the edges to create a 'ring beam'. Reinforcement will be what is called 'nominal', ie a mild steel mesh made up of 6mm mild steel welded together at 100mm centres. You may be asked to put some 8 or 10mm mild steel bars in the ring beam. None of this is very complicated or expensive.

You will be using a coarse mix (*see* p 11); an average-sized garage of 2.4 × 5.0m will need about 1.5 cubic metres of concrete, which is not really enough for you to consider ordering ready-mix, unless you combine it with a driveway (*see* p 31) or other project.

You will need the usual concreting tools: concrete mixer; shovel, spade, fork and perhaps a pick-axe if the ground is very hard; an ordinary claw hammer and saw for making the timber shuttering, and a wooden hammer for driving in supporting pegs; wheelbarrow and several mixing buckets; a steel and a wooden float; spirit level; lines and pegs; tape measure; tamping board.

To begin, clear the ground of top soil and tree roots to a depth of at least 150mm. If the soil is very soft or made up of clay, you may need to go down another 50mm or so to make room for a hardcore layer. The 250–300mm nearest the edge must be taken down a further 80–100mm in order to form the ring beam.

If a hardcore layer is needed, make sure that the bits of brick and concrete you use are entirely free from plaster. The hardcore layer should be about 50mm thick and the pieces rammed into the ground using either a heavy roller or a home-made rammer.

At this point a decision must be made on the position of the damp proof membrane (DPM). You will definitely need one if you are going to avoid a damp floor, but the position of the DPM will be decided by two factors:

(1) Whether the concrete floor will be left as it is — perfectly all right for garages and potting sheds — or whether it will be finished with a screed to obtain the perfectly smooth surface usually required for living areas.

(2) Whether the walls will be built with a damp proof course (DPC) and in cavity construction — the standard treatment for extensions — or whether the walls will be built in single brick, a more economic design for garages.

Generally speaking, the home extension with a screeded floor and cavity walls should have its DPM laid between concrete and screed, with the DPM taken up and tucked into the brickwork to join the DPC (Fig 164). The garage will have no screed, and the DPM will be below the concrete (Fig 165).

If your DPM is to be below the concrete, then cover the hardcore with a layer of sand to soften the rough surface. Over this layer of sand, lay the thick polythene sheeting to form the DPM, weighed down temporarily with brickbats. (If the DPM is to be between concrete and screed, the sand can be omitted.)

Now start sawing and nailing the shuttering together using the usual softwood floor boards (*see* p 29). Make sure that the top edges of the shuttering boards are all at the same level.

169

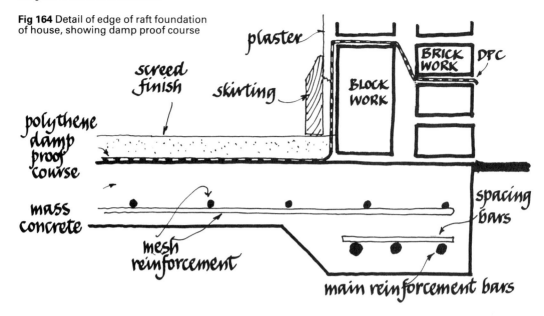

**Fig 164** Detail of edge of raft foundation of house, showing damp proof course

plaster

screed finish

skirting

BRICK WORK DPC

BLOCK WORK

polythene damp proof course

mass concrete

mesh reinforcement

spacing bars

main reinforcement bars

Now put in the mesh reinforcement (*see* p 29), using extra reinforcement bars in the ring beam as necessary (p 30). Concrete spacers will make sure the reinforcement is kept 25–35mm clear of the bottom of the concrete slab.

Since the slab as a whole is reinforced with mild steel mesh and often with bars on the perimeter ring beam, there will be no need to allow for movement joints at 2.5–3.0m. However, floor slabs much greater than 5 square metres could probably be handled more easily if poured in bays.

Mix and pour the concrete as prescribed (*see* p 31) making sure that the boards marking intermediate bays are withdrawn before starting the next bay. Finish off the concrete, after tamping, with a wooden float to get a

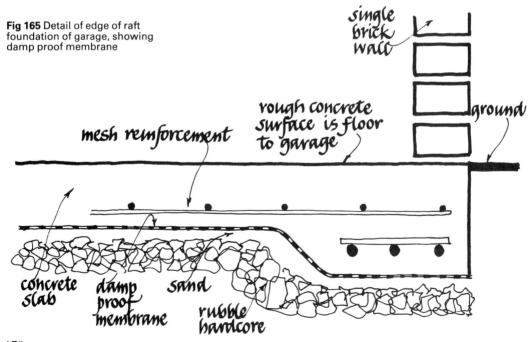

**Fig 165** Detail of edge of raft foundation of garage, showing damp proof membrane

single brick wall

rough concrete surface is floor to garage

ground

mesh reinforcement

concrete slab

damp proof membrane

sand

rubble hardcore

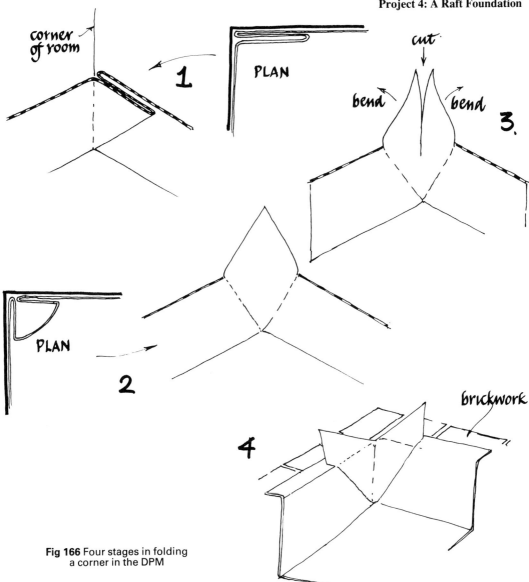

**Fig 166** Four stages in folding a corner in the DPM

reasonably flat surface. If the concrete floor is to be left without a further screed, make sure that the float is used sparingly; too much use brings up the cement/water component of the concrete which produces dusty floors.

The concrete should be covered with plastic sheeting and/or an insulating layer of straw or polystyrene and allowed to cure a week or two before embarking on the next stage, which will be either:

(1) The building of the brick walls to the garage or shed. This work is described in detail in Project 8.

(2) The laying of a DPM and screed. Most architectural drawings show the DPM being neatly turned up to meet the DPC sitting some 150 or 225mm higher. How this is exactly done at the corners and door openings is usually left to the builder's imagination and experience. Let us look at the whole operation in somewhat greater detail.

Assuming that you are building the walls using cavity brickwork, begin by laying two or three courses of the inner leaf. Special care has to be taken at all door openings; a sheet of polythene some 500mm wider than the

171

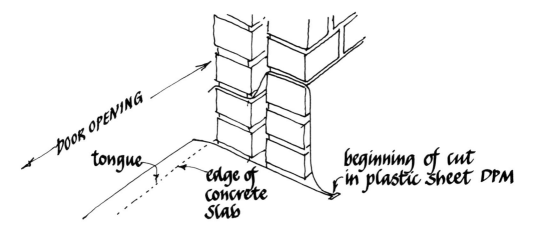

**Fig 167** Detail of DPM at door opening

door opening and about 500mm deep is laid on the concrete floor before the brick inner leaf is built.

When these three courses of brickwork are laid, the whole floor is covered in polythene sheeting. This is normally sold in rolls 6 or 9 metres wide. If you have to join two pieces because your floor is larger, make sure that sheets overlap by at least 150mm and are double-folded and held in place temporarily with adhesive tape. The sheet is taken to the edges and folded up and over the brickwork and held in place by loose bricks.

You will find that at corners the plastic will need quite a bit of folding before it sits in place (Fig 166). Do not cut any of the plastic if you can avoid doing so; on internal corners fold it carefully and make use of more adhesive tape. Only at door openings is the plastic slit so that a 'tongue' pokes out between two brick reveals (Fig 167).

Now you can place battens on the plastic in the usual way to form bays approximately 1.5 metres wide. The bays are screeded (*see* p 35) using the usual sand/cement mix. The screed is taken right up to the surrounding brickwork.

After two or three days' curing, the poly-thene is taken up and over the bottom three courses of the inner brickwork leaf and can now be trimmed to finish neatly some 30–40mm in from the room side of the brick-work. Underneath the plastic and on top of the third brick course is laid a thin bed of mortar; the plastic is now pressed onto this layer and held in place by a proprietary DPC and some mortar. Finally, the fourth row of bricks is laid on top to hold the DPM and DPC in place.

You have now a completely damp proof junction and can continue building up the brick inner and outer leaves in the normal way.

# Project 5: A Solid Base to Your Kitchen

Like many other people, I live in a house built before World War 1. It has solid brick walls (no cavity to insulate or keep the rain out) and suspended timber floors on first and ground floors (Fig 168).

The house, luckily, is not too damp, so that the joists and floor boards of the ground floor are still sound. The people next door were not so lucky; they have had to replace most of their ground floor.

However, while the kitchen of the back extension in my house had a suspended ground floor, the scullery did not. I took down the wall in between the two, and finished up with a very uneven surface. Obviously something had to be done.

The answer, both for my neighbour and myself, was a new solid ground floor. Besides being an economic replacement, it also meant that damp could no longer penetrate into the ground floor rooms from underneath.

The project was discussed with the local building inspector, who checked certain things like head clearance, gave instructions as to the concrete mix he felt was required, and gave advice on the DPC.

We started off by clearing away all the furniture and fittings; by the time we had cleared away the sink and other built-in furniture most of the weekend had gone. We did manage to get the skirting boards removed (carefully, since we wanted to put them back later on) but left the rest of the work for the next weekend.

My neighbour's floor, which was indeed rotten, was ripped out by a gang of three people in the course of a day; the wood was thrown into a skip to be burned (or dumped). The timber in my floor was still sound, so I spent the evenings with a crowbar levering off the floor boards, removing the old nails and setting the boards to one side for later use as shuttering. Getting the joists out meant sawing them through at one end; even

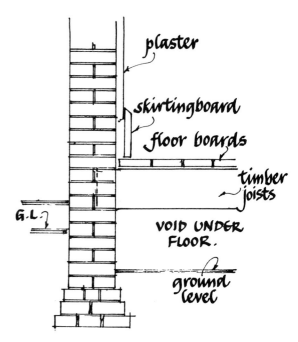

**Fig 168** Section through existing suspended timber floor

so, I was left with some nice timber as a bonus.

I then had to break up the old solid floor in what had been the scullery. A large sledge hammer did the trick, but quite a few times I wished I had thought about hiring an electric (or even pneumatic) drill.

The next stage involved clearing the site. The area under the floor was littered with old bricks, bits of wood and copper pipe. The first 120–150mm proved to be soft loose sand; this was also removed, and I finished up with a clear and level surface.

I had decided to use this opportunity to lower the level of the kitchen floor (Fig 169). As the soil was quite firm, there was no need to lay down hardcore first; I could pour concrete directly onto the ground. My neighbour did not want steps down into his kitchen, and so had to make up the difference between the ground level under the suspended ground

173

**Fig 169** Section through solid ground floors

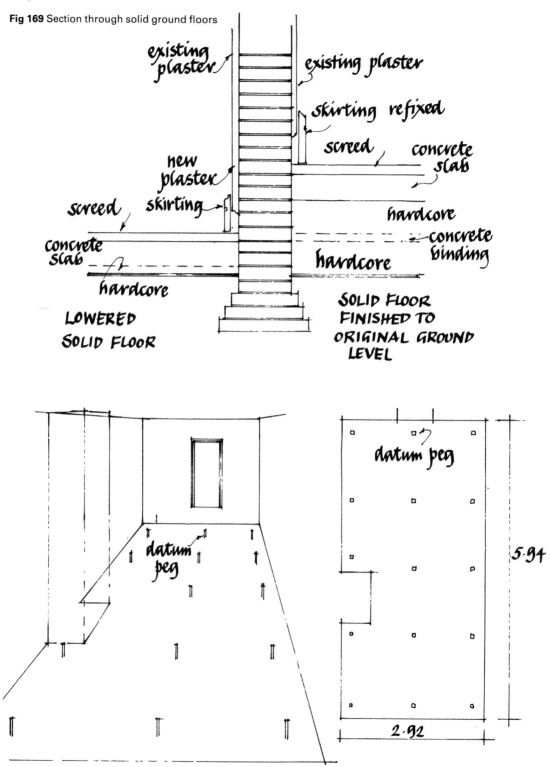

existing plaster

existing plaster

skirting refixed

new plaster

screed

concrete slab

screed

skirting

hardcore

concrete slab

concrete binding

hardcore

hardcore

LOWERED SOLID FLOOR

SOLID FLOOR FINISHED TO ORIGINAL GROUND LEVEL

datum peg

datum peg

5·94

2·92

**Fig 170** Layout of pegs to solid floor

174

floor and a new level some 160mm below the surface of his solid floor.

To make up this difference in concrete would have meant pouring some 9 or 10 extra cubic metres. A cheaper solution was to make up most of this with hardcore, compacted every 150mm or so. This resulted in a hardcore layer of about 400mm, and in fact we decided that it might be a good idea to consolidate the hardcore with a very weak concrete halfway through. We mixed a 1 : 4 : 8 cement : sand : aggregate mix and laid this over a 200mm thickness of hardcore, let it dry for a day or so before laying a second hardcore layer of 200mm, making a total of 400mm (Fig 169).

To achieve a perfectly level floor in the kitchen, I drove in levelling pegs at 1.5 metre intervals throughout the room (Fig 170). These pegs, made from 40mm square softwood and pointed at one end to facilitate driving in, were hammered home firmly into the ground.

The peg nearest the door was accurately marked to show the finished floor level, and the top of the peg sawn off to this mark. Using a 2 metre batten and spirit level, all the other pegs were similarly marked and sawn. Pegs alongside a wall were kept some 200mm away from the wall to make tamping (see below) easier. I also drilled the tops of the pegs to take the coach-screw handle (*see* p 27) to facilitate pulling out after pouring the concrete.

This is also the time to sort out your drainage. Most old kitchens have a sink near a window, partly to allow daylight to fall on the sink, but mainly because the old building regulations insisted that as much drainage as possible was kept to the outside of the building (Fig 171). Consequently, most kitchens in older buildings are a little limited in layout. If you want your new sink to be put along an inside wall, you will have to run drainage pipes in the solid floor (Fig 172).

This is not all that difficult. Use 40mm diameter PVC pipes with glued joints, and run these in the thickness of the concrete floor. Before the concrete is poured, assemble the pipes, taking them through the external wall (and into a gulley or manhole) at one end, and bringing them out 150mm above finished floor level at the other end. Glue the joints together, and shut off the ends with waste paper covered with sticky tape. Prop the pipes up with lumps of concrete along their length to allow a slope of 1 in 40 (or steeper); make sure there are no 'low' bits in which water (and rubbish) can collect to slow down and eventually block drainage (Fig 173).

As my neighbour and I were renewing our floors more or less simultaneously, we decided to pool resources, labour and material. We needed about 6 cubic metres of concrete for our kitchens, and felt this was enough to enable us to order ready-mixed concrete. A local company was found that was prepared to deliver this small amount; it was up to us to make sure we had adequate labour and wheelbarrows.

On the day, we cleared the passages of furniture and floor coverings, and laid down planks on steps to make the movement of wheelbarrows easier. Shovels, rakes, floats, brooms and tamping boards were all to hand. Thermos flasks of coffee stood ready.

The lorry arrived; three wheelbarrows were at the ready, and we started trundling. The concrete had to be poured quickly — partly to avoid holding up the lorry (actually the driver did not mind) but mostly because concrete does not keep for long. We concentrated on one floor at a time; the concrete was transported by three people, a fourth person pushed the concrete into place and a fifth did the levelling.

The person responsible for finishing off tackled the floor in bays; each bay was the width of the room and the length equal to the distance between successive rows of pegs (Fig 174). Each bay was poured, tamped, levelled and floated in turn before the next bay was started.

The tamping board was first moved in a saw-like fashion between the tops of the levelling pegs. Once the floor was roughly level, the tamping board was lifted and dropped, using both hands to keep the board parallel to the surface it was tamping. After tamping the concrete, the pegs were shaken loose and lifted out using the special peg-

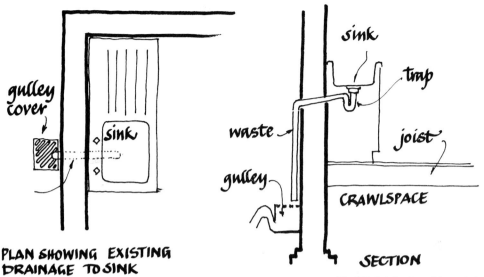

**PLAN SHOWING EXISTING DRAINAGE TO SINK**

**SECTION**

**Fig 171** Original position of sink

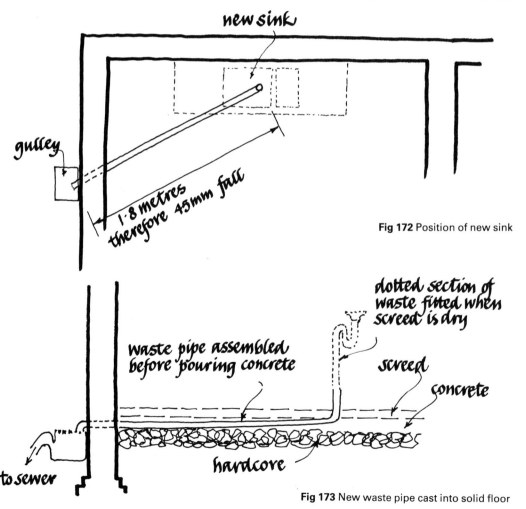

**Fig 172** Position of new sink

1·8 metres therefore 45mm fall

**Fig 173** New waste pipe cast into solid floor

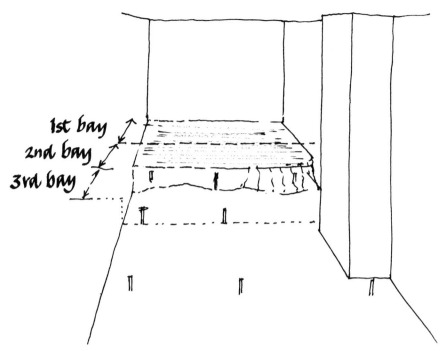

1st bay
2nd bay
3rd bay

Fig 174 Pouring the concrete into bays

lifter (*see* p 27), and the hole filled with a little extra concrete.

Lastly, the wooden float was used to smooth out the concrete surface, and the next bay could be started. Bay after bay was completed; the last part of the last bay was floated while the person holding the float was kneeling in the doorway.

While the first floor was being finished, the wheelbarrows were moving the concrete to the second work area and dumping the mix over the whole floor area without waiting for the concrete to be levelled, tamped and smoothed. Any surplus could be removed at a later stage, but this way the lorry could be on its way.

In fact, we ran out of concrete, and had to mix the last few buckets by hand. Knowing this might happen, we had kept a little sand, cement and ballast in reserve. We knocked up the extra concrete on an old sheet of plywood and finished the second floor.

Well, that was a busy day, and we were not yet finished. We spent another few hours cleaning up and covering the floors with building plastic to make sure that the setting concrete retained enough water to allow it to cure, and cleaning up and returning hired and borrowed tools.

We left the concrete to cure for two weeks while we got on with other things, and then came the time when we could deal with the DPM. As already explained, the DPM should be continuous with the DPC to ensure a really damp proof ground floor room. The surveyor acting for the building society through which we obtained our mortgage had insisted on an injected DPC. We now had to make sure that the DPM on the floor would be taken up and tucked into the brickwork over the DPC.

I first painted the brickwork with a silicone water proofer. I then cut the first horizontal mortar joint above the DPC back some 20mm all the way around the room (Fig 175). Into this joint was tucked the top of a 700mm high sheet of thin polythene. The polythene was kept in place by filling the rest of the joint with 1 : 3 sand : cement mortar. The skirt was allowed to hang down onto the concrete.

Special attention was paid to the corners, where the polythene was folded and taped together. I certainly did not want to cut the polythene if it could be helped. Any overlaps along the length of the skirt were folded over twice and the folds taped.

**Project 5: A Solid Base to Your Kitchen**

A local builders' merchant supplied me with sheets of Expamet metal lathing (Fig 175). These were cut to a height of 500mm; the top was screwed (using plugs) to the brickwork at 250mm intervals. The bottom of the Expamet would eventually be retained by the screed floor.

Finally, building plastic (polythene) was laid over the main floor area, and taped firmly to the skirt at the edges, any joins being firmly overlapped and taped down (Fig 176). All was ready for screeding.

**Fig 175** Taking the DPM above the DPC

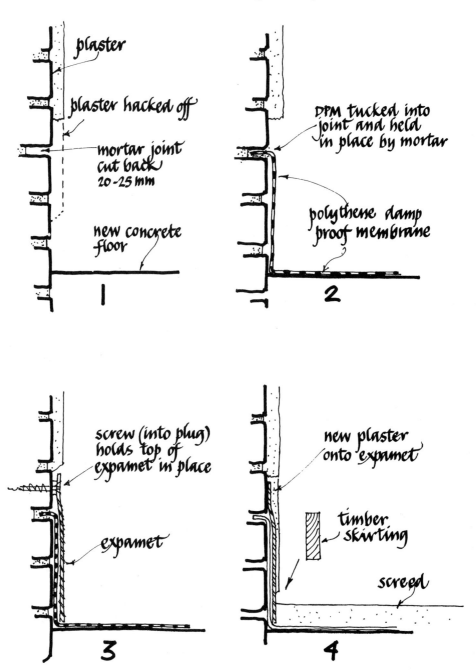

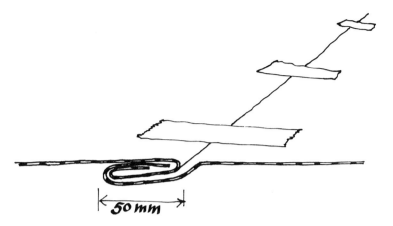

**Fig 176** Folding and taping a join in the DPM

Timber battens, 50 × 25mm softwood, were laid on the floor at 1.2m intervals, parallel to the walls of the length of the room. A small (hired) electric mixer outside knocked up a 1 : 3 sand : cement mortar which was carried inside using plastic buckets. We emptied the contents onto the floor between the battens, and then propped up the battens with generous pats of mortar to each side.

Once the battens were propped up, the rest of the mortar was spread out over the floor between the battens. A levelling batten was used to 'saw' the mortar flat between the battens. As with the concrete sub-floor, the mortar was laid in bays about 1 metre deep and the width of the room. Each bay was levelled, and then the battens were slid about half a metre forwards out of the screed. The void thus left was filled with a little more mortar, and the whole area smoothed with the steel float.

Then the next bay was laid, levelled and smoothed. While my wife mixed the mortar and carried it in, I levelled the floor and used the float to smooth it. I made sure that the mortar was pushed right up to the Expamet which in turn was held firmly against the brickwork.

The screed was left to cure for a week, by which time it was quite safe to walk on although it was still far too wet to think of laying any floor covering. However, I wanted to 'make good' the plasterwork.

Using browning mixed in a plastic bucket, a hawk and the same steel float, I was able to push on the undercoat to the bottom 450mm of the walls. The browning stuck well to the Expamet, and I finished up with a layer of plaster ready to take the finishing coat a day or two later. The wall above the skirting area served as a guide for my tamping batten. The bottom 100mm was left unplastered, as this was to be covered by the skirting board.

The skirting board was fixed using large screws driven into plastic plugs let into the brick wall at 800mm intervals. It meant breaching our elaborate DPM, but the DPM was designed to resist a moderate amount of damp, not all of it. It would have been different if the floor had been below the water table. A few screw holes may have allowed a small amount of damp to penetrate, but not enough to make damp patches.

About a week later, the kitchen furniture was moved back, the sink connected up and the floor covered with some old rush matting. The matting (which likes a certain amount of damp) allowed the floor to breathe and dry out, while at the same time keeping our feet reasonably warm and dry. At the end of six months, I judged the floor to be dry enough to lay vinyl tiles.

All in all, we were unable to use the kitchen for about five weeks. Not that we worked solidly for five weeks to get the job done — but it did mean washing up in the bathroom and cooking on camping gas stoves for that period. All the same, at the end of a lot of upheaval, we had a clean, warm and tidy floor, plus a little more headroom.

# Project 6: Openings in Existing Brickwork

Making a new opening in existing brickwork creates three problems:

(1) The existing structure must not be allowed to collapse whilst lintels, beams or arches are being inserted.

(2) The beam, lintel or arch has to be inserted or cast *in situ*.

(3) The brickwork around the hole has to be tidied up.

The first problem is serious only if loads such as floor joists or beams rest on the brickwork inside the critical triangle. By 'critical triangle' I mean an area of brickwork whose base is the top of the new opening and whose height is 0.9 times this base (for the older, solid 225mm thick brickwork walls) or 0.5 times the base for the newer cavity walls (Fig 177).

If the opening is going to be much more than about 1.25 metres wide, or if there are loads resting on the brickwork in the critical triangle, you will need Acrow props, supporting baulks of timber and possibly needles. All this gets a little beyond the scope of the beginner; but once you have helped or watched a professional tackle it you may decide to try your hand.

The simpler jobs, however, needing only a lintel to hold up the brickwork itself can be completed by you. You will need to discuss the job with the local building inspector; he will probably tell you the size of the lintel required.

If you are going to make the new opening look convincingly like part of the original

**Fig 177** Area of brickwork supported by arch/lintel

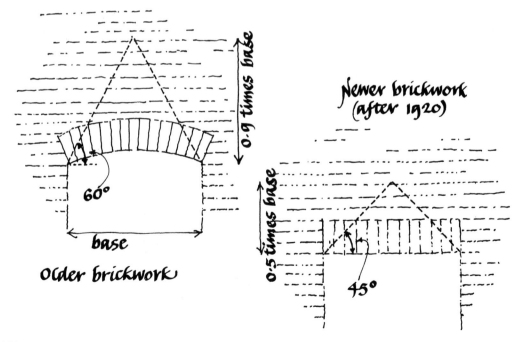

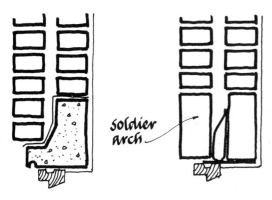

**Fig 178** Boot lintels

design, you will need to try to copy the brick-work support used elsewhere in the building. The support — usually some sort of arch or lintel — can take several forms:

(1) Most modern houses (ie houses with cavity walls) use either concrete or steel boot lintels (Fig 178).

The lintels are usually covered by a 'soldier' arch, made up of vertical bricks or brick slips (bricks the same length and height as an ordinary brick, but only 20 or 25mm thick) stuck to the face of the concrete or steel lintel doing the actual work. Occasionally, of course you will come up against an exposed concrete lintel.

(2) Mass housing built before World War 1 will usually have almost flat arches on the face of the building and a timber or concrete lintel on the inside. The stones of the arch, known as voussoirs, will be the same as the main wall, and the joints between adjacent voussoirs will be a shallow wedge (Fig 179).

(3) Better-class older houses will have really flat arches using special bricks called rubbers. The rubbers were made of a very soft clay, and were rubbed together till the stones were very slightly wedge-shaped. Thus the joints between adjacent voussoirs are parallel (Fig 179).

You can, of course, try to copy the high-class flat arches of the older Victorian and Georgian houses, but this book will stick to modern soldier arches and the somewhat cruder 'flat' arches of older housing.

**Fig 179** Victorian brick arches

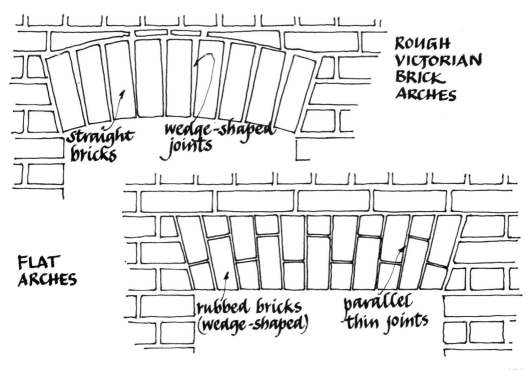

ROUGH VICTORIAN BRICK ARCHES

straight bricks

wedge-shaped joints

FLAT ARCHES

rubbed bricks (wedge-shaped)

parallel thin joints

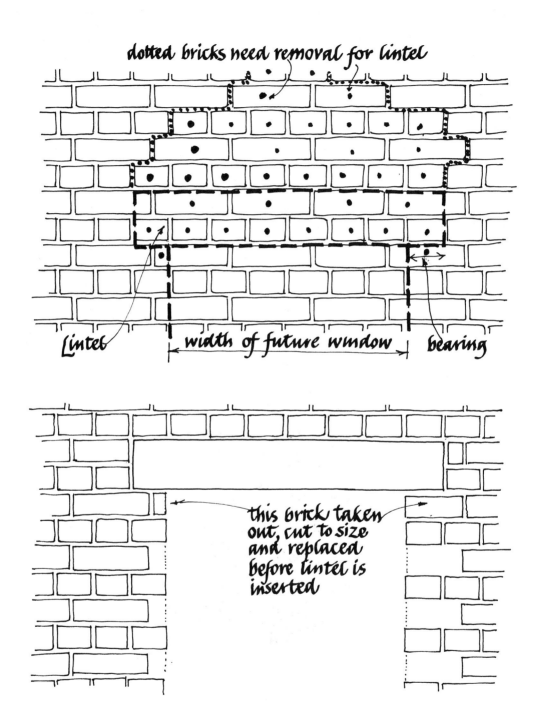

**Fig 180** Building in a lintel to 225mm solid brickwork

Once you have decided on the position of the new opening, and have discussed the project with the building inspector, the first job is to create an opening in which the new lintel will sit. The lintel will need at least 100mm bearing at each end; you will need to make an opening some 150mm wider than the width of the window and between 4 and 7 courses of brickwork high (Fig 180).

It is most likely that the first brick will be damaged as you try to get it out. Start by using a bolster chisel and hammer along the joints on all four sides to loosen the mortar. Then use the bolster chisel upright some 30mm from one end of the brick, and use the hammer to try to crack the brick. Once cracked, this end of the brick can be pulverised using a smaller chisel, and eventually the bits broken out.

Once the first bit is out, the rest of the brick is easier. And once the first brick is out, the other bricks are easier. Each brick should have the mortar on all sides cracked using the bolster chisel; alternate ends of the brick are hit by a mallet on a piece of wood to cushion the blow to try to loosen the brick. Once loose, it can be pulled out in one piece. Try to keep as many bricks whole as you can; they come in very useful at a later stage.

When the opening is large enough to install the lintel, clear away all mortar from the remaining bricks. Check that the 'shoulders' (the two bricks that take the weight of the lintel) finish on a perpendicular joint in line with the reveal of what will be the opening. If they do not, it may be necessary to take out a whole brick and lay two half-bricks.

### Pre-cast lintel in cavity brickwork

For this you will be using either a pre-cast concrete boot lintel or a much lighter steel equivalent. You will need to check with the local building inspector if the steel version is permitted; many local authorities insist on concrete lintels because these do not weaken so quickly in a fire. The steel lintels, when heated by intense flames, soften and allow the structure they support to collapse. Not a very likely event, but it might make a difference in an emergency.

Knock up a small batch of 1 : 3 cement :

**Fig 181** Boot lintel with DPC

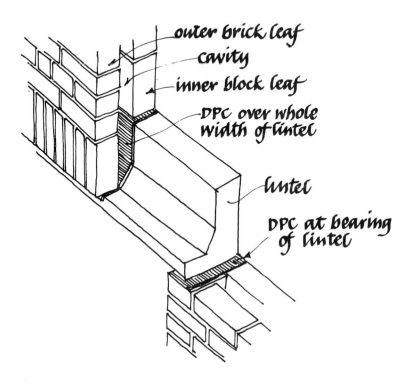

outer brick leaf
cavity
inner block leaf
DPC over whole width of lintel
lintel
DPC at bearing of lintel

## Project 6: Openings in Existing Brickwork

**Fig 182** Replacing the last brick in existing brickwork

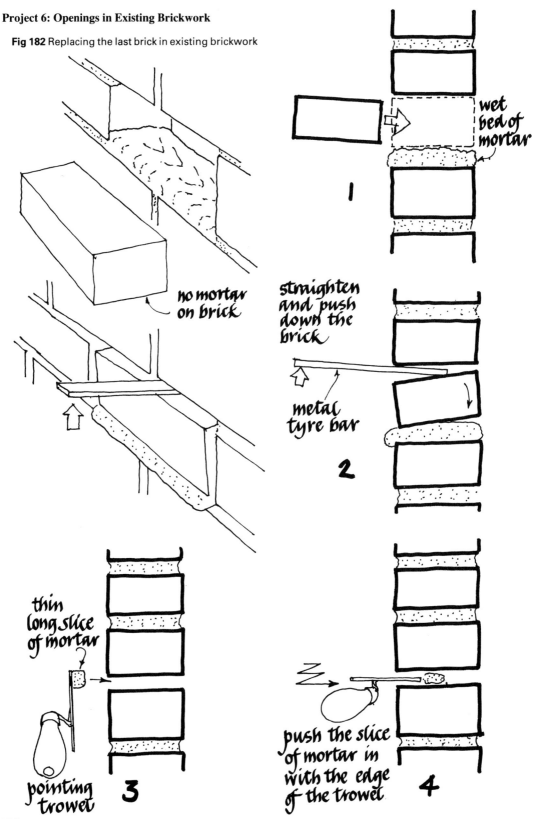

no mortar on brick

wet bed of mortar

**1**

straighten and push down the brick

metal tyre bar

**2**

thin long slice of mortar

pointing trowel

**3**

push the slice of mortar in with the edge of the trowel

**4**

sand mortar to lay on the two shoulders that will take the ends of the lintel. The lintel is hoisted into place; check that it sits in the correct position with regard to the face of the brickwork and that it rests truly horizontal.

The next day a DPC is laid over the lintel (*see* Fig 181). The brickwork over the lintel can now be built up. This is quite a ticklish little job, and some of the skills built up when learning to repoint will come in very useful now.

The inner leaf will be built up in the normal way; the only real problem is getting the bricks into place and making sure enough mortar goes around the joint. The bed joint of each brick is supplied with mortar in the normal way, except the bed is flattened with the blade of the trowel till it is almost as thick as a normal mortar joint and spread the full length and width of the brick it is about to support. The brick in question is buttered one end in the normal way and then placed in position.

If there is enough space (ie there are still two courses open) the brick is lowered in the normal way, the mortar pressed down and the brick tapped into position. However, if this is the last brick, then the brick is scraped home with its top edge hard against the underneath side (or soffit) of the existing brickwork. When it is in the right position it is levered into place using perhaps an old and large screwdriver (Fig 182).

When this brick is in its place, the mortar to its top and sides is pushed in place using pointing techniques (*see* p 65). There will have to be quite a bit of 'chopping' to get the mortar to sit all the way to the back of the joint, but it can be done, even if quite a lot of mortar falls onto the ground.

The brickwork to the front of the lintel is more difficult, in that it can be seen and therefore needs to be tidy. The upright soldiers of a soldier arch are comparatively simple, and are built in to rest on the toe of the boot lintel.

## Solid brickwork with an *in situ* lintel

If you are dealing with solid brickwork, you will probably be taking the load of the brick-work using a 190 × 225mm lintel with a brick slip arch in front.

Begin as before by making an opening in the existing brickwork. The opening will have to be high enough to allow you to build the shuttering as well as be able to place the reinforcement and prod the cement into place. It is enough to remove brickwork for about three full courses of bricks plus the height of the lintel.

Shuttering bottom and sides can be made using either old floor boards or shuttering-quality plywood. The sides will have to be of a width equal to the height of the lintel; the bottom must be equal to the thickness of the wall less the thickness of the brick slips (and of course the mortar joint).

Fig 50 (p 55) shows the combined frame-work and support to the shuttering. Make sure the supporting 'legs' are strong enough; use wood of either 50 × 50 or 75 × 40mm section. When both framework and shutter-ing are in position tight up to the brickwork, use putty to seal the gaps between the timber and the brickwork to stop the cement slurry of the concrete leaking through and thus weakening the concrete and staining the brickwork.

The lintel needs to be reinforced. As suggested earlier, the position, size and amount should properly be calculated by an expert, alternatively, the building inspector will tell you the amount he deems to be necessary. Possibly the reinforcement may have to be placed before completing the shuttering if the opening above the lintel is too small.

Finally the concrete — a coarse mix — is poured into the shuttering, and prodded into place under and between the reinforcement with a broomstick. The concrete is left to 'cure' for three weeks before the brickwork over the lintel can be completed.

The front of the shuttering can be taken away after a week or so to allow you to get on with building the arch. Building a brick arch is much less difficult than you think. Start by constructing a 'foot-rest' (Fig 183), using a piece of timber batten planed to a curve. Next, using whole and cut bricks, construct the two 'springs' (the point where the arch starts).

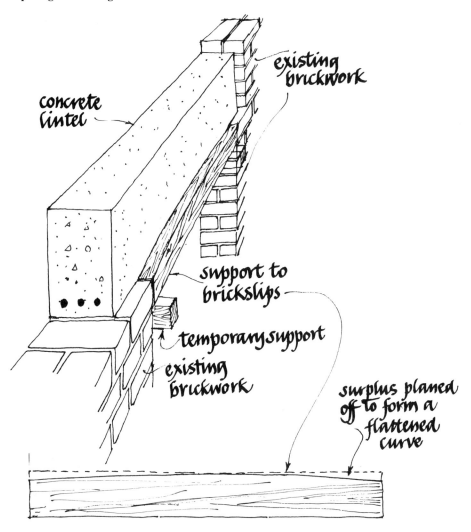

concrete
lintel

existing
brickwork

support to
brickslips

temporary support

existing
brickwork

surplus planed
off to form a
flattened
curve

**Fig 183** Temporary support or 'foot-rest' to brick-slip arch

You can now start laying the voussoir brick slips (Fig 184). The mortar joint of each has to be judged by eye to get the brick slips to change direction as the arch progresses from left to right. You may possibly have to add a little mortar to some, and take a little away from others till the arch looks just right. Finish off by using pointing techniques (ie 'chopping' in more mortar) to fill the joints solid.

The brickwork above the lintel or arch is now filled. The last few bricks of the opening will prove the most difficult, but again your skills built up by repointing the house will

come in useful. Make sure that each brick sits level; you may have to use an old screwdriver to lever the brick straight, since you cannot tap it into place. Occasionally you will find that you have to add mortar to the bed as well as to the head joint of the brick in question.

Having dealt with the top, next turn to the bottom or sill. Most modern houses will have a timber sill integral to the timber frame; older houses may have a tiled sill, or more often a stone sill or a sill built up from brick specials. These brick specials are almost impossible to obtain; so you must decide either to use cast concrete imitations or have a non-matching window or door opening.

Stone sills are copied more easily — just

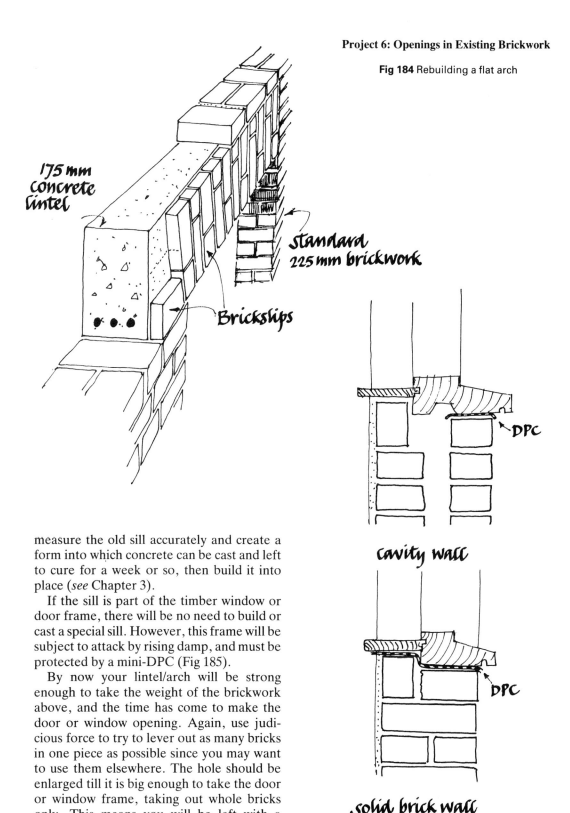

**Fig 184** Rebuilding a flat arch

175 mm concrete lintel

standard 225 mm brickwork

Brickslips

**cavity wall**

DPC

**solid brick wall**

DPC

**Fig 185** DPC under a sill to brickwork

measure the old sill accurately and create a form into which concrete can be cast and left to cure for a week or so, then build it into place (*see* Chapter 3).

If the sill is part of the timber window or door frame, there will be no need to build or cast a special sill. However, this frame will be subject to attack by rising damp, and must be protected by a mini-DPC (Fig 185).

By now your lintel/arch will be strong enough to take the weight of the brickwork above, and the time has come to make the door or window opening. Again, use judicious force to try to lever out as many bricks in one piece as possible since you may want to use them elsewhere. The hole should be enlarged till it is big enough to take the door or window frame, taking out whole bricks only. This means you will be left with a ragged edge (Fig 186).

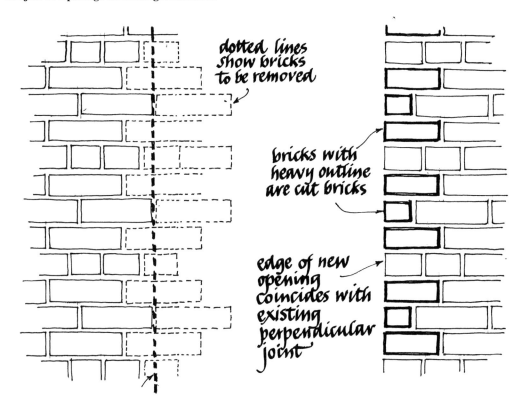

**Fig 186** A new opening in existing brickwork

Try the frame for fit, and mark the places accurately where horizontal mortar joints allow you to fit retaining lugs to the frame. Take the frame out, screw the lugs on and, after cutting back the mortar in the existing brickwork, push the window (with lugs) into place. This may entail a certain amount of hurried chipping as you manoeuvre the frame into place.

Mix up some more cement using a lime : cement : sand mix (1 : 1 : 6 will do nicely) and chop this into the space around the lugs. Then, using brick bits and pieces, close up the space between frame and the inner leaf of a cavity wall (or the inner part of a solid wall).

Then finish the outer leaf (or outer part of a solid wall) in a neat way. Start by hammering in two masonry nails into the brickwork above and below the opening in such positions that a line stretched between the two will mark the exact vertical line of the reveal.

Now cut bricks to size, using the 'whittling'

technique (*see* p 76) and build them in one by one using the pointing techniques described earlier (chopping in the mortar). There is a tendency to put in more mortar on the bed away from the reveal so that the bricks sag down towards the frame; watch this, and if anything, add a little too much mortar on the part of the bed nearest the opening.

The final job, after the mortar has had a chance to dry for a week or so, is to seal all gaps between the frame and the surrounding brickwork with a mastic sealant. The result should be a new opening that looks like part of the original design.

These techniques should also enable you to tackle the task of bricking in an existing opening. Too often this is done leaving a very obvious 'patch'; again, by taking out the half-bricks of what was the reveal and building in new whole bricks you should be able to achieve what appears to be continuity. Your only real problem will be finding matching bricks!

# Project 7: A Small Conservatory

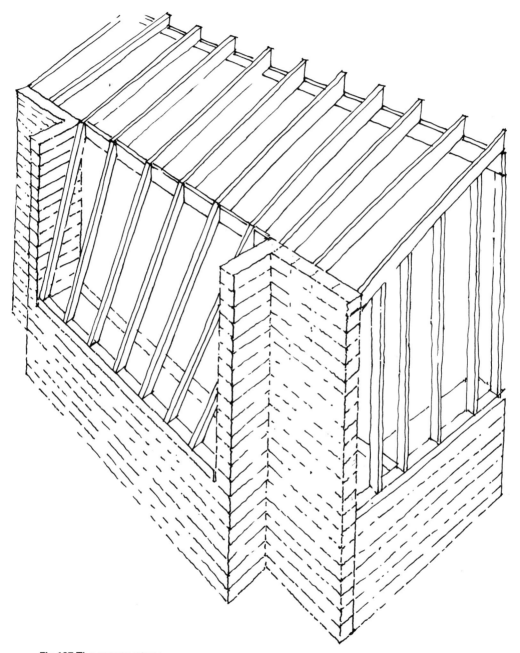

**Fig 187** The conservatory

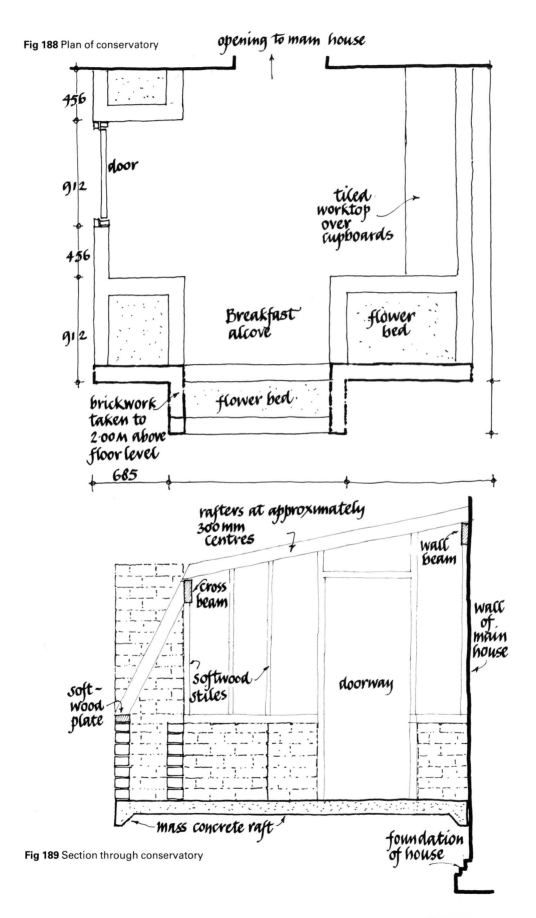

**Fig 188** Plan of conservatory

opening to main house

456

door

912

tiled
worktop
over
cupboards

456

912

Breakfast
alcove

flower
bed

brickwork
taken to
2·00M above
floor level

flower bed

685

rafters at approximately
300 mm
centres

cross
beam

wall
beam

soft-
wood
plate

softwood
stiles

doorway

wall
of
main
house

mass concrete raft

foundation
of house

**Fig 189** Section through conservatory

A small conservatory (Fig 187) attached to the house has many advantages. Generally speaking, the advantages have to be paid for — getting a conservatory built by a regular builder is not a cheap exercise. If you are able to build it yourself, it may be cheap enough to afford, especially if you can use second-hand materials.

In most cases a conservatory does not need planning permission. Obviously, you would need to check with your local planning office, but by and large, as long as the conservatory does not exceed 10 per cent of the total volume of the house, it will not need planning permission (this applies to any additional structure, including garages) as long as it is built to the back or side of the house.

If it is emphasised that the structure is a conservatory for the growing of plants (ie it is not going to be used as an extension to the house) you may even be able to exceed the 10 per cent rule. This would probably not be the case if you indicated a desire to enlarge existing openings such as doors and windows.

The great advantage of a conservatory, of course, is the way in which it can extend the space available in the house. It will create a very airy living room, a pleasant dining room or even a play area for the children. All this while still growing tomatoes, lettuces or other vegetables or flowers, all the year round.

A second great advantage of the conservatory, especially if facing south or southwest, is that it will act as a heat trap. In winter, the rays of the sun will penetrate the glass, but be unable to get out. Any rooms in direct communication with the conservatory are warmed up at no expense. If you create a large opening between conservatory and living room, and leave this open in the daytime while shutting it at night, you will find your fuel bills cut!

Of course, the cut in fuel bills must be offset against the capital cost of the conservatory, which is why such a trade-off only really becomes economic if you build the structure yourself.

Although you probably will not need planning permission, you will need building regulations approval. This may be quite

sticky, since the glass used is classed as a fire-hazardous material (remember Summerdale on the Isle of Man). A co-operative council official may be able to steer you through and around all sorts of regulations. Again, remember that you are building a conservatory, and not an extension to your house. If, at a much later stage, you wish to convert an existing window between living room and conservatory into a doorway, this is a totally different matter.

Having negotiated your way through a thicket of regulations, you can now start on the project itself. Begin by making the relevant drawings — plans, elevations and the like — and estimate quantities and calculate costs (Figs 188 and 189).

The materials for the base will of course be new, but for the timber frame extensive use can be made of second-hand timber, both sawn and planed (*see* p 143). A coat or two of dark stain/preservative will transform the assorted timber into what appears to be uniform material.

For the glass, a lot of money can be saved by using 'agricultural quality' glass. This is not as uniform as ordinary window glass (objects seen through this glass may be distorted a little) but it is a lot cheaper. Again, you may well use a variety of odd thicknesses and shades if you happen to find undamaged second-hand glass.

The base of the conservatory will be either a raft foundation (*see* Chapter 2) or an ordinary strip foundation. The raft foundation (Fig 190) will give you a relatively quick flat floor suitable for 'interior' finishes such as wood strip, vinyl tiles, carpets or matting. The use of concrete footings is perhaps more suitable if you are planning to lay rougher finishes such as bricks or paving stones.

Chapter 2 and Project 4 should provide enough information on how to construct the base of the conservatory. Once this is in place, you can turn to the walls.

Of course, the walls can be simple dwarf walls up to a height of, say, 300mm above floor level — enough to stop the base of the timber construction from rotting with the rising damp. However, you can do so much more than this.

191

For instance, the walls can be used to form built-in flower/vegetable containers so that the conservatory yields a year-round supply of vegetables and flowers, and provides a pleasant decor to your extended dining or living room.

The walls can be used to support tables and benches if you want to make a dining/breakfast area (Fig 191); you could even make built-in seating for a living area/conversation pit (*see* Project 1). Naturally, each design will have to take into account the amount of room available, and the purpose to which you want to put the conservatory.

The conservatory framework is formed from timbers, generally starting with a framework of 50 × 100mm, although if you can come by other sizes cheaply, do not hesitate to go for a more chunky design. Walls of a conservatory can be vertical or sloping. The combination of a 75° slope with a deep flower/vegetable bin can lead to pleasant results.

The main frame should be so constructed that a standard width of glass can be accommodated. This standard width obviously depends on what sort of glass you are buying, so check the glass measurements before setting out the timber.

To each side of the timber (roof and walls) are nailed small battens on which the glass will rest. The pieces of glass overlap at the trailing edge going down-slope, rather the way tiles or slates do. The glass is held in place by further battens or by putty (Fig 192).

Where the glass joins up to the main body of the house, it butts up to a timber beam drilled and bolted to the main house wall (Fig 193). From the wall to the main beam there should be some flashing. Officially and properly, you should use metal flashing sunk into the brickwork joint immediately above the timber and this may indeed be necessary on

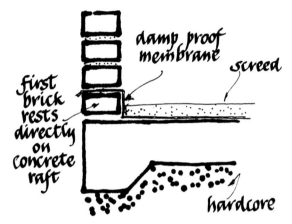

damp proof membrane

screed

first brick rests directly on concrete raft

hardcore

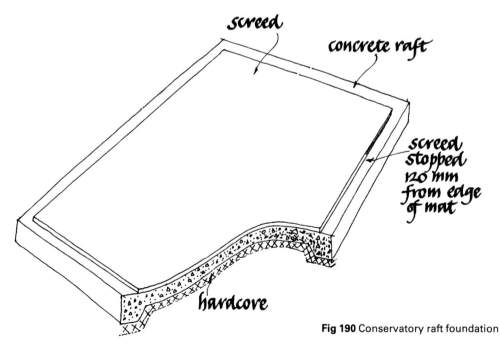

screed

concrete raft

screed stopped 120 mm from edge of mat

hardcore

**Fig 190** Conservatory raft foundation

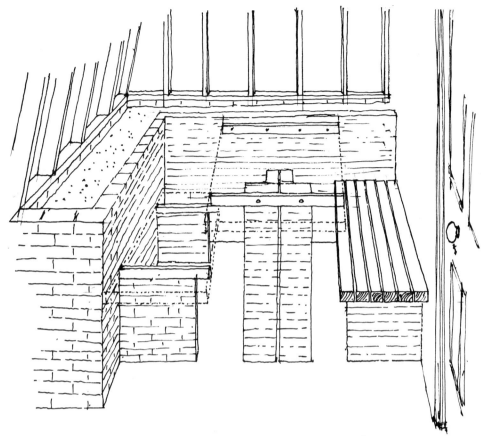

**Fig 191** Flowerbed, table and benches, creating a breakfast corner in a conservatory

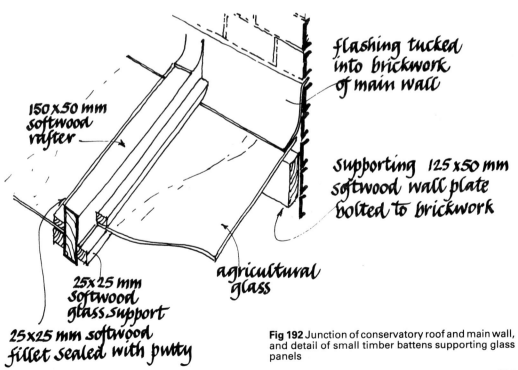

150 x 50 mm
softwood
rafter

flashing tucked
into brickwork
of main wall

supporting 125 x 50 mm
softwood wall plate
bolted to brickwork

agricultural
glass

25 x 25 mm
softwood
glass support
25 x 25 mm softwood
fillet sealed with putty

**Fig 192** Junction of conservatory roof and main wall, and detail of small timber battens supporting glass panels

**Fig 193** Detail of conservatory roof

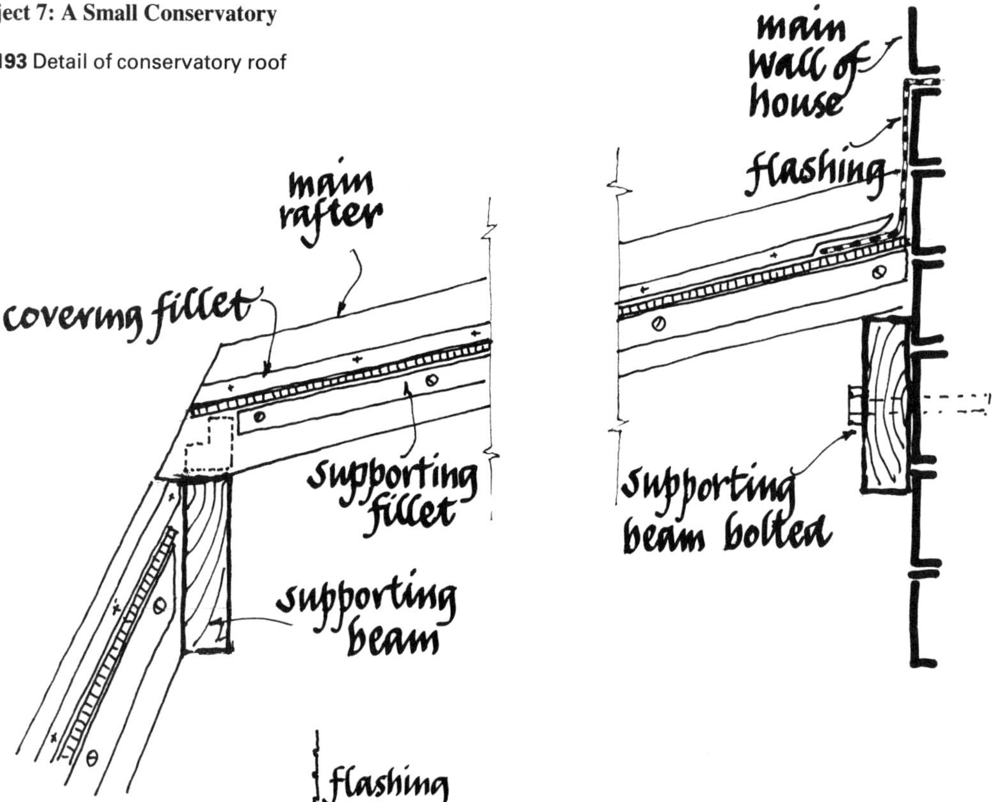

main
wall of
house

flashing

main
rafter

covering fillet

supporting
fillet

supporting
beam bolted

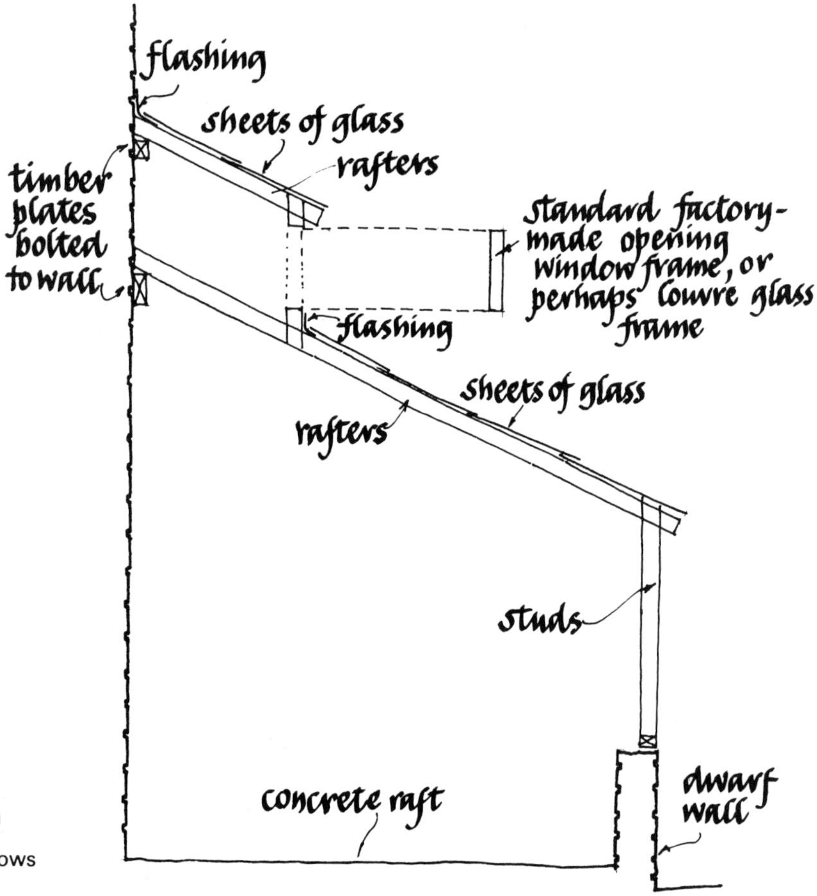

supporting
beam

flashing

sheets of glass
rafters

timber
plates
bolted
to wall

standard factory-
made opening
window frame, or
perhaps louvre glass
frame

flashing

sheets of glass

rafters

studs

concrete raft

dwarf
wall

**Fig 194** Section through
conservatory showing
vertical high-level windows

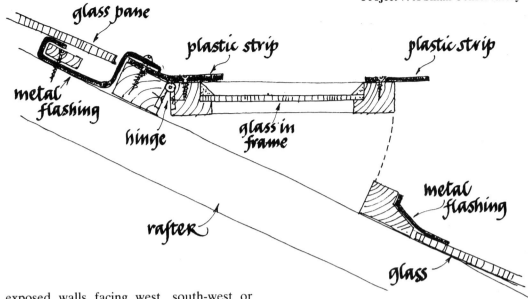

*glass pane*

*plastic strip*

*plastic strip*

*metal flashing*

*hinge*

*glass in frame*

*metal flashing*

*rafter*

*glass*

exposed walls facing west, south-west or north-west. If the wall is more sheltered, you may well get away with a roll of proprietary stick-on sealant strip.

When designing the conservatory, remember to allow for ventilation. Because of the extensive amount of glass used, summer temperatures can become extremely uncomfortable. Hence proper ventilation is most important. This is best done by allowing cooler air to enter at the bottom of the structure, and hot air to leave at the top. You should therefore allow a number of opening lights as near to the foot of the structure as possible. Since the windows will be in a wall which is either vertical or fairly nearly so, this should give no real problems. The windows near the top, however, can cause design problems.

Two alternatives are suggested. First, the conservatory can be designed in such a way that there are mini-walls near the top (Fig 194). Secondly, the opening windows can be constructed to open in the sloping roof (Fig 195), but you must then accept that it will not be perfectly watertight and windproof. Such a defect might not be acceptable in an ordinary living room, but if you have a tiled, paved or brick floor to your conservatory, and do not plan to make much use of it when the weather is cold, then this will not be too great a problem. Such a sloping window only lets in a few drops in a really bad storm.

**Fig 195** Opening window in conservatory in plane of roof

Another suggestion to make the conservatory pleasant in the summer is to shade it all by growing vines or by the use of horizontally drawn blinds. This should be borne in mind when designing the main timber structure.

The internal brickwork could well be enlivened by features not suitable for brickwork exposed to the elements in the normal way. For instance, the joints, especially the horizontal ones, could be well raked out. Alternatively, the brickwork could be laid in unusual patterns, eg keeping all the perpendiculars in line.

Other possibilities are to form elaborate copings to the flower bins and to slope the brickwork backwards or even forwards. Wavy forms on plan are possible, although a great deal of care must be taken that it does not all degenerate into an 'artistic' mess.

Once the conservatory is finished, it can be inspected by planning and building regulation officials from the local authority. Should you happen to decide, perhaps a year or two later, to convert the windows between living room and conservatory into doors, you could make extensive use of the information in Project 6, although of course you would not necessarily have to build in new lintels.

195

# Project 8: Building a Garage

Building a garage is one of the first major projects undertaken by most people. A garage adds to the value of the house, protects your car against theft and the weather, and gives space to put away things like bicycles, lawn mowers and all your tools, not to mention the deep-freeze.

Such a list provides some clues to the design of your garage. When you buy a house with garage, or if you have a garage built by a small builder, the final cost will depend very much on the size of the structure. Hence most garages have room enough for the car and an odd corner for squeezing in other items. If you are building yourself, you might as well make it roomy enough for all your needs. It costs a little more in terms of cement, sand, mortar and bricks but those are not all that expensive.

Before starting anything more than a back-of-the-envelope sketch, make your way down to the planning department of your local council. An informal discussion about what you can and what you cannot do may make life much smoother at a later stage.

By and large, as long as you keep the wall nearest the road in line with the front of the house, do not build higher than the house, and keep the volume of the garage to 10 per cent of the volume of the house, you do not need planning permission at all. This is very worth while, since it means:

(1) You do not have to have drawings prepared to submit to the council.
(2) You do not have to wait six months or longer while the slow wheels of bureaucracy grind exceedingly fine.
(3) You can build the garage to look the way you want it and which suits you, rather than the way the planning department feels it ought to be built.

If, though, you do exceed 10 per cent, or the garage has to stick out a few inches in front of the house, then planning permission becomes important. Getting planning permission is a matter of getting a draughtsman to draw plans and elevations, filling in numerous forms, and waiting a long time to get an answer. However, it might all be worth while if you want to go in for a little more than just a minimal garage.

Having sorted out the planning side, the next step is to deal with building regulations. This is an entirely different department — literally — and full of technical rules about quality of materials and construction, sizes etc. Again, a visit to the local council and an informal discussion about what you plan to do will probably be sufficient. The local council is responsible for the stability and standard of any structure within the borough, and that includes a humble garage.

You do not have to produce professional sets of drawings showing all the details (although if the local authority insists it might be politic to do so). A verbal description is usually enough as long as the whole project is kept simple. If you are planning to build a combined garage, rumpus room, hobby den and guest suite, it might be another matter.

Now comes the stage at which to sit down and make a few amateur drawings (Figs 196 and 197). You want to be able to work out the size and shape (on plan) of the garage. Obviously you will need a space large enough for your car (and any future car) to stand. You need space to one side that will allow you to open the driver's door to get in and out. A space to store car tools, cans of oil and anti-freeze, and other car items is probably indicated, especially if you are the sort of person who builds his/her own garage.

Making the garage a little bigger to accommodate garden tools and bicycles will not cost a great deal, and might make a lot of sense. Again, enough space to accommodate a freezer might be well worth the extra cost of bricks and cement. You have to balance the larger garage with the resulting smaller

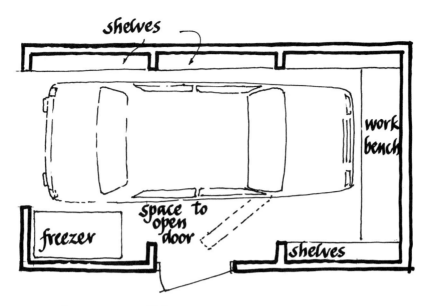

shelves

work bench

space to open door

freezer

shelves

garden and with the extra cost. Take your time in thinking this over. Above all, remember that it costs much more to build a garage in two bites than one big one.

When you have your plans sorted out, the time comes to start estimating quantities. For help on estimating the amount of concrete required, *see* p 11, and p 56 for the number of bricks.

In general, the cheapest and quickest way of dealing with the foundations is to lay a raft

**Fig 196** Plan of garage showing use

foundation (*see* Chapter 2) reinforced at the edges for extra strength, and at least 120mm thick, laid on a hardcore bed. This will certainly be strong enough for any ordinary car (or even a small van). The finish of the concrete raft will also be adequate for the garage floor.

**Fig 197** Plan of garage showing dimensions

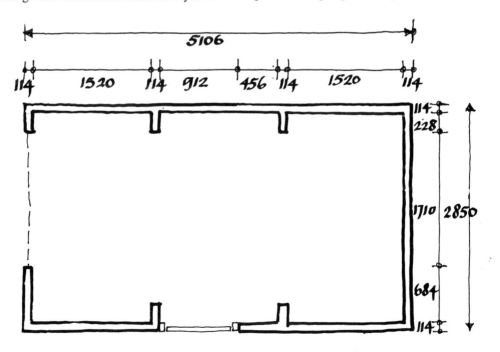

## Project 8: Building a Garage

Most garages are built with walls of a single brick thickness, ie some 112mm. This saves on materials and labour, and most people do not feel any need to make the garage wall any thicker. Of course, it does mean that the long walls will need one or two piers. However, if you are building the garage yourself, there is nothing to stop you building it using cavity wall construction with a block inner wall. It is somewhat more expensive in materials, but it has the advantage of cutting down on condensation inside the garage (which will be beneficial for your car) and also allows you to convert the garage to an extra room at a later stage if you are ever stuck for space.

Most of the front of the garage will be taken up by the doors; generally speaking, the quickest and cheapest method of shutting off the garage is to buy a ready-made metal up-and-over door set and build it in as you go. However, if you prefer making your own timber stable-doors, why not? Only this book will not deal with such refinements!

Letting some natural daylight into the

garage is a good idea; and ventilation is also important. However, you will not need as much light as for a living room, and security is always a problem; the best solution might be a couple of small, long, opening windows fairly high up; I would suggest something in the order of 300 × 100mm near the roof. That leaves room for shelving below (for tools, onion sets and cans of paint), and allows light and air to get in.

Depending on the use to which your garage is put and the relationship between house, garage and garden, it might be useful to plan for a second door. Again, you can buy standard door frames, fitted with a door and ready for building into your brick wall.

After the concrete floor is well and truly laid (*see* Chapter 2), put up the door frames. If these are timber, first treat them with preservative at all vulnerable points, especially near the foot. Timber frames are supported in their place by a temporary timber batten nailed to the top and stretched diagonally to the concrete floor (Fig 198). Metal frames are a little more difficult (unless they have timber subframes) and you may have to drill a hole

**Fig 198** Building in a door frame

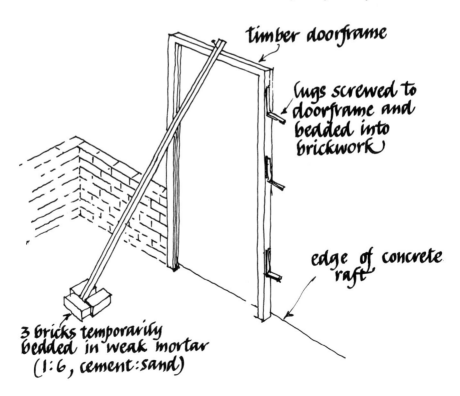

timber doorframe

lugs screwed to doorframe and bedded into brickwork

edge of concrete raft

3 bricks temporarily bedded in weak mortar (1:6, cement:sand)

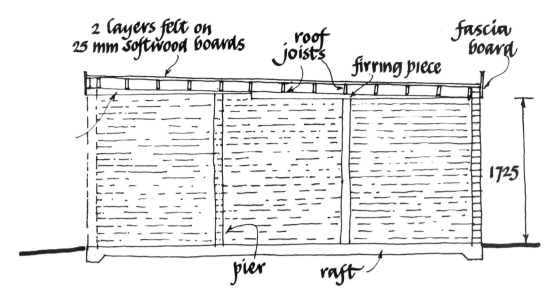

**Fig 199** Section through garage showing firring pieces

through which a screw is driven into a temporary supporting batten.

Now lay the brickwork, referring to Chapter 6 for more detailed advice on how to start setting out and laying the first course of bricks, how to build up the corners and fill in the intervening stretches. Depending on the standard you have set, you may or may not have to incorporate a damp proof course. In any case you will be taking up your brickwork, and inevitably will come to the problem of dealing with the lugs to door and window frames.

Metal frames are of two types:

(1) The type that is meant to be screwed to a timber subframe.
(2) The type that is meant to be built into the brickwork using lugs.

These lugs are metal strips that can slide up and down along a special 'track' of the pressed metal frame. They usually have to be slid in before the frame is set down onto the concrete floor.

Wooden frames or subframes can also be held by lugs, but these lugs have to be screwed to the frame at the point at which you want to build them into the brickwork.

Whichever type you use, make sure that each door frame is held in place by at least two, and preferably three, lugs to each side (or jamb) of the frame. Window frames should also be held in place with two lugs to each side.

With timber window frames it is always a good idea to sit the frame on a strip of plastic polythene to act as a DPC. The brickwork immediately below the sill is always damp, especially with a single brick wall, and a piece of plastic here may mean that your window will last fifty years instead of thirty.

The roof of a garage is partly a matter of design, partly of taste. Generally speaking, you will be using timber beams or trusses over which are laid either timber boards and two or three layers of roofing felt, or a layer of building paper followed by tiling battens and then the tiles themselves.

We start with the simplest sort of roof, the 'flat' roof. In actual fact it must slope by at least 1 in 60, but it is safer to make it slope 1 in 40 to avoid any chance of water building up. That means that if you are making the left-hand side of the garage the 'high' point, the right-hand side of the roof on a 2.5 metre wide garage would be about 60mm lower. That is not a great deal, but not everyone likes having a lop-sided garage. What can be done?

First of all, we could make the roof slope from front to back (or vice versa). This makes a difference of some 120–130mm, approximately the height of two bricks. In order to deal with this, the rafters are laid on 'firring' pieces, which are simply pieces of

199

wood sawn as a long triangle. If you make the long slope in two steps (Fig 199), then each firring piece would have to be about 40mm thick at the narrow end, rising to 100mm at the wide end.

Such a firring piece could be sawn out of standard 100 × 50mm softwood and held down onto the brick wall by galvanised mild steel straps, about three per length of wood. The 125 × 50mm softwood joists are then nailed to these firring pieces — some local authorities like to see these rafters bolted, screwed or strapped to the firring piece. Both firring pieces and rafters should be treated against rot. The rafters should project over the edges of the firring piece by at least 50 or 75mm to provide sheltering eaves.

The rafters should be laid at intervals not much greater than 400mm and in such a way that the first and last rafters both sit with the outside face flush with the wall below. To these last rafters should be nailed 50 × 50mm offcuts, and to the offcuts a 150 × 25 (or 40mm) softwood board that will form the fascia. The fascia is continued on the cut ends of the intervening joists to provide a level trim all the way around.

On top of the rafters is laid either a softwood timber (boards) deck, or you can use chipboard, plywood or other decking material. Once you have a firm and stable, reasonably waterproof and rotproof decking, you can

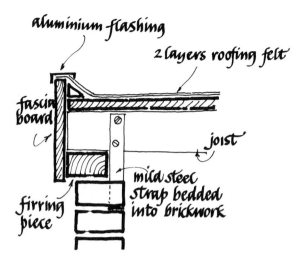

Fig 200 Section showing junction of flat roof at side

finish it off with building paper and two or three layers of roofing felt (Figs 200 and 201).

For a tiled roof, the rafters will slope at angles greater than 30°. Thus there will be no need to slope the brickwork. The rafters are laid on 100 × 50mm sawn softwood firring pieces bolted to the top of the brickwork walls. The rafters themselves will be 100 (or 125) × 50mm sawn softwood spiked to the firring pieces at their lower end, and to a 125 × 25mm sawn softwood ridge plank at the higher end. A 100 × 25mm sawn softwood tie should be bolted to each pair of rafters to

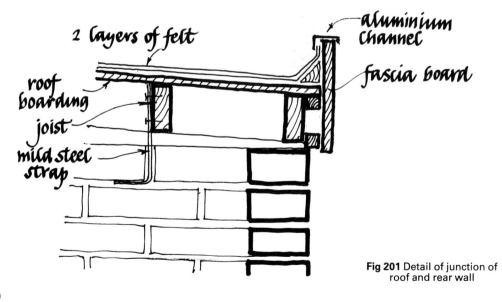

Fig 201 Detail of junction of roof and rear wall

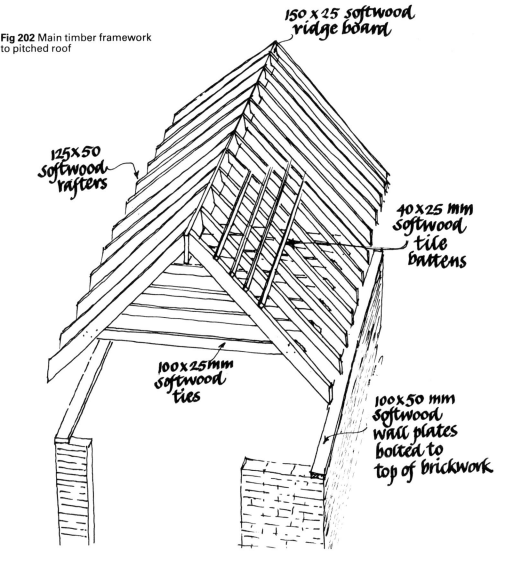

**Fig 202** Main timber framework to pitched roof

150 × 25 softwood ridge board

125×50 softwood rafters

40×25 mm softwood tile battens

100×25mm softwood ties

100×50 mm softwood wall plates bolted to top of brickwork

stop the roof collapsing under the weight of the tiles (Fig 202).

The gable ends of the garage will need to be built up to meet the rafters. The rafters themselves should be spaced so that the first (and last) set of rafters sit right next to the brickwork and yet the space between adjoining rafters is never more than 450mm.

Once the rafters are in position, they are covered with building paper, and then tiling battens. The battens, usually 40 × 25mm sawn softwood, will need to be nailed to the rafters at intervals advised by the tile manufacturer; be careful not to step through the building paper when you nail the battens down.

The tiles are now nailed to the battens, starting at the bottom and working up to the ridge. Most tile manufacturers have special ridge tiles to cap the roof; if not, you will have to buy specials — the builders' merchant will help.

The roof will be finished with barge boards at the gable ends: 150 × 25mm PAR (planed all round) softwood fixed directly to the brickwork on the outside. The eaves will have another board, usually 125 × 25 PAR, nailed to the ends of the rafters; this eaves board supports the guttering, which can be simple PVC half-round, leading to a soak-away or even directly to the drive or the road if the local authority permits this.

201

# Project 9: Tiling the Bathroom

Almost every medium-priced home built during the past twenty years or so will have had a modest quantity of tiling installed over the bath and wash basin in the bathroom. This is the splashback, designed to stop the wallpaper (and the plaster behind it) from getting soaked as you splash about. Soaked wallpaper looks nasty and comes off over a period of months; soaked plaster becomes soft and crumbles away in a few years.

One project you may well decide is worth doing is to tile your bathroom in a slightly more wholesale fashion. Rather than have two or three small areas of very basic white or avocado green 6 inch square tiles and the rest of the bathroom in water-resistant vinyl wallpaper, you could splash out on some really pretty tiles all around the walls up to waist height. It will unify the bathroom, and in any case, a splashback never seems quite sufficient.

Start by measuring all the wall surfaces very, very accurately. I would suggest you make scale drawings, using graph paper if necessary, of all wall surfaces you want to tile, showing exactly where any fixtures and fittings sit. Now go to the showroom and start looking at tiles.

If you look back to Chapter 8 on basic tiling, you will see how each length of wall virtually dictates its own tiling pattern in terms of cut tiles. I also mentioned there the idea of choosing a different tile to take the place of the cut tile.

If you choose to tile the majority of the wall in a light-green tile of 150mm wide, and use a border of small (40mm square) dark-brown mini-tiles, it will mean that, with a little bit of judicious juggling with the vertical joints, that you can virtually accommodate any wall length above 2 metres without having to cut tiles.

Such a mixture of two colours and two sizes may not be to everyone's taste, but it is an idea that may save you a lot of difficult work

and may even be preferred for its looks.

However, assuming that you are going to do everything in tiles of one width, it becomes important to decide exactly where the centre joint of each tiled surface will sit, and which tiles need cutting.

Calculate the number of tiles required, add a margin of 5 per cent (for tiles damaged in cutting) and order the whole lot: ordering additional quantities at a later stage may mean disappointment, as importers stop importing, factories discontinue the range or the shade changes slightly.

Before applying the tiles, make sure all surfaces are bare and clean: no wallpaper, old paint, loose plaster or grease. Paint the surface with a bonding agent (*see* Chapter 8) and when it is dry start marking out the lines where the tiles are to go. As described in Chapter 8 start with the top horizontal line, and then mark out the vertical joint nearest to the centre.

Start work at the centre line along the bottom of the first wall. Continue laying tiles to each side of the centre till you come to the tile that has to be cut.

Lay all the whole tiles before beginning to cut or to lay any cut tiles. And remember: the house with perfectly straight walls or floors has yet to be built. This is something that will hit you time and again if you are dealing with tiles.

When the time comes to lay the cut tiles, start by sliding each tile over the full tiles till it hits the wall or reveal. Mark where the tile is to be cut, and cut it using one of the three methods described in Chapter 8. Lay this single tile and start on the next.

Pipes coming out of the wall form a special problem. Cutting the hole is a matter of technical skill, but fitting the tile round the pipe is the real problem. The professional tiler solves this by cutting the hole, snapping the tile in two and then laying the two parts of the tile butting together along the snapped

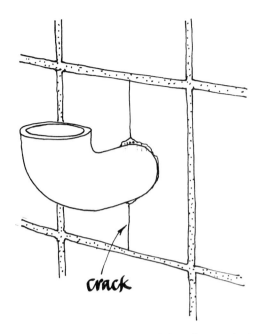

**Fig 203** Fitting a tile around an existing pipe: method used by professional tiler

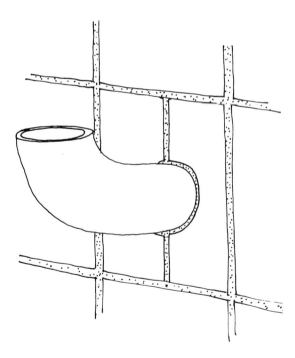

**Fig 204** Fitting a tile around an existing pipe: more noticeable but purposive joints

joint (Fig 203). You see a thin line running away from the pipe. This is a fairly quick and easy solution, and most people are not overly disturbed by the crack, but a proper joint the same thickness as the other joints and running either vertically or horizontally might be a better solution (Fig 204). The joint is more noticeable, but looks purposive rather than furtive. It is all a matter of taste.

Of course, the neatest solution, should you have the skill and the time, would be to make a hole in the tile, and fit the tile over the pipe and onto the wall. This means disconnecting the pipe (and very often the whole fitting) before the tile can be slipped into place.

Start by cutting a cardboard template. Take a piece of cardboard the exact size of a tile, and cut a quadrant out of one corner. The internal corner of the quadrant should be roughly at the centre of the protruding pipe. Now enlarge this internal corner, little by little, till it fits neatly and snugly around the pipe. If you have cut too much, stick some masking tape over the hole; gradually you should form a template. You can check by accurately copying this template onto a second (and much thicker) piece of cardboard, and seeing whether you have got it right.

Once the template is correct, disconnect the pipe and/or the fitting to a stage where a tile could be fitted over the pipe and slid along till it hits the wall.

Using a slow-speed electric drill and a masonry drill, cut a hole starting at the back of the tile. The tile is laid on some old carpeting to cushion the vibrations. Do not exert too much pressure or you will crack the tile. Once you are through, you will need to enlarge the hole.

You can buy special files designed to cut through bricks and tiles; alternatively, you can use old rough wood files for the job. At first you will have to 'worry' the file through the relatively small hole left by the masonry drill, but gradually the whole file can get through. File from the front (glazed) side of the tile, and check, using the cardboard template, that you're making the hole the right size and in the right place. If you can, use an offcut from the pipe to check the hole.

Allow a little tolerance if the tile has to slide around a bend in the pipe.

Eventually the hole is the right size, and the tile can be slipped over the pipe and into place. If all is correct — but be prepared for disappointment — the tile can be glued or cemented into place, and the pipe (and fitting) reconnected.

This is exactly the sort of job only a DIY man can afford. If it were to be done by a contractor, it would mean that the plumber would have to come in on the job twice (once to disconnect, once to reconnect) and that the tiler would have to fiddle around for half an hour or an hour just for one tile. Far too expensive for most people, and yet exactly the fiddly sort of job you can do.

Having tiled your bathroom walls to waist height, what else can you do? What about tiling the bath-surround (the panel that hides the bottom and sides of the bath)? It is perfectly possible to build yourself an extremely luxurious bathroom; the bath and vanitory units are all set into tiled surrounds, and the tiles are taken to ceiling level. In one design of mine, the bath was let into a tiled top to a wooden structure tiled top and sides; the piping was run below this top and, though the tap controls were within easy hand reach of anyone sitting in the bath, the water actually entered the bath at the foot end where really hot water had less chance of scalding the bath's occupant. A tiled access hatch allowed for repairs to the piping — the joints of the hatch were at the tile joints — an almost invisible hatch.

# Index